Wildlife Conservation in India—4

Besides Loving The Beasts

HS Pabla

2021
First Edition (Updated in 2023)
Publisher: H.S. Pabla
Printed by: Kindle Direct Publishing
Cover Design By: Pratiksha Gupta.

Paperback and e-book available with Amazon and other e-tailers.

Dedicated to the countless, nameless, and helpless victims
of our aimless wildlife conservation policies.

Table of Contents

List of Abbreviations

Abbreviation	Full Form
AU	Animal Unit
BEW	Burning Early-Winter
BMW	Burning Mid-Winter
CBNRM	Community-Based Natural Resource Management
CEC	Central Empowered Committee (of the Supreme Court)
CFR	Community Forest Resource
CII	Confederation of Indian Industries
CITES	Convention on International Trade in Endangered Species of Wild Fauna and Flora
CM	Chief Minister
CSR	Corporate Social Responsibility
CWLW	Chief Wild Life Warden
DFO	Divisional Forest Officer
DPM	Disc Pasture Meter
DPR	Detailed Project Report
FAC	Forest Advisory Committee
FCA	Forest (Conservation) Act, 1980
FD	Forest Department
FDI	Fire Danger Index
FICCI	Federation of Indian Chambers of Commerce and Industry
FMP	Fire Management Plan
FRA	Forest Rights Act, 2006.
FRI	Fire Return Interval
FRL	Full Reservoir Level
GCF	Grass Curing Factor
GMAs	Game Management Areas
GoI	Government of India
HWC	Human-Wildlife Conflict
HWS	Human-Wildlife Symbiosis
IFA	Indian Forest Act, 1927
IFS	Indian Forest Service
JFM	Joint Forest Management
MFP	Minor Forest Produce (Same as NTFP)
MoEF&CC	Ministry of Environment, Forest & Climate Change
MoTA	Ministry of Tribal Affairs

MP	Madhya Pradesh
MPFD	Madhya Pradesh Forest Department
MPTF	Madhya Pradesh Tiger Foundation
NBWL	National Board for Wild Life
NFP	National Forest Policy
NGT	National Green Tribunal
NHAI	National Highways Authority of India
NPV	Net Present Value
NTCA	National Tiger Conservation Authority
NTFP	Non-Timber Forest Produce (Same as MFP)
PA	Protected Area
PIL	Public Interest Litigation
PM	Prime Minister
PTR	Panna Tiger Reserve
SBWL	State Board for Wild Life
SDTF	Seasonally Dry Tropical Forest
UP	Uttar Pradesh
WII	Wildlife Institute of India
WLPA	Wild Life (Protection) Act, 1972
WTI	Wildlife Trust of India

Acknowledgements

I am deeply indebted to several individuals for assisting me in putting this book together. Without their help, this book would not have been half as useful.

When I was struggling to find Indian research articles on forest fires, a chance conversation with Prof. R. Sukumar and Dr. Sandeep Pula of the Indian Institute of Science opened the door to a treasure trove of information. Rajeev Mathew patiently worked with me to develop the model hunting rules for mammalian pests and to estimate their economic potential. He also read the manuscript several times and sent me some very encouraging comments about the value of the book. My colleague Ram Gopal Soni helped me with up-to-date statistics about the Ken-Betwa river linking project. Ms. Upma Darwal of the Wildlife Institute of India turned over to me her entire collection of research papers on human-wildlife conflict. Dr. Sanjay Shukla provided the latest remote sensing data on forest fires in Madhya Pradesh.

Dr. AJT Johnsingh painstakingly reviewed the manuscript and suggested some very important changes. My senior colleague and friend Ramesh Dave also went over the draft very carefully and made some very valuable suggestions.

Lastly, I thank all the authors whose work I have used in writing this book. Most have been mentioned but I might have missed as many. Without their work and toils, this book could not even be conceived.

Thank you, everybody, from the bottom of my heart.

Preface

I was in the middle of finishing my last book, "Laws At War", when Covid-19 struck. When the book came out in June 2020, everybody said, "So, you have utilised the lockdown well". Even before the flood of customary congratulations died out into a trickle, I started wondering, "now what?"

The answer was not far to seek. I had some good stuff left over from the last book as it did not fit with the overall theme of "Laws At War". This pertained to the question of the viability of wildlife corridors in India and the controversial Ken-Betwa river linking project. I was wondering about a suitable parking place for these essays as I did not want to waste them. Incidentally, I was working with a group developing a national strategy for human wildlife conflict management under a project of the Central Government. There seemed no takers for my kind of solutions in that group. While continuing to implore and cajole my friends into accepting some of my thoughts, I started thinking of putting my version of the story out into the public domain myself. Thus, the book started taking shape in my mind.

But those few essays would not have amounted to be a full book. It is here that my life-long romance with forest fires came into use. For many years, I had been thinking that, like hunting, we have a totally wrong approach to forest fires. So, I thought it would be a good idea to bring the science of forest fires, and the way the rest of the world uses fire in conservation, to the attention of the Indian conservation community. However, the subject became so vast that I had to reserve most of the matter for another book. Only glimpses of how the world handles forest fires are given here.

While I was still contemplating the book, I read that the Chief Wild Life Warden of Gujarat was in trouble with his own government for saying in a webinar that the lion management in the state was on the wrong lines. Although the Gujaratis think that the lion is nobody's business but theirs, I thought it was necessary to tell them that there was a way to have lions without having to feed them cows and, occasionally, people.

Ever since the inception of the Forest Rights Act 2006, I have been advocating that the forest departments must reinvent themselves to stay relevant in an era when most of the forests will be controlled by the communities and the foresters will not have the power to supervise or advise them. Although I have dealt with that Act extensively in my last book, the thought that I had not provided the full suite of solutions was still rankling me. So, I decided to give the issue further thought and the chapter "Living with the Forest Rights Act" was born.

As I have dealt with the subject extensively in my earlier books, wildlife tourism was not in my thoughts right up to the day when I thought I had said what I had in mind. One day, I came to know that the Central Government was relaxing the restrictions on ecotourism imposed under the Forest (Conservation) Act, 1980, but was unable to come out of the old mindset completely. So, I sent them a quick draft of the guidelines that could remove the shackles on ecotourism without violating the Act. I thought it will be useful to share my thinking with the public and a new chapter was born.

Thus, matter kept piling up and finally acquired the shape you have in your hands. It acquired a name only after hundreds were rejected by Jagpreet and Akshara, my son and daughter-in-law, for being too academic or preachy. Now that it is in your hands, I eagerly await to know that you liked it as much as I enjoyed writing it. Like all its siblings, **"Besides Loving the Beasts"** is also an exhortation to the country to look beyond the current conservation strategies and create an environment of symbiosis between people and wild animals, rather than letting them continue to be at each other's throats. I know some people are not going to like what I say. I respect their views but keep wondering why the same facts teach me lessons that others miss. The reason, perhaps, is that I do not accept any religious, moralistic, ideological, or political constraints on my professional beliefs. Somehow, I tend to look at the questions straight in the eye and try to find answers within them. I want wild animals to be around forever and am convinced that they can survive only if they are seen by man as an asset instead of a threat. Especially in places like India where men and dangerous animals have to live as close neighbours.

H.S. Pabla

Bhopal (August 2021).

Introduction

Conservation of wildlife is a sweet, romantic, and pious idea for a lot of people. While that is most welcome, they hardly realise the complexities of this job and the costs borne by remote, rural communities. The preservation of large mammals is particularly problematic as they are often a threat to the lives and well-being of local people. Hundreds of men, women, and children die and thousands suffer crippling injuries in animal attacks each year. Lakhs, perhaps crores, suffer losses of livestock, crops, houses, and sleep, at the hands of these animals. Crores of people lose their livelihoods because their traditional foraging grounds (forests) are converted into protected areas (PAs) for wild animals. The utilisation of these animals in any form is illegal. Even the criticality of the ecological role of big mammals, in keeping natural ecosystems healthy and balanced, is questionable in the modern context as men or machinery can perform most of their functions. We still love and protect them. So much so, that even shooing them out of our fields or homes needs official permission.

But, plain love can take things only so far. At some stage, the cost of feeding your love and its tantrums starts hurting. That is where we are now with regard to wild animals. Even more serious problem with this love affair is that the people who love animals and those who pay the price are different. This scenario can be sustained only by reducing the costs or by generating significant benefits, preferably both, for the suffering lot. Conservation is not only about providing food and water to the animals. It is also about bearing the pain and losses they cause. In order to be able to protect them, we need to make animals desirable to the people, despite the difficulties of having to live with them. Conservation also means warding off what the world throws at wild animals and wild lands in the name of development. Thus, conservation is much more complex than simply loving wild animals.

The first thing that the animals need is adequate space, which is reasonably well-stocked with food, water, and cover for breeding, feeding, and resting. As these requirements can vary from species to species, conservation practitioners need to know how to provide for the needs of all the species that share a common habitat. Although it is a tough ask in itself, we also need to know how much is enough as providing too much for one species may harm the interest of others.

Not only this; managers also need to know how many animals are too many for an area as they also compete with local people for everything i.e., food, water, and space. They spill into the human habitat if there are too many. Provisioning for wildlife has to be often done at the cost of local people. Moreover, animals are always a threat to human life and property. While preserving dangerous animals at the cost of human well-being and safety in any case makes no sense, it may just be impossible in the teeth of public and political opposition that human suffering can trigger.

While the nuances of the conservation versus development debate are well known, we often see the respective protagonists expecting the other side to make compromises. We often forget that there is a limit to the adjustments that one can make without compromising one's own mandate. As development provides for the immediate needs of the society while conservation is for the vague and distant future, conservation is always the loser in this tug-of-war. Although conservation lobbies have to continue to fight the development juggernaut in order to retain whatever little of the wilderness remains in the country, they must also recognise that conservation will always be at the mercy of development. This mercy may not always be forthcoming or be enough. Therefore, it is important to ensure that whatever lands are dedicated to the protection of wildlife, i.e. the PAs, are able to produce and hold viable populations of all native species and that their efficacy is not entirely dependent on the kindness of the development agencies.

As if the pulls and pushes between conservation and development, particularly in the face of continually shrinking land availability in the country, were not enough, we now have a law that says that wildlife habitats, i.e. forests, no longer belong to the government. According to the Forest Rights Act, 2006 (FRA), the forests belong to the local communities and they can claim them as and when they so desire. This has virtually outlawed the way forests and wildlife have been conserved in the country so far. Conservation was so far done either by physically withdrawing people from wildlife habitats or by restricting their use. This is going to become more and more difficult as communities' control over forests progressively grows under the influence of FRA, with no incentive for tolerating wild animals. In fact, this law gives the impression that our love for wildlife is a phony claim.

This book explores all these challenges, and more, in search of viable solutions.

In no other country, so many people live so close to wild animals. The principal challenge in the conservation of wild animals is to minimise the difficulties and dangers that they inflict on local communities. However, the desirability of having wild animals in the neighbourhood is not completely dependent on how little danger they pose to the people. It also depends on what benefits they confer on them. Therefore, the reduction in human-wildlife conflict (HWC) is not only about keeping animals and people reasonably separated, it is also about generating sustainable incomes from wildlife, either through ecotourism or through hunting. Although it is quite fashionable these days to use the expression "human-wildlife co-existence" instead of HWC, the real solutions lie in the realm of human-wildlife symbiosis (HWS). Living with wild animals despite the discomfort and difficulties is co-existence. But, protecting animals for clear-cut economic benefits is symbiosis. That can take conservation to an entirely new level. Our current legal and policy framework is based on the premise that wild animals need human mercy, tolerance, and compassion to survive. It does not make any provision for wild animals improving people's well-being. It does not make adequate provision even for the removal of difficulties caused by wild animals to local people. In fact, in the rush to protect dwindling wildlife, we even forgot that this kind of conservation infringes the constitutional rights of the people to life and property. Even more surprisingly, it never occurred to anyone that letting protected animals cause human death and destruction is a crime under the Indian Penal Code, 1860. This has to change.

Although some ways of creating HWS within the existing regulatory framework are also suggested, the chapter "Living with Predators and Pillagers", advocates substantial changes in the Wild Life (Protection) Act, 1972 (WLPA) in order to make conservation of wildlife really sustainable in the country. This chapter sets the stage for the rest of the book and suggests a strategy to convert conservation into a profitable pursuit from being a liability.

Conservation of wildlife, leading to all the ecosystem services we expect from wild spaces, can become a profitable pursuit if we integrate hunting and tourism into our conservation paradigm and try to make conservation less of an obstacle to other human pursuits. I know that is easier said than done, but this attitude itself can strengthen conservation.

I know very few people will heed my advice to treat hunting as a natural corollary of wildlife management, at least for the time being.

However, there is less reluctance to accepting wildlife tourism (ecotourism) as a means of protecting nature. Despite this acceptance, we have made little headway in spreading and scaling up ecotourism in the last decade or so. The reason is not WLPA, as we would perhaps naturally think. We have deliberately blocked the march of ecotourism in the country by misusing another law, the Forest (Conservation) Act, 1980 (FCA). The law itself has nothing against ecotourism, but the minds that implement it were dead against people enjoying nature until last year. Although there are indications that this attitude is changing, as the amended FCA Rules indicate, it appears the government has still not thought through the whole issue. This is why, despite the recent reforms, ecotourism is unlikely to go far unless we facilitate the active involvement of the private sector. But the new reforms do not address this issue. I have tried to show here that FCA should not come in the way of developing ecotourism if interpret it with a positive mindset. In fact, I use the metaphor "Milking Wild Life" to bring home the point that ecotourism can produce huge benefits for society without having to kill wild animals.

The second challenge is to produce sufficient numbers of all species in the limited space dedicated to their conservation and provide for the requirements of all the species within these protected areas. This challenge needs to be dealt with in two ways. On one hand, we need to know how to create the diverse habitats required by all the species resident in PAs so that sufficient food and shelter (cover) is available to all. On the other, we need to ensure that the wild animals produced in PAs stay in PAs rather than being poached or killed in the conflict in the so-called wildlife corridors. This suggestion is in contradiction to our current conservation model in which we expect PAs to populate adjoining forests through spill-over of animals. My premise is that animals should be allowed to spill over into human-dominated forests only if they can generate any benefits for people as these are the very animals that make conservation unpalatable to the common man. The chapter entitled "Wildlife Corridors: Necessity or Luxury?" examines the conflict between PAs and wildlife corridors and proposes a conservation model in which the efficacy of PAs is not compromised by interconnecting corridors.

The amount of food and cover available in a habitat can be modulated through management. While we use protection as a primary habitat management tool, the world uses prescribed fires. While we treat forest fires only as a destructive force; the rest of the world recognises their creative role as much as their power to consume life and its remains. In this process, fire creates a diversity of habitats, entailing changes in food and cover availability, which multiple animal species can exploit. We have never taken this role of fire into account in wildlife management. I am now sure that we also need to adopt a more nuanced approach towards forest fires rather than putting out even good fires along with bad fires.

The third challenge for conservation is to ensure that the change in the ownership of forest lands ushered in by FRA does not result in the decimation of forests and wildlife. I have dealt with the observed and likely impact of FRA on forests and wildlife in the preceding volume of this series (Laws At War). I had lamented there that the law does not have sufficient checks and balances to ensure that our forests will survive this upheaval. Although I had suggested a "Way Forward" in that book, it was mostly focused on how to align FRA and other forest laws, through amendments, to remove confusion and ensure positive synergies. In the chapter "Living with the Forest Rights Act", I delve deeper into how the forest department and forest management need to reconstruct themselves in a legal environment dominated by FRA as it is today. As it is unlikely that the forest laws and FRA shall be brought into proper alignment any time soon, given the political implications of the subject, I think foresters need to find ways of staying relevant through adaptation rather than keeping their eyes closed to the gathering storm. Irrespective of the fact whether forests and wildlife survive the FRA, forest departments, as we know them today, are certainly doomed. They will have no role in future forest management. This chapter discusses how forest departments can reinvent themselves into desirable service agencies before their managerial and law-enforcement role disappears completely.

"Living with Asiatic Lions" discusses the looming disaster in Gujarat. The situation in Gujarat is completely in line with the uniquely Indian stupidity of people having to live with predators without the freedom to defend themselves. However, I am totally at a loss to understand why the Gujarati people and politicians do not realise the simple fact that they just do not have space for so many lions. Certainly, not for any more. They will have to regularly kill or sell their lions in order to ensure the well-being of the people as well as of the species. Even if better sense prevails and Gujarat allows half a dozen lions to be translocated to Kuno in Madhya Pradesh, as the whole world desires, it is not going to solve the lion problem of Gujarat. They need to remove many more and every year. The sooner they realise it, the better it will be for all stakeholders. They can easily convert their lions into a welfare machine for the state by selling surplus lions to hunters, zoos, or sanctuaries. This chapter explores these options in some detail in the vain hope that it might bring the lion lovers of Gujarat, and India, to their senses. Gujarat government asked its own Chief Wild Life Warden (CWLW) to shut up when he suggested a way out of this mess. It was then that I thought of speaking up for the lions although I am not a lion expert by any measure.

The Chapter entitled "Linking Ken and Betwa: Bane or Boon?" illustrates my own evolution as a conservation practitioner. Perhaps, this happens with everyone. At least it should. I opposed a dam in the heart of Panna National Park when I was its director in the eighties but am now ready to accept it if it comes with all the environmental safeguards and mitigation measures floating around. At that time, there was no law to save the environment if a destructive project was to be located in the middle of a forest. Even FCA was a little helpless baby. Now FCA and WLPA are together a formidable conservation force. The Supreme Court of India has also struck some terror in the hearts of development maniacs in the last two decades or so. As a result, we have started seeing thousands of crores being spent to preserve wildlife corridors likely to be destroyed by highways and railways. As the construction of this dam is a writing on the wall, and it will also be a template for the future, I have come to believe that now our approach should be to extract maximum concessions for nature rather than stubbornly opposing the project. This chapter discusses the evolution of this project in the last 40 or so years and how my own thinking about it has evolved over time.

This book is different from the previous ones although the theme is common. There I have mostly raised questions, while here I am focusing mostly on answers and solutions. If I suggest that new rules need to be made to control mammalian pests, I actually draft these rules. If I think WLPA needs to be modified, I rewrite the relevant sections. I have even drafted the circular which the Central Government can consider issuing to free ecotourism from the contrived clutches of FCA. I hope the authorities will take a serious look at these instruments in order to make the conservation of wildlife a sustainable way of life rather than just being a moral imposition on society. If they do decide to do something, these documents will provide them the prototypes for preparing the conservation policies of the future.

I had originally planned just one book on "Wildlife Conservation in India" but soon I had to announce a trilogy. When the trilogy was done, I still could not stop and this book was born. Perhaps, there will be more. I started writing these books because I seriously thought we should do our conservation differently. However, I have not seen much impact so far perhaps because our mandarins have no time to read anything but their own files. I hope someday someone who matters shall take notice. I wish it happens before I say goodbye to the world. Because nothing matters after that.

CHAPTER-1

Living with Predators and Pillagers

Managing Human-Wildlife Conflict

Competition and conflict between organisms, even of the same species, are fundamental to life on earth. This competition is primarily for space, food, and water. Human beings are as much a part of this struggle for survival as other animals. In fact, human beings are at loggerheads with all other species, particularly in densely populated countries like India where people have to live cheek by jowl with wild animals.

Throughout history, wild animals have been human food. Man was also food for some animals. This relationship has continued to evolve, with human beings gradually going off the menu of carnivores. However, their livestock and crops started attracting animals as agriculture and animal husbandry became major human occupations over time. As long as men were free to hunt animals attracted by their crops, this conflict also had an element of symbiosis. But, with the advent of modern conservation and consequent prohibition of lethal means for dealing with wild animals in the country, the symbiosis element has been dismantled. As a result, all ungulates living near human habitations are now seen as a threat by local communities. On the other hand, a large part of the food of carnivores is domestic livestock, primarily taken when grazing in the forests. Although human beings are no longer the staple of any predator, thousands of them still fall prey to chance encounters as well as deliberate attacks from, carnivores, elephants, bears, pigs, crocodiles, etc. Occasionally, some large cats and wolves just forget that human beings are no longer their food and turn what we usually call man-eaters. Millions more suffer because their bread winners are killed or because their means of livelihood are destroyed or degraded by wild animals.

Apart from the actual damage caused by wild animals, the vulnerable communities have to incur huge expenses on the protection of their crops and other assets through fencing and guarding. The loss in the quality of their life, with having to spend hundreds of sleepless nights out in the open guarding their crops, mostly in the worst of weathers, is almost immeasurable.

While wild animals harm human interests or lives as it naturally comes to them, thousands of them are killed by the victim communities through retaliatory or preventive actions, such as electrocution, snaring, and poisoning. Many thousands also perish in road accidents. Thus, human beings and wild animals usually live as bickering and warring neighbours. However, we call it HWC when an animal kills a man, not the other way round. It is also important to note that killing of animals for profit is not considered HWC, but killing to reduce their threat to human interests is. Quite often, however, the two objectives are intertwined.

In fact, conflict between conservation and local communities runs much deeper than just the losses incurred by people through physical encounters with animals. Thousands of people lose access to their traditional resources when their neighbourhood forests are converted into PAs. Although relocation of people to create PAs is meant to be voluntary or consensual, relocation itself is an admission that people and animals cannot coexist happily. Shared habitats, i.e. the forests outside PAs, where local people graze their livestock and obtain their forest produce from, are even more active theatres of human-wildlife conflict as most of the human and livestock casualties take place there. The ambit of conservation is further expanding in the form of buffer zones and eco-sensitive zones around PAs, extending even further into wildlife corridors and conservation landscapes crisscrossing the country. This often obstructs energy and infrastructure development projects far away from PAs and impacts a much larger section of the society than just the rural communities.

Thus, the popular concept of HWC, that it "arises when animals pose a direct threat to the livelihood or safety of people and this results in persecution of that species" (IUCN) does not fully express the vast spectrum of the ways HWC can express itself.

Patterns and Extent of HWC in India

The nature and intensity of HWC varies from state to state, even within states. Elephants, blue bulls, wild pigs, and monkeys are the most important crop depredators in the country. Species like rhinos, gaur, some deer and antelopes, bears, bats, etc. also cause significant crop damage in some states. Birds like parakeets, crows, peacocks, ducks, geese, etc. perhaps do as much damage, if not more, to crops, as other wild mammals, but these losses seem to have been internalised by the society to a large extent. While people affected by the mammalian depredations are often angry and vocal, we rarely notice popular anger against bird damage.

Apart from damaging crops, elephants extensively destroy houses and infrastructure, and kill or maim nearly a thousand people each year. Carnivores like leopards, tigers, lions, bears (all species), wolves, and crocodiles also earn "man-eater" tags off and on. Jackals sometimes become a serious threat to human life when affected by rabies. Bears cause most non-fatal human injuries, while leopard attacks in Uttarakhand are almost a daily affair.

Along with crop losses, loss of livestock to carnivores is the commonest manifestation of HWC across wild India. Tigers, lions, leopards, wolves, wild dogs, bears (mainly Himalayan black and brown bears), and snow leopard regularly prey on livestock. Lions, leopards, and snow leopards entering cattle sheds or sheep pens and killing dozens of animals in one go is also not uncommon. Our wildlife conservation strategies must take into account the potential for these conflicts in order to ensure sustainable success.

Herbivores raid crops because of lack of fodder and water inside their habitats as well as because agricultural crops are often more attractive and nutritious. Livestock is generally killed by predators while grazing in forests and pastures. Attacks in their pens are less common but not rare. Predation on livestock is often attributed to the lack of natural prey. However, some animals just become habituated to killing domestic animals, perhaps because they are easier to kill. Human beings often get attacked by predators while out defecating or collecting fuel wood, fodder, or non-timber forest produce (NTFP). These attacks come usually when people are in crouching positions and can be confused with ungulate prey, often at dawn or dusk. Some animals may lose the fear of man due to frequent exposure and may also learn to deliberately stalk human beings over time. Man-eaters looking for human prey in villages is much rarer now than depicted by hunters like Jim Corbett in their fabled books. The rarity of attacks on humans by carnivores living with humans in some places, as, for example, leopards in Mumbai and lions in Gujarat, goes to show that these animals are perhaps as concerned about avoiding HWC as we humans do.

Wild animals are killed by man either because they are dangerous and harmful or because their meat and trophies are valuable. Despite

HWC being the principal sticking point for wildlife and people in the country, no data is actively collected by any government agency which may help in creating a national picture of the situation. Therefore, the only way to get some sense of the extent of HWC in the country is to glean through research papers, media reports and questions asked in various legislatures. Although sketchy, the following scenario emerges on the basis of the information found here and there:

- Anand and Radhakrishna (2017) reported that 90% of the country is affected by HWC, involving 88 species belonging to nine taxonomic groups.
- Thomassen, *et al.* (2011) reported the following picture of HWC, for a two-year period (2006-07 and 2007-08) on the basis of a national survey:

Table 1: Human-Wildlife Conflict in India.

Category of Loss	Number	Compensation Paid (million Rupees)
Human Deaths	888	75.2
Human Injuries	7381	34.0
Livestock Deaths	14144	37.4
Crop Damage (Complaints)	80956	100.0

In the above survey, 622 forest divisions from 25 states, out of 804 in 28 states, responded to the questionnaire. This makes it perhaps the most comprehensive HWC survey undertaken so far. Elephant was found to be responsible for the largest number of human deaths while jackal was found to be the culprit for most human injuries, mainly in Madhya Pradesh (MP).

- Rangarajan *et al.* (2010) mention that elephant-related conflict alone damages 0.80 to one million hectares of crops, affecting over 5,00,000 farmers and destroys 10,000-15,000 properties, apart from killing over 400 persons annually.
- In a survey of 735 households from 347 villages surrounding Kanha Tiger Reserve, Karanth *et al.* (2012)

report that, "Seventy-three percent of households reported crop loss and 33% livestock loss in the previous year, but less than 8% reported human injury or death."

- Karanth *et al.* (2017) also report that in a survey of 5,000 households around 11 tiger reserves, "Crops were lost by 71% of households, livestock by 17%, and human injury and death were reported by 3% of households (losses attributed to 32 species)."

- In another study, Karanth *et al.* (2018) report that "In 2012–2013, a total of 78,656 conflict incidents were reported from 18 states with complete data. Of these incidents, 73.4% were crop loss and property damage, 20% livestock predation, 6.2% human injury, and 0.4% human death."

- According to The Corbett Foundation (2017), 1456 cases of human injury have been recorded in the Kanha-Pench Corridor between 2001 and 2015, of which 41% were caused by wild boar, 24% by sloth bear, and 22% by jackal. Other animals, including tiger, leopard, and langur amounted to 13% of the attacks. Outside PAs, attacks were predominantly more by jackal (57%), followed by wild pig (16%), and sloth bear (13%). Within PAs, documented attacks were more by langur/macaques (24%), followed by wild pig (22%), and sloth bear (19%). Fatal incidents amounted to 47 in the past 15 years, most (16) because of sloth bears, followed by wild boar, tiger, and jackal. In terms of the number of human fatalities, sloth bear (30%) caused highest number of deaths in non-PA, followed by jackal (29%) and wild pig (16%). Tiger (64%) caused the highest number of deaths in PA, followed by wild pig (16%), leopard (8%), and sloth bear contributed 6% of fatalities.

Apart from such research reports, online media also provides glimpses of the state of HWC in the country. The following reports are note-worthy:

- "With 17 people killed by tigers in the past five weeks in the four Indian states of Uttar Pradesh, Karnataka, Tamil Nadu, and Maharashtra, angry residents of affected areas are threatening to take the law into their own hands."

<https://www.bbc.com/news/world-asia-india-25755104>(January 20, 2014)

- "A man-eating tiger on the prowl in northern India has claimed its ninth victim, defying hunters and wildlife officials who have been trying to gun down the animal, an official said Friday.
Since December 29, the same big cat is believed to have been on a killing spree in a densely forested area near Jim Corbett National Park in the northern state of Uttar Pradesh."   <https://www.businessinsider.in/Man-Eating-Tiger-Still-At-Large-In-India-After-9th-Kill/articleshow/30001067.cms> (February 07, 2014)

- In a piece entitled 'Why do leopards kill humans?' *The Hindu* published the following account of man-eating leopards in Maharashtra in its June 2, 2016 edition:
"After years of hardly any man-eating incidents, leopards suddenly started targeting people in the verdant valley of Junnar, Maharashtra, where farmers grew sugarcane, maize, and bananas. In 2001, leopards attacked 50 people and killed 29. The usual speculations were bandied: lack of forest, lack of wild prey animals, disturbance from a dam, and extensive sugarcane fields. But the problem lay elsewhere.
A research project by Kaati Trust uncovered that several months before man-eaters struck, the forest department (FD) began a programme of trapping leopards from sugarcane fields and releasing them in the nearest forest. By the time nearly 150 relocations had taken place, attacks on people became frequent. Villagers were nervous wrecks. Released man-eaters attack people in the new area. A leopard suspected of killing seven people in March-April 2013 was trapped on the edge of Tadoba Tiger Reserve and released inside the forest. Within a week, six people in a nearby village were killed."
(https://www.thehindu.com/news/cities/chennai/chen-columns/why-do-leopards-killhumans/article5124009.ece)

- Nagpur edition of the Times of India, dated 14th May 2019, reported that, "In over three years (2016-2019), 34 human deaths and 304 cases of human injuries have been officially reported in wild animal attacks in Brahmpuri division alone. The government paid Rs. 16.52 crore compensation which includes for cattle kills and crop damage".

- *The Hindu* again reported on 22nd April, 2017: "The Ministry of Environment, Forests, and Climate Change has recorded 98 human deaths due to tiger attack from April 1, 2013 to March 31, 2017. As per the report, the number of human deaths due to elephant attacks from April 1, 2009 to March 31, 2016 was 2,804."

- A report published in *The Guardian* on August 1, 2017, gives the following figures on HWC in India:
"Statistics released this week by India's environment ministry reveal that 1,144 people were killed between April 2014 and May 2017. That figure breaks down to 426 human deaths in 2014-15, and 446 the following year.
Of the 1,052 lives claimed by elephants in the last three years, many had simply been in the way when the pachyderms wandered out of jungles in search of vegetation and raided farmers' crops."

- Another report in *The Hindustan Times*, dated June 13, 2018 gave the following account of the cases of human deaths and injuries caused by wild leopards and tigers in Uttarakhand:
"The mountain state has in the last 13 years declared 182 big cats, including 166 leopards and 16 tigers, as man-eaters. In the last 13 years, 45 leopards have been killed after being declared man-eaters. As many as 15 leopards and three tigers were declared man-eaters in 2016. In 2017, officials found that 16 big cats were declared a threat to human life. Of the 10 animals declared man-eater in the first six months of 2018, seven are leopards, one is a tiger, and two elephants.
Going by the official figures of the forest department, in the past one decade, the highest 24 man-eaters were declared in 2009. They included 20 leopards and four tigers.
As per the RTI (Right to Information Act) reply, between 2006 till 2016, hunters gunned down 45 leopards that were declared man-eaters. Officials close to the matter said that nearly 50% of the big cats declared man-eaters were rescued and released in other areas to contain conflict. Even the department does not want to kill these animals----."

- *The Tribune* of September 18, 2018 reported that, in Himachal Pradesh, "The wild animal nuisance has been a major cause of concern and it causes a loss of Rs 229 crore per annum to farmers as per government estimates, but a survey conducted by an NGO, Gyan Vigyan Samiti, has put the loss between Rs 400 and Rs 500 crore."

- According to a Marathi newspaper, *Sakaal* dated 17th September 2020, an astounding 53 persons lost their lives in human- wildlife conflict in Maharashtra in the first 9 months of 2020.

- In a report entitled "Human-leopard conflict rises in Uttarakhand, over 10 people killed in 2 months", Suparna Roy reported in the October 14, 2020 issue of *The Hindustan Times* that "75 leopards have been declared dangerous to human life (or declared as 'man-eaters') this year till August. Last year, 55 leopards were declared dangerous to human life."

- "Till October 30 this year (2020), 50 people have already been killed (nearly half of them by leopards) and 214 injured in attacks by wild animals in the state (Uttarakhand) (*Times of India*, Dehradun, November 22, 2020).

- The Nagpur edition of *Times of India* mentioned on 3rd December 2020 that 28 persons had been killed by tigers and leopards in 2020 in Chanda (Chandrapur) district of Maharashtra alone. Four of them were killed by leopards.

- "Responding to a query in Lok Sabha, Minister of State (MoS) for Environment, Babul Supriyo said 2,398 people have died since 2014 up to March 31, 2019 due to human-elephant conflict---- 516 in 2017-18 and 494 in 2018-2019 --- tiger-human conflict has killed 224 persons in India in the last five years" (*PTI*, New Delhi, 28 June, 2019).

The list of such horror reports is unending.

The state of Madhya Pradesh is attempting to create an online database on HWC although the entries in the database are lagging seriously behind. A glimpse at the current state of the data leads to some very interesting inferences.

Table 2: Human deaths and injuries caused by wild animals in MP.

Species**	2014		2015		2016*		2017*	
	Deaths	Injuries	Deaths	Injuries	Deaths	Injuries	Deaths	Injuries
Jackal	15	628	10	505	0	275	0	23
Wild Pig	12	297	5	211	7	185	1	22
Sloth Bear	8	207	10	153	0	84	0	7
Monkeys	2	203	1	68	0	75	0	7
Fox	4	148	2	47	0	11	0	13
Wolf	2	27	3	21	1	44	0	1
Panther	13	47	3	20	4	8	1	2
Hyena	1	36	1	19	1	10	0	5
Tiger	8	10	5	6	3	7	0	0
Nilgai	1	?	0	7	1	3	0	0
Unknown	0	12	0	2	0	0	0	0
Wild dogs	0	6	1	3	0	0	0	0
Gaur	0	3	0	2	1	3	0	0
Mugger	0	3	3	0	0	2	0	0
Chital	0	3	0	1	0	1	0	0
Elephant	0	1	3	0	0	0	0	0
Sambar	0	0	0	0	0	2	0	0
Blackbuck	0	0	0	2	0	0	0	0
Unidentified	0	7	0	2	0	2	0	0
Total	66	1640	47	1069	18	712	2	80

*Data for these years seems to be particularly incomplete.

It is clear from the above table that it is major carnivores are not the only ones that kill and injure people. The jackal has been the principal tormentor of people in Madhya Pradesh for many years now, while the pigs, sloth bears, monkeys (mainly rhesus), and wolves also cause more casualties than tigers and leopards. Even hyenas seem to attack more people than tigers. The number of persons affected by HWC is huge as seen from the data for the years 2014 and 2015. MP did not have wild elephants until recently but the species is becoming almost residential in eastern MP now and regular casualties by elephants are being reported.

HWC and Crop Losses

Apart from the single report from Himachal Pradesh about the level of crop damage mentioned above, there is no assessment of the extent of damage done or the cost of guarding crops in any other state despite the fact that this is the biggest element in HWC. As a result, the country does not know and understand the full gravity of the situation, despite the blood-chilling reports mentioned above.

Once I tried to get some sense of the situation in Madhya Pradesh through a very crude exercise. The year was 2002. I asked three divisional forest officers (DFOs) of the state to give me their assessment of the quantum of losses caused by wild animals in their divisions. A common methodology was suggested to them. The assessment was to be done along transects radiating from the forest boundary, passing through the adjoining croplands, in terms of percentage loss, determined ocularly, in consultation with the owners. The average loss came to be Rs. 1,067 per hectare, up to a distance of two kilometres from the forest boundary. Even more significant than the actual loss, which often varied with the level of effort invested by the farmers in guarding their crops, was the cost of crop guarding and fencing. Farmers spent at least 100 days and nights guarding their crops in the worst of weather (monsoon and winters). We did some rough calculations as to how much cropland will fall within the vulnerable zone and how many farmers would involve. We found that while the actual loss was nearly Rs. 94 crores only, the cost of crop protection in terms of labour and materials came to around Rs. 528 crores per annum. Converting these figures into current prices, the total comes to around Rs. 1,872 crores, on the basis of the cost inflation index (CII) for 2020-21 (The CII notified for 2020-21 is 301 with 2001-02 as the base year). As the forests of Madhya Pradesh are roughly 10% of the forests of India, the all-India figure may be taken as Rs. 18,720 crores. An important point to be noted is that this cost is borne by the poorest of our farmers in the remotest parts of the country where agriculture is often a subsistence activity. Although these figures are very crude underestimates, they do give some idea of the scale of HWC in India. In fact, the actual scale of the problem must be many times more as HWC has now spread to many more areas since 2002 and the damage is also prevalent far away from forest boundaries. I was surprised to learn from my own relatives in Punjab about the resurfacing of wild pig and nilgai menace in areas where they had not seen them for generations.

To compound the matters, damage perceived by people is often much more than the damage actually caused by wild animals. In a recent study by the Wildlife Institute of India (WII), Pandav *et al.* (2021) the decrease in wheat yield in the fields damaged by wild pigs in the study area was only 2.5% while the farm owners believed it to be 23.4%. However, perceptions are as important in a democracy as the reality.

The above reports are extremely horrifying, to say the least. It is obvious that the intensity and spread of HWC in India are unbelievable. The quality of life of the people who live under constant fear and discomfort and suffer loss of life and livelihoods cannot even be imagined by the rest. India is a very special country where wild animals are tolerated despite causing so much havoc. It happens nowhere else.

Wild Life and the Constitution of India

The Directive Principles of State Policy state that "The State shall endeavour to protect and improve the environment and to safeguard the forests and wild life of the country" (Article 48A). The obligation to "protect and improve the natural environment including forests, lakes, rivers, and wild life, and to have compassion for living creatures" has also been included in the Fundamental Duties of the citizens of India {Article 51A (g)}.

Prima facie, these provisions look natural for any civilized society. However, if these provisions mean no control or management of the populations of wild animals, as the country seems to interpret them, they are obviously a danger to human life and property, as both can be food for wild animals. This puts these provisions in conflict with two other important features of the constitution, namely, the right to life (Article 21) and the right to property (Article 300A).

Article 21 says that "No person shall be deprived of his life or personal liberty except according to procedure established by law". Article 300A states that "No person shall be deprived of his property save by authority of law". Thus, whether the deaths and losses caused by wild animals protected by law amount to the deprivation of life and property by the state in violation of Article 21 and 300A should be an interesting question to examine. Surprisingly, nobody has asked the courts to ponder this question so far.

Further, the obligation on the part of the state and citizens to "safeguard" and "protect" wild life, or to "have compassion for living creatures" cannot be fulfilled as long as wild animals are a threat to the well-being of the people. In fact, people have a natural right to kill animals in order to protect themselves against their depredations. This right has been taken away by WLPA as even driving wild animals out of your property amounts to hunting which cannot be done without a permit. If people are not allowed by the law to defend themselves against protected animals, they should be entitled to suitable compensation for any losses suffered by them, although some losses just cannot be compensated. Although most states do provide financial assistance to the victims of animal depredations, there is no law that obliges them to do so. It is paid as an *ex-gratia* assistance i.e. as a favour or out of a sense of moral obligation rather than because of any legal requirement. An alternative approach to protect and safeguard wild life, as mandated by the constitution, without infringing the right of the citizens to life and property, could have been to manage wild life as a natural resource for the benefit of the people rather than protecting it only by the force of law. Any loss of life or property, in that case, would be incidental to people's livelihoods, more like any other occupational or civic hazard. Thus, it is important to make all-out efforts to keep HWC down to tolerable levels and even find ways to transform the human-wildlife relationship into a mutually beneficial one in order to enable the state and the people to meet their constitutional obligations.

HWC and Wild Life (Protection) Act, 1972

Fencing, killing, capturing, or driving are the only means of keeping menacing wild animals away. All these solutions, except fencing, are defined as "hunting" by the Wild Life (Protection) Act, 1972 {Section 2 (16) (b)}. The law also specifies the conditions under which problem animals can be hunted. Broadly, wild animals can be hunted:

(a) If they become dangerous to human life or property (Section 11);

(b) For scientific management, education, scientific research, and collection of specimens for zoos and museums. Snakes can also be captured for the collection of snake venom. However, animals cannot be killed for the purpose of scientific management. They can only be captured and translocated (Section 12).

(c) For "improvement and better management" of wild life in sanctuaries (Section 29) and national parks {Section 35 (6)}.

(d) When a species is declared vermin in a specified area (Section 9).

Strangely, animals cannot be killed in the name of "scientific management" but we can "destroy" or "exploit" them in the name of "improvement and better management of wild life" in a PA although both expressions mean the same thing. Our law is full of such contradictions.

Although all these provisions can be used to manage HWC, section 11 is specifically tailored for this purpose. The Chief Wild Life Warden (CWLW) of the state is the authority to issue permits for hunting problem animals. His authority under Section 11 is absolute while he needs to go through a series of approvals, depending on the species and the legal status of the land involved, if he wants to allow hunting under any other provisions.

The law has classified Indian wild animals into two groups (schedules) and has specified the HWC conditions under which they can be hunted. Species belonging to schedule I can be hunted *only* if they become dangerous to human life {Section 11 (1) (a)}. Other animals can be hunted if they are a threat to human life *or* property, including standing crops {Section 11 (1) (b)}. Hunting cannot be done without a permit from the CWLW or any other officer authorized in this regard, although killing an animal in personal or another person's defence is not an offence {Section 11 (2)}.

Interestingly, "driving" away wild animals and "every attempt to do so" is also defined as hunting in the Act {Section 2 (16) (b)}. This has created a strange situation as even shooing dangerous animals away also requires official permission. Thank God, nobody has yet been prosecuted for pushing wild animals out of his house or crops. Otherwise, every farmer would have been a criminal.

Animals hunted under Sections 11, 29, or 35 are state property (Section 39). This means they can be consumed, transferred, or traded by the hunter only if permitted by the government. The practice of burning or burying the carcasses, even of vermin, prevalent in most states, is not mandatory under the law.

Section 44 provides for issuing licenses for setting up businesses in manufacturing of wildlife articles and dealing in live animals, trophies, meat, etc. Species (or their parts/derivatives) belonging to

Schedule I of the Act cannot be traded. However, no such licenses are actually being issued at present, except, perhaps, a few taxidermists in Karnataka and Maharashtra. Thus, as no licensed dealers exist in the country and because the public is obliged to purchase any wild animals or animal products (meat, trophies, etc.) only from a licensed dealer (Section 49), no animals hunted under Sections 11, 12, 29, or 35 can be sold, transferred, or traded. Therefore, animals killed in the name of managing HWC can be self-consumed if permitted (being state property), but they cannot be transferred or sold to anybody else. Punjab is the only state that allows the hunter consumption of hunted animals (only wild pigs) at present. Although the order specifically prohibits the sale of meat, pork is widely available in the Punjab countryside now.

While our conservatism about allowing hunting liberally is understandable, doing it at the cost of people's lives and well-being is utterly nonsensical. Perhaps this is being done under the notion that the law (although the laws are not cast in stone) allows hunting only when an animal has *actually* done some damage to human life or property. Its consumption is prohibited because all animals, dead or alive, are state property. I think both these notions are wrong. Section 11 says that the CWLW has to be *satisfied* that an animal or a group of animals has become dangerous before allowing its hunting. He/she is not required to wait till the damage has been actually done. His/her satisfaction can be based on several factors, such as the aggressive behaviour of an animal, its inability to hunt its natural prey due to age, disease, or injury, its foraying dangerously close to human habitation, its overpopulation in areas frequented by people, and so on. Similarly, the state as the owner of dead animals can very well decide what to do with them. They can be given away to poor people as food rather than ordering their destruction through burning and burial. Another notion that restrictions on hunting and consumption of wildlife will eliminate the demand for wildlife is also misplaced. It is now well-established that bans and restrictions do not curb consumption; they just push them underground. Liquor is the well-known example.

Wildlife Conservation an Official Crime?

Causing human death or injury or loss of property, willfully or negligently, is a crime as per the Indian Penal Code 1860 (IPC). As wild animals are the property of the State (Section 39 of WLPA), any death, injury, or loss caused by them amounts to having been caused by the State. The depredating animals are only the instruments (weapons) with which the crimes are committed by the State. When the country decided to protect wild animals without taking responsibility for protecting people against their depredations, it inadvertently decided to commit a variety of crimes against its own people. As the State knows that these animals can cause death, injury, or loss of property, and still does not take adequate steps to prevent these dangers, these offences perhaps fall in the willful category rather than those committed by negligence. Taking away people's right to private defence against intruding animals further compounds the gravity of this crime (You cannot kill or expel wild animals on your property without official permission). The sections of the IPC violated by the government in causing human death, injury, or property losses through wild animals are as follows:

- Section 289: Negligent conduct with respect to an animal (knowingly or negligently omitting to take such order with any animal in one's possession as is sufficient to guard against any probable danger to human life, or any probable danger of grievous hurt from such animal).
- Section 299: Culpable Homicide (unintentionally causing bodily injury or death but with the knowledge that the act is likely to cause it).
- Sections 321 and 322: Voluntarily causing hurt/grievous hurt.
- Sections 336, 337, and 338: Endangering life or personal safety, causing hurt by endangering life or personal safety, and causing grievous hurt by endangering life or personal safety, through rash or negligent acts.
- Section 378: Theft (wild animals eating crops and livestock).
- Section 425: Mischief (to knowingly cause destruction of any person's property or diminish its value).

I always had an uncomfortable feeling that imposing such severe costs on poor people in the name of conservation was unfair and immoral. It never occurred to me that conservation can be a plain and simple crime. The realisation that I was part of a crime machine for 35 years is very unsettling, to say the least. This also makes all the conservationists, conservation NGOs, and researchers abettors in this crime. It is unbelievable that a nation can carry on an immoral, unconstitutional, illegal, financially unviable, and ecologically unsustainable agenda for half a century without anybody ever questioning it. *Mera Bharat Mahaan* (My India is Great)! It is obvious that we run a serious risk of conservation, the way we do it, being outlawed in the country by some court. It is just a question of someone filing a PIL.

Current Approaches to HWC Management in India

The primary responsibility to deal with the threat from wild animals in India is of the affected individual or community. The law does not allow the public to kill or capture threat animals without a permit, which is difficult to obtain and costly to operate. Therefore, most vulnerable individuals and communities use fences and guarding as their primary defence against animal depredations, apart from electrocuting, snaring, and poisoning the marauding animals illegally. Incidentally, nobody knows that even driving animals away without official permission is also a crime.

Fences are primarily used to protect crop lands and can range from simple thorns, brushwood and barbed wire to wire mesh (chain-link) and electric fencing. Private chain-link and power fences are still uncommon as they are expensive to install and need continuous maintenance. Quite often, farmers connect barbed wire and chain-link fences to power transmission lines, rather than using proper pulsating-current fences. This results in the deaths of thousands of animals, including the non-threat species.

Although guarding practices vary from area to area, depending upon local cropping practices and threat species, almost everywhere farmers in the vulnerable areas have to spend 100-150 days a year watching their crops day and night, often in chilling winters and pouring rains. Apart from severely affecting their quality of life and imposing severe financial strain, the practice also has severe social costs. Many families cannot send their kids to school because they have to guard crops. Death or injury to an earning member of a family in HWC may impact the future of his/her children even more seriously. Quite often a single breach of the fence, or a day's slackness in guarding, may result in very serious losses to farmers.

In some places, farmers in vulnerable areas cultivate crops that are repugnant to problem animals. Mustard cultivation is popular in Madhya Pradesh partly because it is not liked by nilgai and pigs, while tobacco, chilli, and ginger fields are less damaged by elephants in South India.

Government Interventions for HWC Management

Although the law imposes no obligation on the state to protect the public against wild animals, as mentioned before, most states still have policies to assist people in coping with HWC. State interventions in HWC are primarily of three kinds, namely:

- Compensation or financial assistance, often called *ex gratia* payments, to victims;
- Permitting killing or capture of threat animals; and
- Erecting fences on forest boundaries or subsidising individual/community fences for crop protection.

Karanth *et al.* (2018) report that out of India's 29 states, "22 (76%) compensated for crop loss, 18 (62%) for property damage, 26 (90%) for livestock depredation, and 28 (97%) for human injury or death in 2012-13." The average expenditure per incident worked out thus: For crop and property damage, Rs 3,406; for livestock, Rs 5,363; for human injuries, Rs 7,465; and human death, Rs 233,715. Maharashtra paid the most for human injuries, Rs 1.15 crore, followed by Madhya Pradesh, Rs 1.12 crore. (original figures in US dollars).

Although compensation schemes are mostly state-funded, subsidised marginally by the Centre, some NGOs also run compensation programmes that are often locality or species specific.

Although subsidised agricultural insurance schemes have existed in India since 1985, forest departments or conservationist lobbies never tried to use them for managing HWC. However, the revised (2020) Operational Guidelines of the current crop insurance scheme, called Pradhan Mantri Fasal Bima Yojna (PMFBY), have a provision for "Add-on coverage for crop loss due to attack by wild animals" for a "notional premium" which may be further subsidised by the states.

Carnivora are often ordered to be hunted (killed or captured) by the states when these animals show tendencies to deliberately attack human beings. As mentioned before, Uttarakhand alone orders the hunting of more than 15 man-eaters, mostly leopards, every year. The number was 55 in 2019 and an astounding 75 (and counting) in 2020. Animals branded as man-eaters or habitual cattle lifters are often captured and kept in captivity. Maharashtra and Gujarat translocate hundreds of leopards to distant forests each year but they are often reported to come back to their native ranges.

Many states, such as Madhya Pradesh, Maharashtra, Gujarat, Uttar Pradesh (UP), Punjab, Telangana, Haryana, etc. have permit systems in place for hunting crop-raiding *nilgai* and wild pig. However, virtually no hunting has been done under these rules/orders as the states, except Punjab, generally do not allow the consumption of their meat. Religious beliefs against the killing of animals, particularly *nilgai*, also come in the way. Himachal Pradesh has been allowing hunting of rhesus macaque for many years but virtually no animals have been killed due to religious reasons. The Government of India (GoI) has also been declaring wild pig, *nilgai,* and rhesus macaque as vermin in certain areas of Uttarakhand, Bihar, Karnataka, Himachal Pradesh, etc. from time to time. However, very few animals are killed under this arrangement as well, perhaps, because hunting is expensive and enormously difficult, and time-consuming. For this reason, Bihar used the services of hired hunters to kill problem animals. The Government of Telangana, under advice from GoI, recently empowered the village *sarpanchas* (Village Heads) to allow the killing of wild pigs. But no funds for burning and burying the carcasses or for paying the hunters have been provided. Obviously, the order is likely to be futile.

In addition to allowing killing, some states, namely, Himachal Pradesh (HP), Uttarakhand, Chhattisgarh, have also set up sophisticated facilities for controlling rhesus monkeys through sterilisation. Despite neutering thousands of monkeys, the problem is not anywhere near a solution although the growth rate seems to be coming down in HP.

Mass translocation of crop-raiding animals like *nilgai*, blackbuck, and wild pig is rather rare, especially because the numbers involved are too large and the Indian expertise in mass capture methods is almost non-existent. However, Andhra Pradesh has translocated thousands of blackbucks from croplands to forest areas with the help of traditional hunting communities (*Chenchu* tribals). Most of these animals die soon after translocation due to shock. Recently, Madhya Pradesh tried to develop a capacity for mass capture of *nilgai* based on the South African technique of driving animals into a boma (enclosure). They used even helicopters and horses to drive the animals in. But the effort seems to have been abandoned in view of the high cost of such operations.

Mass translocation of animals also suffers from the fundamental handicap that there are virtually no places to receive these animals and it often amounts to relocating the problem rather than solving it. Of course, most animals return to their native ranges in due course.

States erect fences, even walls, around forest areas to prevent encroachments and illegal grazing. These fences also prevent animal depredations to various degrees. Their impact is limited because most wild animals can easily jump over (e.g. *nilgai*) or pass through or under (e.g. wild pig) these fences, which are often vandalised by local people. Most states with wild elephants and rhinos have found solar-powered electric fences on forest boundaries effective in controlling depredations. Fences consisting of old railway tracks are reported to be quite effective against elephants in Karnataka, although they are very expensive to erect. Elephant-proof trenches, which used to be popular in the past and still exist, are no longer a favoured solution perhaps due to the risk of triggering soil erosion, among other things. Innovative technological interventions to control elephant movements are also being tested in some places. These include the use of electronic diverters on railway lines, drones and imitation of bee-humming, etc.

Governments also erect fences of various kinds on PA boundaries to prevent crop losses by herbivores. These include chain-link fences, power fences, or just rubble walls. Rajasthan has built extensive masonry walls on forest boundaries. The city of Hardwar in Uttarakhand has a masonry wall around it to prevent elephant depredations. Madhya Pradesh has erected a fence to keep tigers out of the capital city of Bhopal. Interestingly, villagers often resent fences around forests, sometimes even those erected for crop protection, as fences also cut off their access to the forests.

Some states, namely, Himachal Pradesh, Rajasthan, Gujarat, and Punjab, have recently started schemes to provide subsidies on crop fencing. Although the states provide 50% to 85% subsidy, these schemes are still not popular as the burden on the beneficiaries is still quite substantial.

"Mitigation of Human-Wildlife Conflict" is a part of the National Wildlife Action Plan (2017-2031) of India. It gives a list of measures to be undertaken in this regard and prescribes the "scientific management" of wildlife populations and the participation of affected communities as the principal strategies (among others) for HWC management. It also provides a list of "Priority Projects" along with the names of the organisations responsible for various actions. While all the actions proposed in it are important, it does not address the core issues of generating benefits from wildlife to make HWC less painful and the legal and administrative hindrances in mitigating HWC.

Global Experience in HWC Management

As expected, a variety of approaches to HWC management are prevalent in the world. Some salient features of these approaches are as follows:

- In South Africa, wild animals have to be kept within fenced areas. If a dangerous animal escapes a fenced area, it is the responsibility of the landowner to kill it.
- Animals causing damage to crops or property in most African countries can be killed by the landowner or by government agencies. Killing animals in self-defence, including in the defence of crops, livestock, or other property, is legal in many countries although government agencies try to minimise autonomous action by affected people by intervening as soon as possible.
- Although many countries pay compensation for losses, these payments are aimed more at species conservation (preventing killing) rather than an obligation to compensate wildlife damage. Many African countries do not pay any compensation on the premise that it does not address the root cause of the conflict. Many countries and NGOs run compensation programmes in kind, such as providing livestock, food, equipment, job opportunities, hunting opportunities, etc. rather than providing cash compensation.
- In the USA and Canada, wild animals on private property can be hunted with the permission of the landowner. However, compensation for crop losses or property losses can be claimed if non-lethal methods are used to prevent damage, and, if the landowner has enrolled in a wildlife damage prevention programme (systems vary from state to state) (Wagner *et al.* 1997). Quite often the loss verifying and paying agencies are separate.
- In Europe (e.g. Scotland, Germany, Holland), the conflict between farmers and the grazing needs of migratory geese is managed by an integrated approach, consisting of hunting, compensation, and providing alternative feeding grounds (Boere *et al.* 2006).

- Government-managed compensation schemes are generally considered unsustainable in Africa because of: Bureaucratic inadequacies • Corruption • Cheating, Fraudulent claims • Time and costs involved • Moral hazard • Practical barriers that less-literate farmers must overcome to generate a compensation claim • Difficult to manage • Require reliable and mobile personnel and logistics to verify and objectively quantify damage over wide areas • Delayed decisions, low rate of irregular and inadequate payments or rejection of compensation claims {Lamarque *et al.* (2008) and Muruthi (2005)}. These conditions are equally applicable to Indian schemes as well.

- There are private (e.g., Spain, Finland, Austria, Minnesota) as well as public (e.g. Greece, Canada) insurance companies for damage caused by wildlife in Europe and North America. There also are locally run insurance schemes funded by a mix of donor and private funding in combination with participant premiums (e.g. Baltistan, Namibia). It is well established that any successful insurance scheme must have the following critical features: Randomness of loss; low probability of occurrence; independence of risk, uncontrollability of loss or damage; unequivocal and verifiable loss (Morrison *et al.* 2009). However, many of these criteria are difficult to meet for insurance against wildlife damage, especially in the case of crop damage.

- Management of threat populations through culling, sport hunting, subsistence hunting, poisoning (e.g. strychnine) has been practiced in many African countries, with varying degrees of acceptability and effectiveness.

- Immunocontraceptives have been found to be expensive and generally ineffective to reduce populations quickly but are being tried as a tool to slow down population growth in many countries (e.g. Zona Pellucida on elephants).

- Many kinds of chemical (touch or olfactory irritants), physical and acoustic deterrents are being tested across the globe.

- The fencing industry is highly developed in most countries in Africa, Europe, and North America. While power fence is often the tool of choice, hybrid fences (combination of wire mesh and power fence) are also commonly used. Fences are often customised for particular target species as animals can jump over or burrow under fences if not tailored to their bodily and behavioural characteristics. In view of the impact of fences on animal migration and corridors, they need to be planned very carefully so that their adverse impact on ecology is minimal.

- Community-based natural resource management (CBNRM) involving tourism, sport hunting, collection of crocodile eggs for breeding farms, etc. is being used in many African countries to make people tolerant of losses.

All these interventions are used in combination with the traditional methods used by affected communities such as crop guarding, herding of livestock, and use of guard animals (e.g. dogs, donkeys), which are being further refined by research and education. Many NGOs and governments run programmes to educate people about how to avoid animal attacks and how to react in case of attacks.

HWC Management Strategy for India

India is different from most other countries. The number of people suffering from HWC in India is much larger than in any other country. Therefore, the scale of HWC management required in India is very different from other countries. Our raucous democracy and general reluctance to kill problem animals also limit our choices. Despite these constraints, our HWC management strategy has to be guided by global experience and Indian realities. Some of these guiding facts are:

- HWC is inherent to the conservation of large mammals. It is particularly severe in India because of our high human density in rural areas and our relative success in the conservation of large mammals. It is likely to intensify further unless HWC management is made central to wildlife conservation.

- Our current conservation ethos severely limits the options available to the affected people to protect themselves against wildlife depredations. Even the law does not impose any obligation on the state to protect the vulnerable people against, or compensate them for, the losses caused by wild animals protected by the State.

- In most countries, wild animals are not protected outside protected areas. Affected people are free to deal with wildlife threats as per their capacity, often with the help of the state. Compensation programmes primarily aim to protect valuable species rather than the people.

In contrast, wild animals (except vermin) are protected everywhere in India, and compensation programmes are primarily meant to mitigate the losses caused by wild animals.

- In other countries, wildlife is managed as a natural resource and generates significant economies from hunting, culling, or photographic tourism. People are willing to tolerate losses and dangers because of the incomes generated by wild animals. In fact, HWC management and the generation of economic benefits from wildlife are two sides of the same coin.

  India, in contrast, does not see wildlife as a natural resource and even photographic tourism is allowed reluctantly.

- The National Wildlife Action Plan (2017-2031) provides for "scientific management of wildlife populations" as the primary solution to HWC. Management of wildlife populations essentially means removing a certain proportion of the target population on a regular basis through hunting, culling, translocation, or birth/fertility control. While technologies for birth/fertility control have not yet matured anywhere, the other solutions are exorbitantly expensive unless the killed/captured animals have an end-use.

  As India does not allow wildlife utilisation, implementation of the full range of HWC management options, including those recommended in the National Wildlife Action Plan, is not possible under the current legal regime.

- Although wildlife populations within PAs are also managed, protected areas in many countries are either fenced or they interface with wildlife utilisation areas which are often managed by communities or companies. In India, in contrast, PAs are neither fenced nor are they surrounded by wildlife utilisation areas. As a result, wild animals spill out of PAs and other forests directly into conflict zones. Therefore, HWC in India is more intense and widespread than elsewhere.

- There is virtually no HWC management industry in India. There are no private companies involved in the business of capture and transportation of wild animals. Only a limited range of fencing materials and animal capture/transportation equipment are available in the country.

In the light of these critical realities, the following HWC strategy is proposed for India.

1. Strategic Goal

The national strategy on HWC management shall aim at achieving the following long-term goal:

"To transform human-wildlife conflict (HWC) into human-wildlife symbiosis (HWS)."

2. Objectives

The strategy shall aim to achieve its goal in terms of the following specific objectives:

> 2.1   To reduce the losses caused by wild animals to the people living in and around wildlife habitats;
>
> 2.2   To generate sustainable benefits from wildlife for the vulnerable people, particularly from damage-causing species;
>
> 2.3   To assist vulnerable people in coping with HWC where conflict reduction and/or benefit generation are not technically or administratively feasible.

3. Strategic Initiatives

In accordance with the HWC management goal and the determining facts mentioned above, the basic approach to HWC management in India must be to prevent the losses along with the generation of economic benefits from wildlife for the vulnerable communities. Apart from this core strategy, additional mitigative measures should be taken and assistance to the victims should be provided on a site-specific basis where the core strategy is not applicable. Additional steps can be taken as necessary to facilitate the implementation of the core strategy. Following initiatives should be launched by the Government of India, in collaboration with the States and other stakeholders, to achieve the goal and objectives of this strategy:

3.1   Establishment of the National Centre for Monitoring and Research in HWC.

As mentioned before, there is no institution in the country that keeps track of HWC, despite it being the main hindrance in the conservation of wildlife. Therefore, an adequately resourced National Centre for Monitoring and Research (NCMR) in HWC should be established in the Ministry of Environment, Forest & Climate Change (MoEF&CC) or any of its institutions. The Centre shall develop and maintain a national database on HWC events such as human deaths/injuries, livestock deaths, houses/property damage, crop damage, etc. The database shall also incorporate information on animal mortalities and HWC mitigation strategies employed by the states. The web-based database can be populated by the states on the basis of compensation claims, as most states pay compensation for losses incurred in HWC, and shall provide species-wise HWC scenarios at various administrative scales (the state, regional and national, etc.). Special studies shall be launched by this Centre where necessary in order to plug data gaps, quantify losses, or study aspects not covered by available data.

The Centre shall also undertake and support research and training in all aspects of HWC, including the development of tools, technologies, and strategies for its prevention and mitigation.

3.2 Community-Based Wildlife Management

As mentioned before, hunting of wild animals which become dangerous to human life or property, including standing crops, can be allowed by the States. This provision can be used to manage the populations of crop-raiding species outside forests while generating significant economic returns for the victim communities. Only the species in schedule II of the Act can be hunted if they become dangerous to standing crops. Thus, if any species belonging to Schedule I is considered dangerous to standing crops, it will have to be transferred to schedule II to enable its hunting. The states can then make rules for the introduction and regulation of hunting of such species, and for transferring any income accruing from these operations to the affected communities. This can be done by exercising their rule-making powers provided under Section 64 (2) (h). These rules shall be, broadly, on the following lines:

- The state shall notify the list of species that can be allowed to be hunted in accordance with these rules.
- Any community (i.e. gram sabha) suffering crop damage and having significant populations of notified species resident in the village commons can apply to the divisional forest officer (DFO) to constitute a hunting block on its cropland.
- Any person desirous of hunting notified species shall require a hunting permit and shall hunt in accordance with the conditions specified in the rules, for a specified fee.
- The hunter shall be entitled to the meat, skin, and other parts of the quarry but shall not be allowed to sell it (The law does

not allow it unless he is an authorized dealer). He may, however, donate any of these goods to the concerned gram sabha who shall be deemed to be a dealer appointed under Section 44 of the Act.

- The annual hunting quota for each block shall be determined as a proportion of the estimated population of the species, based on the desired population level and sustainability of harvest.
- The rules shall specify the proportion of the income accruing from hunting fees to which the affected communities shall be entitled.

Draft rules on the above lines are given in **Appendix-1 (Rules for Hunting Crop Raiders)** at the end of this book. These rules are almost in a ready-to-implement condition. All the forms and a subsidiary notification of huntable species and hunting fees are also included.

The Central and State governments should develop suitable schemes to assist such initiatives with technical, financial, and managerial support as appropriate.

3.3   Community-Based Ecotourism

The process to generate community benefits from wildlife management, based on the utilisation of wild animals living outside government forests has been provided above. An alternative approach for communities to generate benefits from wildlife living on their lands (adjoining natural forests) is to set up a wildlife tourism programme, rather than harvesting. This approach shall normally be applicable in areas where communities especially want to set up wildlife tourism programme on their lands because agriculture is not profitable or where exclusion of wildlife from their lands by fencing is not possible because of difficult terrain. Or, because hunting is unacceptable on religious grounds. Maharashtra has already taken the initiative to encourage landowners adjoining protected areas to convert their lands into community or private conservancies for tourism through incentives and priority entry into tourism zones of PAs (Government Circular No.: WLP 0315/ CR 56/F-1, Date: 21 October, 2015). A similar approach may be followed by other states. The general procedure for setting up a community conservancy for ecotourism may be as follows:

- Farmers owning lands adjoining forests shall convert their lands, along with other common lands of the village, into wildlife habitat by keeping it fallow and developing adequate fodder, cover, and watering points. Wildlife shall be free to move between this land and adjoining forests uninhibited by fences of any kind.

- This land shall be called a wildlife conservancy to be duly recognised by the forest department through a prescribed procedure.
- The conservancy shall develop an ecotourism business based on wildlife viewing/photography on conservancy lands as well as the adjoining government forests.
- Communities may run their ecotourism businesses in partnership with a competent business house with experience and capacity in developing, marketing, and operating ecotourism operations, under a benefit-sharing arrangement.
- Conservancies shall be allowed to extend game drives and hiking trails into the adjoining forests and shall also be allowed to develop other low-impact ancillary structures (viewpoints/hides/*machaans*, toilets, etc.) therein. However, no residential facilities shall be developed on the government forest land.
- Ecotourism in joint forest management (JFM) areas and community forest resource (CFR) areas (the latter granted under FRA 2006) shall be encouraged as a conservation strategy for wildlife corridors by aligning them with community conservancies.
- The Central and State governments shall develop suitable schemes to assist such initiatives with technical, financial, and managerial support as appropriate.

The concept of community conservancies in partnership with private business has already taken roots in Maharashtra. A company called Bamboo Forest Safari Lodge (BFSL) has developed a concept called "Community Owned, Community Operated Nature Conservancies and Habitats" (Cocoon Conservancies). One of their initiatives is already operational in the village Alijhanjha on the border of Tadoba Andhari Tiger Reserve and another initiative is taking shape in the village Gothangaon on the border of Umred Karhandla Paoni Wildlife Sanctuary. 37 farmers of this village have allowed forest to return to their 100-acre farmland where wild animals and birds now reside. The company has provided the capital for the construction and operation of world-class hospitality facilities in which the landowners are employed. The landowners also get compensation for their land contribution at a rate much higher than the agricultural income. Many former poachers, like a man called Gheenaji (even a tiger has been named after him), are also working as community rangers. The Alijhanjha camp is already receiving high-profile visitors. BFSL intends to hand over the facility to the land owners after 30 years. (Source: Sunil Mehta, Owner of BFSL and Sanctuary Nature Foundation). Nepal has been promoting community-based ecotourism on the outskirts of its national parks for decades now.

3.4 Building Capacity of Vulnerable Communities in Dealing with HWC.

The participation of victim/vulnerable communities in HWC management is of critical importance, both as first responders as well as in assisting professionals in implementing more sophisticated HWC solutions. Therefore, a programme for mobilising and equipping identified communities to perform an important role in dealing with emergency situations (e.g. presence of a rogue elephant or man-eating tiger) or persistent threats (e.g. crop-raiding) in coordination with local authorities, must be launched. Apart from preparing the vulnerable communities to protect themselves against possible wildlife threats, the programme shall aim at creating well-trained and equipped response teams who shall actively deal with the threat in coordination with other agencies and experts.

3.5 Compensation for HWC Losses

As human life and property are constitutionally protected, the government is legally obliged to compensate any loss of life or property caused by animals protected by law. Following strategies can be employed to compensate these losses:

- *Ex-gratia* payments for human deaths and injuries as per the rates and procedures determined by the states from time to time. In case of the death and permanent disability of the earning member of a family, states should also evolve suitable mechanisms to look after the education and sustenance of their dependents.
- Compensation for the loss of livestock at rates linked to the estimated market value of the lost animal.
- Loss of housing and other property should be compensated as

per the estimated cost of reconstruction.

- The current system of compensation of crop losses based on physical verification is prone to corruption and delays. Loss of agricultural and horticultural crops should be compensated through annual grants to cultivators within the area determined to be vulnerable to crop depredations. The amount per unit area may vary depending on the degree of vulnerability of a tract. The vulnerable area can be determined on the basis of periodic assessments linked to the "All-India Estimation of Tigers, Co-predators, Prey and Habitat" conducted by NTCA and WII every four years. This exercise may be suitably modified to make it possible to estimate changes in the degree and areas of vulnerability to crop losses. If this does not work out in some places, as in the case of non-tiger states, special studies may be commissioned for this purpose. (Note: These grants need not be available to those who avail crop fencing subsidy proposed ahead).
- Collaborations with national and international conservation NGOs should be sought to improve the effectiveness of schemes as well as to raise additional resources.

Note: Crop losses caused by wild animals have been included as an add-on item in the Pradhan Mantri Fasal Bima Yojna (Prime Minister's Crop Insurance Scheme) with effect from 2020. As the bulk of the premium is going to be paid by the government, this may provide some relief to the farmers. Small and marginal farmers, however, are unlikely to benefit much as penetration to that level will be slow and difficult. Corruption related to assessment processes will further inhibit wider adoption. Crop insurance in any case does not fit this category of losses. This is because insurance companies basically operate on the basis of low probability of claims while in this case, the claims are almost certain within the vulnerable areas. Even the government will not be able to afford the expenses if all the victims adopt crop insurance.

3.6 Management of Carnivores and Elephants

Any animal, particularly a big cat or an elephant, which has become a danger to human life, or is showing the tendency to do so, must be eliminated at the earliest, without any other considerations. After an animal has been determined to be a threat to human life, the field officers must have the freedom to use every means at their disposal to capture or kill the animal at the earliest. The captured animal may be euthanized unless there is a demand for display (i.e. in a zoo) or for conservation breeding. Such aberrant animals should in no case be released in the wild without ensuring complete control of their movements and behaviour.

Big cats and elephants can also become a threat to people's lives due to their overpopulation close to human habitations. Such populations need to be kept at safe levels by regularly destroying or capturing animals, unless they are fenced. Draft rules for managing life-threatening animals are given in **Appendix-2 (Rules for Hunting Predators)** at the end of the book. It provides a framework for the hunting of dangerous carnivores and elephants. Although the text of these rules is complete, the necessary forms for issuing and managing permits will have to be developed by the implementing authorities.

3.7   Wildlife Barriers and Deterrents

The use of barriers and deterrents is an integral part of wildlife management, particularly HWC management. However, fences are reluctantly used in India due to their cost, the potential to fragment habitats and landscapes, negative effects on non-target species, and the limited variety of materials available. The use of chemical, visual, olfactory, or acoustic deterrents is almost non-existent in the country, except some traditional practices (e.g. scare-crows, beating of drums, etc.). The Government of India should support the development and promotion of species-specific and site-specific ecologically and socially acceptable wildlife fences and deterrents. Following steps should be taken to optimise the use of wildlife barriers and deterrents in managing HWC in the country:

- Progressively erect fences on all external forest boundaries interfacing with human habitation or croplands, except where the existence of community conservancies obviates the need for a fence.
- Develop suitable subsidy schemes for supporting crop fencing in vulnerable areas. The rate of subsidy may vary on the basis of the degree of vulnerability of an area (tract) to wildlife-related crop losses, determined periodically for the payment of compensation as mentioned before.
- Promote research in cost-effective and customisable wildlife barriers (physical as well as electric) and deterrents.

- Collaborate with the industry bodies/federations to encourage the production of modern fencing/deterrent materials within the country (e.g. Bonnox fences of South Africa).

3.8   Improve Effectiveness of Protected Areas.

As of January 2019, India has a network of 668 sanctuaries and national parks, covering an area of 1,65,088.10 sq. kms. (5.02% of the total geographic area), mostly over reserve or protected forests. This amounts to approximately 23.30% of the total forest cover and 40.61% of all the dense and very dense forests of the country (although all PAs are not necessarily in dense forests). Besides preserving *in situ* wildlife populations, the PAs are also seen as the source of animals for populating areas beyond their boundaries. These spill-over populations are the principal source of HWC in the country as their habitat is interspersed with human habitat and infrastructure nearly everywhere. A natural approach to curbing HWC should, therefore, be to keep wild animals within PAs as far as possible and develop PA management strategies that ensure that populations within PAs are ecologically viable and genetically diverse. This is also important because most of the animals spilling out of PAs get poached or perish in HWC, without contributing significantly to the genetic robustness of their species. Moreover, our land-starved country cannot afford to let the management of all her forests be guided by only wildlife considerations, already having dedicated 23% of her forests solely for wildlife. The much-vaunted wildlife corridors are in fact the sinks rather than the sustenance for wildlife due to HWC and risk of poaching. There is also a limit to which the ever-expanding linear infrastructure can be made wildlife-friendly, although efforts in this direction must continue. In the light of this background, the following PA management strategy is proposed to minimise HWC while improving their effectiveness:

- Possibilities for enlarging the PAs should be continuously explored in order to accommodate viable populations of migratory (e.g. elephants) and territorial animals (e.g. tigers).
- Boundaries of all PAs should be fenced, wherever possible, unless the PA interfaces with an ecotourism area or a community conservancy. This will reduce poaching as well as HWC. The buffer zones of tiger reserves must be managed under one of the latter categories in order to generate

significant community benefits from wildlife. Instead of fencing the core area, the boundaries of the villages situated in the buffer zones, or their croplands, should be fenced as may be practical. External boundaries of the buffer zone forests should be fenced following the same approach.

- Fences should be designed in a way that they are permeable to harmless species and the chances of injury due to the animals hitting a fence running is minimum (i.e. make them flexible and shock absorber).
- Scientific management of the populations of large mammals inside PAs, particularly if fenced, should be encouraged in order to keep them in balance with the capacity of the available habitat and the populations of other conspecifics.
- Active exchange of breeding individuals between confined populations in different PAs should be carried out in order to maintain their genetic vigour/diversity.
- Villages situated within PAs should be encouraged and helped to relocate outside by providing them attractive relocation packages.

3.9   Development of Unpalatable Crops

Wildlife research institutions should be encouraged to partner with agricultural research institutes to develop cropping systems that are less attractive to wild animals and are suitable for local climatic and edaphic conditions.

3.10   Refinement of Traditional/Indigenous Practices of HWC Management.

A large variety of indigenous/traditional HWC management practices have evolved in different parts of the country, some of which may have the potential to be adopted in other parts as well. Such techniques/practices should be examined for refinement with the help of modern science and technology. Any practices with scope for wider application/adoption, with or without further refinements, should be widely disseminated in other relevant regions of the country.

3.11   Development of Non-Lethal *in situ* Population Control Solutions

The Government of India should encourage the development of species-specific chemical and/or surgical contraceptive or fertility control solutions for controlling the growth rates of undesirable populations where lethal solutions are not acceptable and translocation is not technically or financially feasible.

3.12 Development of HWC Management Industry

HWC management is primarily the responsibility of the government. However, the government has limited capacity to implement solutions due to various reasons, such as the shortage of funds, staff, technology, and in-house expertise. Private businesses can play an important role in providing financial, technical as well as managerial support to the government as well as to the community conservancies proposed in this strategy. New business areas can be developed in the fields of conservancy management, animal capture, and translocation as well as in manufacturing suitable equipment and consumables. Industry can also access foreign expertise much more easily through joint ventures than government bodies. Keeping in mind the need to enhance the role of the industry in dealing with HWC, the following steps should be taken:

- MoEF&CC shall coordinate with industry federations (e.g. CII, FICCI) to study the potential market and scope for manufacturing world-class wildlife management equipment and consumables, such as fencing materials, deterrents, capture equipment (immobilisation guns and consumables, traps, cages, nets, etc.), animal transportation vehicles, etc. within the country.

- Rules and procedures shall be developed to facilitate/promote the participation of industry in providing turnkey wildlife management solutions, such as capture and translocation of animals, community conservancy management, etc. Industry can participate in HWC management both as corporate social responsibility (CSR) activity as well as contractual businesses.

3.13 Building Capacity of States in HWC Management

Although mass translocation of wild animals is usually not a viable HWC management option unless the animals are required to populate a new habitat, capture of errant animals remains a critical HWC management intervention everywhere. Moreover, in view of the need to adopt an active management approach to conservation, the country needs the capacity to capture and move around herbivores in large numbers regularly. However, apart from sporadic efforts by some states, the country, at present, has no expertise and wherewithal to undertake large-scale capture and transportation operations.

Recently, we have seen a spate of orders declaring tigers and leopards dangerous to human life (man-eaters), particularly in Maharashtra and Uttarakhand. The governments have to engage private shooters to eliminate such animals because the forest departments neither have the weapons nor the training to deal with such situations. Paradoxically, NTCA has forbidden the use of private hunters for this purpose. While NTCA's order is simply stupid, there is a dire need to train foresters in hunting skills and equip them with the necessary means to deal with such emergencies.

Moreover, WLPA does not allow sufficient freedom to the states to undertake animal capture operations as per their requirement. A capacity-building programme consisting of the following elements should be launched as a part of the HWC management strategy:

- Review WLPA with a view to empower the states to undertake HWC management interventions more autonomously.
- Develop and disseminate species-specific capture and transportation methodologies based on international experience.
- Prepare long-term wildlife capture and translocation plans, based on population management needs of various species and states. Train and equip animal capture teams for each state in accordance with the envisaged workload.
- Develop professional HWC management courses with an emphasis on hands-on experience in the capture and transportation of animals.
- Impart basic hunting training to all foresters and create highly trained and well-equipped shooting and capture squads in all forest divisions to deal with dangerous carnivores and elephants, as required.
- Encourage interaction between states for mutual learning in the field of HWC management.

3.14   Review of Wildlife (Protection) Act, 1972.

As mentioned before, the law imposes no obligation on the government to mitigate HWC or compensate its victims, despite the fact that conservation of wildlife imposes severe costs on a large number of people who are often among the poorest. The Act can also be seen as being in violation of the Constitution of India which guarantees the protection of human life and property (Articles 21 and 300A). In its present form, the WLPA also severely limits our choices for HWC management and there is very little that the states and the victims can do on their own. Therefore, the law needs to be reviewed and amended with a view to providing for the following:

- to make HWC management a mandatory duty of the government;
- to improve the autonomy of the states, local authorities, and local people in dealing with HWC; and
- to facilitate scientific management of wildlife populations, in accordance with global best practices with a view to preventing HWC where necessary.

The sections that need to be reviewed for this purpose occur in Chapter II (Preliminary), Chapter III (Hunting of Wild Animals), Chapter IV (Protected Areas), and Chapter V (Trade or Commerce in Wild Animals, Animal Articles and Trophies). Chapter V A (Prohibition of Trade or Commerce in Trophies, Animal Articles, etc. derived From Certain Animals) should be deleted completely as it contradicts Chapter V and does not fit with the vision discussed here. If revised on these lines, these parts would look the way they are shown in **Appendix-3 (Wildlife Law for the Future)** given at the end of this book.

Economic Potential of Hunting Crop Raiders.

Species like the blue bull, wild pig, and blackbuck are eminently suited for the kind of management suggested under 3.2 (Community-based Wildlife Management) above. Hunters pay up to USD 500 for wild pig and USD 1000 for hunting blue bull in Europe and America. This shows that hunting of these pest species can become a major source of revenue for people, without any investments. The kind of revenues it can generate is illustrated in **Appendix-4 (Economics of Hunting Crop Raiders)** at the end of this book, using Madhya Pradesh as an example. It contains rough calculations of potential hunting revenue from blue bull and wild pig in croplands of the villages situated close to the state forests. The 22,000 villages situated within 5 km of forest boundary have a huntable area of approximately 76,000 km^2. Presuming a conservative animal density of 10 animals per km^2 and a 30% annual take-for both species, the state can generate nearly Rs. 638.40 crore from the hunting of these species only in croplands. If we add the value of crops saved and the multiplier effect of this revenue, it is obvious that the hunting of crop pests can become an important sector of the state's economy. Hunting of dangerous predators can further bolster the economic contribution of this sector as the hunting fees will perhaps run into crores of rupees per animal. Projected at the national level, the potential loss by not hunting these pests would run into thousands of crores. The Animal Use Issues Committee of the International Association of Fish and Wildlife Agencies (2005) calculated that the potential cost of not hunting wildlife in the US would be approximately USD 70.80 billion, in terms of damages and foregone revenues. We are already losing money at a similar scale despite being much, much poorer.

Conclusion

Wild animals, however iconic or sacred, cannot survive a conflict with human beings. Wildlife conservation imposes severe costs and misery on the rural communities without the animals contributing to their well-being in any way. This undermines conservation itself as people try to protect themselves in whatever way comes naturally to them, i.e. by killing the animals. Hunting and fences are the only tools to keep animals away from human habitats and reduce losses and difficulties. Hunting and tourism can also make losses tolerable if the benefits go to the victim communities. However, hunting is simply abhorred by the mainstream society in India, and tourism is only reluctantly allowed. Fences are too expensive to erect and maintain. Most government policies cheekily advise vulnerable communities to learn to live with HWC, rather than proactively trying to mitigate the problem. This is neither sustainable nor desirable as the primary duty of the government is to improve public well-being rather than undermine it by raising dangerous animals in their midst. Everything else the governments do is ancillary to this fundamental duty. Therefore, a paradigm shift in our approach to conservation is required so as to give HWC management the centre stage in conservation. As competition and conflict are inherent in our relationship with wild animals, protecting wildlife would be much easier if wild animals also produced some tangible benefits for society. Thus, conversion of HWC into Human-Wildlife Symbiosis (HWS), not just uncomfortable co-existence, should be the goal of conservation. Only that will save the predators and pillagers in the long run, not our moral jingoism.

I have tried to develop the necessary legal tools required to convert HWC into HWS. These tools are given as Appendix-1 to Appendix-3 at the end of the book. They are presented in this book to encourage the authorities to take the next logical step as well as to save them the labour of having to go through the tedious process of drafting the necessary regulations if they do decide to go that way.

Although I have been pushing the idea of sustainable hunting of crop-raiding species for a long time, I have tried to develop the rules for the hunting of predators and the revision of the WLPA for the first time. They too seem to fall into place equally beautifully. I hope someone, somewhere, shall test them on the ground and show that wild animals can be really welcome neighbours to rural communities in India too

CHAPTER-2

Ecotourism Under the Shadow of the Forest Conservation Act

The year was 1982. I had just joined as the first director of Panna National Park. One day, I laughed at the minister of industries who asked me how much milk a nilgai (literally a blue cow) produced. He was one of the rare visitors to the park and had been dozing throughout the early morning safari. Obviously, he considered nilgai just another variety of the holy cow of India. It was not until 1997 before I regretted my behaviour. Until then I had thought, like most of my ilk, that wildlife had to be preserved without any expectations of return on investment. Obviously, I was ignorant of the fact that a vast majority of the people did not think that way. The minister represented that majority. For them, the animals must produce something in return for our care and protection, like cattle. Although they innately recognised the right of every species to exist, local people often asked me why we were creating the national park at their cost. I had to give them long, convoluted, ecology-centric answers. Why couldn't you do it elsewhere, they would then ask.

By 1997, conservation was floundering and the euphoria of bringing in WLPA and Project Tiger was waning. Although the PA network had continued to expand since the seventies, not many PAs had any significant populations of wild animals. We all thought it was due to the lack of effective protection. Although the concepts of ecodevelopment and joint forest management, aimed at generating benefits for local people in return for their support to conservation, had already become popular by then, the gains were only patchy. This was because these programmes were primarily dependent on outside money with uncertain inflows. The benefits to local people, if any, did not come from forests or wildlife *per se*. They generally came as doles from the government and NGOs. While trees still produced something, even if the cash went to the government treasury, the animals produced nothing. They killed people and livestock. They destroyed crops, and gave sleepless nights. So, why preserve them? I had no straight answer.

The Enlightenment

While writing a piece for a local journal on HWC around protected areas in 1997, I almost had an epiphany, sudden enlightenment. It occurred to me that we would not be able to preserve wildlife as long as it continued to be seen only as a menace by the local people. We had to find a way to generate benefits from wild animals, especially for the victims of their depredations. Hunting and tourism were the only means that came to my mind. Hunting was unthinkable in India, even in the medium term. While I started understanding and exploring sustainable hunting systems prevalent across the globe, tourism offered immediate prospects. I thought if people living around PAs could earn some incomes through tourism, they may start tolerating losses and difficulties caused by wild animals less angrily. They may even actively start protecting animals against poaching, if their incomes are dependent on having animals around. So, the trick was in raising tourism revenues and creating more tourism-dependent jobs, preferably for local people. We must make the nilgai yield something if not milk, I thought.

Suddenly, I had a new respect for wildlife tourism. Until then, like everybody else, I thought we were accommodating tourism in our PAs at the cost of conservation. Now it started looking like a potential conservation tool. Wildlife tourism was now much more than just about raising conservation awareness. It would provide resources for conservation. However, our tourism revenues were negligible back then. We charged only 10 rupees per vehicle (two rupees per person) for safari drives. Although a few lodges had come up around Kanha and Bandhavgarh by 1997, they were still seen as a kind of means to exploit the parks, rather than being treated as allies in a common mission. A lot had to change if wildlife tourism was to become an effective conservation tool, as it had already happened in many countries.

Thus, when I returned to the wildlife wing of the department in 2005, after 17 years, I was burning with the desire to raise tourism revenues and jobs around our PAs. I immediately started working on new tourism rules for our parks. I proposed raising tariffs, opening more areas to tourists, allowing activities like walking, biking, hiking camping, etc. in forests. Above all, we tried to make tourism-based businesses feel welcome. I was sure that only they could create more jobs for the local people. We already had rules that allowed the parks to spend their tourism earnings locally, including on local people. So, even our field managers were excited about these new rules, although some of my colleagues were aghast at my neo-liberal attitude towards tourism. So far, tourism was a necessary evil. Now it was an ally. I was happy with the way things were going. I had even started dreaming of the day when at least a few of our parks could substantially support themselves on their own earnings. That would naturally need a lot many tourists. This means that many more jobs, mostly for the locals. As those jobs would be dependent on having wild animals around, that would naturally mean better conservation. Perhaps the park will earn enough to be able to share a little with local people, apart from creating jobs for them. Although the CWLW, the incomparable Gangopadhyay Sahib, was not a wildlifer, he had a very open and objective approach to these ideas and accepted nearly all my suggestions. I was on cloud nine, literally! Wild animals shall now produce cash, if not milk.

But good times do not last forever. NTCA was born in 2006, in the wake of the Sariska debacle. It was given overwhelming powers to control the management of tiger reserves. The guys running the NTCA somehow believed that tourism in tiger reserves was undesirable. We started receiving directives from NTCA to "phase out" tourism from the core areas of tiger reserves. This pressure continued till 2012 when NTCA was forced, by the Supreme Court of India, to issue guidelines which, though quite regressive in many ways, did not prohibit tourism in tiger reserves (Special leave petition no. 21339 of 2011, Ajay Dubey vs UOI and Others). For details, please see "Wardens in Shackles" by the same author. Although we steadfastly resisted this pressure as long as I was in office, still we were unable to do many things which needed to be done in order to make wildlife tourism a significant contributor to the conservation of wildlife in the state.

Since October 2012, nearly all wildlife tourism in the country has been governed by the guidelines issued by NTCA under the directions of the Supreme Court in the above case. Although these guidelines apply only to tiger reserves, currently 52 in number, that is where virtually all of wildlife tourism happens. There is no national template for other 500 or so PAs yet, although NTCA is pushing that the same framework should apply to them also.

FCA, the New Bogey

With the conclusion of the case for "phasing out" tourism from PAs in the Supreme Court, I thought the major threat to wildlife tourism was over. NTCA's attempts to choke tourism out of PAs by using an obscure expression occurring in WLPA, i.e., "inviolate" areas, had been thwarted for good. As tourism was largely associated with PAs created under WLPA, we rarely looked beyond this law to guide us. However, when we tried to spread tourism outside PAs, by creating the Madhya Pradesh Ecotourism Development Board (MPEDB), we had to read the other forest laws more carefully. That is when we realised that the creation of any ecotourism infrastructure on forest land had been designated as a "non-forest" activity under the Forest Conservation Rules 2003. Therefore, it required prior approval of the Central Government in each case, however small the structure might be. We also saw reports of the Central Government refusing permission to many states when applied for.

The Forest (Conservation) Act 1980 (FCA), under which these rules were notified, provided a list of exceptions that were not to be treated as non-forest works, despite technically being so, if they were "relating or ancillary to conservation, development, and management of forests and wildlife". Ecotourism infrastructure was not one of them. On top of this, the Central Government had specifically provided in the FCA Rules that "*Construction of permanent structures for the purpose of ecotourism on forest land shall be considered as non-forestry activity. In such cases, prior approval of the Central Government under the Forest (Conservation) Act, 1980 is require*d" (clause 11.10 of Chapter 11 of Part B). We tried to side-step this provision by calling every structure we created as *temporary* (non-permanent). Many of our field officers were genuinely worried that we were pushing them to do something not permitted by rules and tried to obstruct the process as far as possible. Thus, ecotourism never made a real headway in the state. The same was the case in other states also.

While we were struggling to give some impetus to ecotourism in the state, the Central Government was telling the states that ecotourism *per se* was an unwelcome activity as far as FCA was concerned and could not be carried out without its prior approval. One letter to the government of Haryana saying so came to be in possession of every divisional forest officer (DFO) who wanted to play safe when we asked him to take interest in ecotourism. So far, we believed that only the construction of permanent structures was the problem. But, now the concept of ecotourism itself started looking illegitimate. Although we were very angry and puzzled at the way the Central Government officers were behaving, little did we realise that their stand was based on Forest Conservation Rules {Handbook of Forest (Conservation) Act, 1980 and Forest Conservation Rules, 2003 (Guidelines & Clarifications) 2019}, (FCA Rules for short) which said, at two places, that ecotourism *was* a non-forest activity as far as FCA was concerned, as shown below:

- *Ecotourism is a non-forest activity requiring prior approval under the FC Act. (clause 1.18 (iv) of Chapter 1 of Part B).*

- ***Eco-Tourism:*** *Ecotourism is a non-forestry activity, and will be allowed in Protected Areas if the said activities are part of the Management Plan/ Tiger Conservation Plan and are duly approved by the Central Government (clause 12.13 of chapter 12 of Part B).*

Surprisingly, I do not remember having seen these two provisions while I was in service till 2012. Perhaps, they were introduced later. If not, it is totally inexplicable that we continued to push ecotourism despite there being clear provisions to discourage it. These provisions also made all ongoing wildlife tourism illegitimate as no PA management plans, other than those of tiger reserves, are approved by the Central Government. There is no provision for that. In fact, I noticed these astounding provisions only in January 2021 while creating a write-up on the legal and policy framework for ecotourism in India for the Responsible Tourism Society of India (RTSOI). I thanked my stars for not ending up in jail, along with so many others, for doing what I thought was critical for the conservation of forests and wildlife in India. For the information of those who may not know, FCA provides for 15 days in jail *for officers* allowing non-forest operations on forest land without the prior approval of the Central Government.

Winds of Change

When I realized the dire situation, I dialed Mr. Satyanand, the CEO of MPEDB that he was likely to go to jail for being the CEO of an organisation involved in doing ecotourism illegally. He immediately called his batchmate in Delhi, who was responsible for implementing FCA in the country, to check whether it was really so. He came back to me with the news that FCA Rules were being amended to open the doors for ecotourism in the country.

In fact, the first inkling of the changing times had already come when the government inserted the words *"Low impact eco-friendly eco-tourism may now be considered as a forestry activity"* in the revised draft of the "Policy for Ecotourism in Forest and Wildlife Areas" in 2020. (This statement was removed from the final version of the policy issued under the title "Guidelines on Sustainable Eco-Tourism in Forest and Wildlife Areas 2021"). I was very happy to see these words in the policy, but was not sure how the government could do it without amending the FCA Rules. Now it was clear that there was a complete change of heart on the part of the Central Government and that it was finally ready to embrace ecotourism as a conservation tool.

The good news Satyanand had promised came in the form of Ministry's circular dated 25th October, 2021 which said:

"i. Para 11.10 of the Handbook of Forest (Conservation) Act, 1980, shall read as: "Development/construction of facilities which are not of permanent nature, in forest areas for the purpose of ecotourism by Government authorities shall not be considered as non-forestry activity for the purpose of Forest (Conservation) Act, 1980."

ii. Paras 1.18 (iv) and 12.13 of the Handbook of Forest (Conservation) Act, 1980, stand deleted."

While the deletion of para 1.18 and 12.13 is a huge relief because no forester will now be prosecuted for permitting people to visit natural landscapes without central permission, the retention of para 11.10, almost in the same form, is puzzling. Although they have changed the language of the para but it still means the same thing, i.e., permanent structures on forest land still need prior approval from GoI. Moreover, even the temporary structures must be developed only by government authorities.

Although this is significant progress, obviously the government is still not looking at the issue of ecotourism versus FCA comprehensively. The critical question of facilitating the involvement of the private sector in ecotourism is not on the government's radar at present. Without harnessing private capital and expertise, ecotourism is likely to go nowhere, despite these reforms. Even communities mean private sector as far as the law is concerned.

Essence of FCA

In short, FCA provides that, without the prior approval of the Central Government, the State authorities cannot order the following:

- Dereservation of a reserve forest.

- Permit the use of forest land for any *non-forest purpose.*
- Assignment (or lease) of a forest land to a non-government entity for any purpose.
- Clearing of a natural forest for any purpose other than reafforestation.

Out of these, the restrictions on the use of forest land for non-forest purposes, and the assignment of forest land to private entities are relevant to ecotourism.

The "*non-forest purpose*" is defined in the Act as "*the breaking up or clearing of any forest land or portion thereof for----any purpose other than reafforestation*". However, the Act does not consider "*any work relating or ancillary to conservation, development and management of forests and wildlife, namely, the establishment of check-posts, fire lines, wireless communications and construction of fencing, bridges and culverts, dams, waterholes, trench marks, boundary marks, pipelines or other like purposes*" as non-forest purpose.

The essence of this definition is that for any work or activity to be called "non-forest purpose" it should involve "breaking-up or clearing" of forest land. However, an activity which is "ancillary to conservation, development and management of forests and wild-life" cannot be called "non-forest" even if it involves "breaking-up or clearing" of forest land. The existence of the words "or other like purposes" at the end of the list of exemptions indicates that any other work which qualifies to be exempted, in accordance with the given criteria, can be added to this list.

Ecotourism, which essentially means allowing people to visit a forest to enjoy nature, does not necessarily involve "breaking up or clearing" of forest land. Secondly, even if there is some "breaking up or clearing" of forest land for development of visitor amenities, ecotourism eminently qualifies to be an exception as the whole purpose of ecotourism is to strengthen the conservation of forests and wildlife. Despite these two obvious indicators to the contrary, the Central Government erroneously designated ecotourism as a non-forest activity. However, this mistake has now been corrected.

But, the way this mistake has been corrected still leaves something to be desired. The government has just withdrawn the reference to ecotourism being a non-forest activity. It has still not been included in the list of exceptions to "non-forest purpose" which would have given ecotourism added recognition as a conservation tool. So, for now, ecotourism in forest lands, along with visitor amenities *"which are not of permanent nature"* and are developed by *"Government authorities"*, can be allowed by the states without the prior approval of the Centre.

FCA and Tourism Infrastructure

Before the recent changes, ecotourism as well as all permanent infrastructure in the name of ecotourism required Central permission. In fact, when ecotourism itself was designated undesirable, the restriction on permanent infrastructure was entirely unnecessary. Now the ministry has authorised the states to carry on with ecotourism in forest areas along with the development of "facilities which are not of permanent nature" without the prior permission of the Central Government. This means central permission will still be required for any permanent infrastructure in forest lands.

It seems the move aims to restrict ecotourism infrastructure on forest land to items like portable toilets, tented accommodation, rain shelters with roofing sheets, etc., which can be removed whenever required and the land can be returned to nature. Perhaps this will prevent the states from developing large high-impact residential facilities on forest lands in the name of ecotourism. This was the fear that had prompted the Central Government to designate ecotourism itself as a repugnant activity in the first place.

However, it will be better to clearly define or list what kind of facilities shall be allowed under this liberalization move. This is because nothing is absolutely of "permanent nature". Even brick, cement and concrete structures can be removed if necessary. Therefore, in the absence of a clear definition or list of items, overenthusiastic or under-pressure officials may allow undesirable developments calling everything not being "of permanent nature". Officials may also face harassment at the hands of rabble rousers claiming some structures to be of "permanent nature" although the officials may consider them otherwise. An indicative list or description will eliminate such possibilities. Simple amenities like toilets, nature trails, day shelters, drinking water, camping grounds, dirt roads, bridges, culverts, etc. can be included in the list. The maximum area to be devoted to such facilities can also be specified. It can be something like 1-5 hectares, depending upon the total area of the ecotourism forest. Anything bigger or different than the norm would obviously need prior approval of the Central Government.

FCA and Private Sector Involvement in Ecotourism

Although the government has unshackled ecotourism considerably through this move, it is unlikely to grow significantly in the country unless the regulations also facilitate the participation of the private sector in it. We generally imagine an ecotourism facility to be a small, basic, and low-impact facility managed by the forest department or local communities. While that is desirable, most such facilities are financially unviable because of low tourist volumes. Volumes are low due to the lack of quality and marketing. Neither the forest departments nor local communities can change all this due to their well-known limitations. Even if service quality, experience, and marketing, improve, operations often take years to break even financially. Neither the government nor the communities have the financial strength to absorb losses for years. However, the private sector has all the qualities required to change all this. Many of our famous tiger reserves now have world-class wildlife lodges. They not only provide high quality hospitality, but also excellent guiding and nature interpretation. They create thousands of jobs for the local people. Although visitors are primarily attracted to the ecotourism product, it is brought to the notice of prospective visitors by the marketing done by these businesses.

Involvement of the private sector in ecotourism is possible in several forms. Firstly, we need their money to develop infrastructure, especially in virgin areas where returns are likely to be delayed. Secondly, a private operator can be engaged to operate a government facility, such as a lodge or a camp, even in upmarket locations, for providing high-quality services. Another way of harnessing the strengths of the private sector is to make the operator responsible for providing a complete experience including logistics, hospitality, guiding, and interpretation. It can either be a simple operations and maintenance (O&M) contract where infrastructure is owned by the government or it may also include the development of necessary infrastructure as well (which the new rules prohibit).

We almost instinctively believe that none of the above can be done without the prior permission of the Central Government in each case which is as good as impossible to obtain. I think this impression is not correct and this mindset must change for things to improve. It is entirely possible to do things despite the restrictions imposed by FCA if we have a positive mindset. This has been happening as long as FCA has been in existence in several other programmes of the forest departments. For example, we have always been assigning forest lands to contractors and communities for various purposes, without the permission of the Central Government, despite FCA forbidding it. For example, all the forests of MP have been assigned to the Primary Minor Forest Produce Trading and Development Cooperative Societies for the collection and sale of tendu leaf. The area, called a unit, consists of all the forests around the cluster of villages that comprise one or more societies. Many of these units are now sold in advance to tendu leaf contractors, although leaves are collected by the societies. Similarly, most of the forests of MP and other states have been divided between joint forest management (JFM) committees also. Large offices and godowns have been constructed by the forest departments on forest lands in almost every forest division in the country. Timber and bamboo sale depots occupy hundreds of hectares of land. All of them qualify to be branded as non-forest purpose as per the Act. But nobody has ever sought or received the approval of the Central Government for these large structures. Nor the Central Government has ever raised any objections to these complexes.

The existence of these assignments (leases, contracts, agreements, etc.) and "non-forest" uses without the permission of the Central Government is a violation of FCA but everybody has ignored it because all this is necessary for the management of forests. However, the proper course should have been not to ignore the law but to find a way to do all this by invoking the law. This can be easily done by providing a generic approval to the kind of assignments (leases and contracts) mentioned above and by declaring the departmental offices, godowns, staff quarters, timber depots, etc. as works "relating or ancillary to conservation, development, and management of forests and wildlife". It should still be done in order to provide legitimacy to all the good work done by the previous generations of foresters. On the same lines, generic approvals can be provided by the Central Government to any contracts or land-uses required for carrying out ecotourism in forest lands.

FCA and the Private Conservancies

Section 36 C and 36 D of WLPA provide for the constitution of community reserves on community lands or private lands. Recent amendments giving better say to the land owner in the management of the community reserves constituted on private land has opened the doors for the creation of private conservancies in the country on the lines of Africa and elsewhere. Although the idea will take time to mature, the creation of large private conservancies, earning their keep from ecotourism, is a real possibility now. Large consevancies adjacent to government forests and PAs can help in significantly increasing the forest cover of the county, especially protected landscapes in the context of agenda 30X30 of CBD. These reserves can also help in imroving ecotourism footprint in government forests by developing permanent infrastructure on private land while offering the experience on forest lands. This can bring real economic and ecological dividends only if the reserve owners are given exclusive access to adjoining forests for ecotourism. They can create limited visitor facilities as permitted under FCA and WLPA inside forests and can be made responsible for the protection of the assigned area. Such assignments can also be done only if ecotourism is treated as a mainstream conservation activity at par with tendu leaf collection, joint forest management etc. If actively promoted, the establishment of private conservancies can be a game changer for conservation of forests and wildlife in India. As India just does not have 30% forest cover to be able to meet the 30X30 goal, our commitment to this goal shall be hollow unless we embrace private conservancies as a mainstream programme. However, it will be necessary to keep the private and community land converted into wildlife habitat free from the shackles of FCA in order to make these ventures economically viable.

FCA and Ecotourism Development Boards

Although Madhya Pradesh was perhaps the first state to set up an ecotourism development board (EDB) in 2005, Kerala has been the real pioneer in ecotourism. Most states are still trying to emulate what Kerala has been doing for decades. Although small operations here and there may be working well, perhaps no state has been able to replicate what Kerala has been doing. This is despite the creation of dedicated institutions, like EDBs, for spearheading the growth of ecotourism in many states. Most EDBs are struggling to justify their creation as they do not have much to show except some small, struggling, low-quality ecotourism initiatives, mostly managed by forest guards in the names of local communities. One reason for the failure of EDBs has, of course, been FCA as neither the board officials nor other forest officers were able to find a way around it. I think the second most important reason for their failure has been that most boards are trying to create their own business operations rather than working to develop an ecosystem in which ecotourism businesses can flourish. Even where they are pushing for the involvement of the private sector, they see private operators operating only facilities, rather than running programmes. They have not been able to convert ecotourism into a mainstream function of the forest department, a process which they were expected to spearhead. An important reason for this failure, perhaps, has also been the fact that EDBs have to compete with the CWLWs for space. CWLWS are the traditional custodians of ecotourism policies and programmes in the states because they control the management of PAs. EDBs are unable to look beyond these existing hotspots of tourism and end up facing resistance. Hardly has any EDB set up a successful greenfield ecotourism project in a virgin area so far. As a result, India continues to be known primarily for 'tiger tourism' in a few PAs (all tiger reserves are not tourism hotspots) despite the existence of dedicated institutions mandated to diversify and expand ecotourism beyond tiger reserves.

With the recent reforms in FCA rules, EDBs should have an easier run in the future. However, significant results will be difficult to achieve if we continue to haggle over silly issues like permanent and temporary infrastructure and if the field is not opened up for the private sector. It is the responsibility of institutions like EDBs to agitate these issues at relevant forums and push for necessary legal and policy changes. Instead of setting up their own business operations, they must focus on creating the necessary facilitation and regulatory framework for the involvement of the private sector.

One important institutional change that can help make EDBs more effective can be to put the EDBs under the supervision of the CWLWs. In fact, CWLWs can be made ex-officio heads of these institutions. This will remove the dichotomy which the creation of the EDBs has created and the CWLWs shall become responsible for the performance of these institutions rather than blocking their growth.

Communities and Ecotourism

One of the core tenets of ecotourism is the well-being of forest-dwelling communities. This happens in several ways. The most direct impact of ecotourism on local communities is in the form of job creation either in the tourism industry or in ancillary services. The staff hired by the tourism industry for housekeeping, cleaning, cooking, guiding, driving, etc. is usually local. Critics often lament that only menial jobs go to the locals, forgetting the fact that even these jobs provide huge relief to the local people. Growth in tourism often creates opportunities for local people to set up small businesses such as tea shops, local foods, handicrafts, motor repairs, and so on. Some can also start homestays. Perhaps the best form of community welfare is where communities themselves run a proper tourism business in the form of residential, catering and interpretation facilities. Governments generally spend a significant part of their tourism earnings on community welfare. For example, MP distributes 30% of the gate receipts in cash among villages situated in the buffer zones of tiger reserves. This is often in addition to the sundry community welfare schemes funded by the gate receipts in various PAs.

Ecotourism or wildlife tourism, as practiced in India, is often criticized for not benefitting the locals significantly. It is alleged that most of the tourism businesses are owned by rich people living in cities and that they take their profits with them. While this is generally true, it hides the fact that a significant part of their operational expenses is incurred locally. Many studies (Chundawat *et al.* 2017, Karanth & DerFries 2010) indicate 70-80% of the staff working in lodges is local. Lodges also procure their groceries, vegetables, milk, etc. locally but are usually handicapped by the lack of suppliers. Even if they shop in nearby towns, that also creates jobs for the locals as it is their produce that the shopkeepers usually sell. Many large lodges also run community welfare schemes of their own, such as, compensation for loss of livestock to predators, grants to local schools and hospitals, solar lights, etc.

However, it is true that current levels of community benefits from ecotourism are often insignificant when seen in the overall context. Therefore, all efforts must be made to increase these benefits in order to justify the claims that ecotourism is a tool for community welfare. We need to adopt a 4-pronged approach to accomplish it, namely:

- Increase the size of the cake by increasing tourist volumes. The larger the cake, the larger shall be the share of local people.
- Build the capacities of local communities to garner the skilled jobs created by tourism and produce goods required by visitors and the service industry.

- Provide incentives to the industry for hiring and shopping locally. This can be in the form of discounts in entry fees, priority access to restricted areas, tax rebates, and so on.
- Encourage the private sector to start greenfield ecotourism businesses in undeveloped PAs and other forests by giving it greater say in product development.

While all this is being already done in several places in various forms, the country has neither seen growth in tourist volumes nor in their spread to new areas. Only a few tiger reserves attract sizable volumes and even there no growth has been seen since 2012 because NTCA has capped the size of tourism zones and maximum intake. Whatever growth in government revenues from ecotourism is seen since 2012 has been primarily due to increased tariff rates. Some growth has come from activities in buffer zones which often are unattractive to visitors. As mentioned before, EDBs have also not been able to start any greenfield projects away from existing tourism hotspots. Thus, community benefits from ecotourism are unlikely to grow significantly unless we adopt some radically different approach.

The only way to increase tourism volumes is to open more areas, both within existing hotspots as well as hitherto unexplored areas. Inviting more visitors to already overcrowded destinations shall be disastrous for obvious reasons. Knowing that the highest wildlife densities in our tiger reserves are found only in areas open to tourism, there is no sense in keeping more than 80% of their areas locked up. And, new destinations must be opened up expeditiously.

The usual way of opening new destinations is to construct a few rooms departmentally, put a few local boys in charge and start expecting visitors. If the first few visitors go back happy, the trickle starts on the strength of the word-of-mouth publicity. However, operating expenses generally grow faster than income as the staff must be paid and facilities must be maintained. If there is no assured income to the staff, they generally drift away. As a result, the facility either closes or deteriorates to the extent that not many would like to venture there. If the wilderness experience is good, people might be ready to tolerate poor hospitality and accommodation to some extent. But new destinations generally do not offer a great experience. As a result, the places may struggle to survive for some time. In due course, the managers and employees get demotivated and start looking for other opportunities.

The Satpura Break

However, we used a bit innovative approach to start tourism in Satpura Tiger Reserve of Madhya Pradesh in 2006. We encouraged a group experienced in running wildlife lodges to build a lodge near the park by signing an agreement guaranteeing to provide the kind of ecotourism experience they would be able to sell to their customers. It included, apart from the usual game drives which are the hallmark of Madhya Pradesh, walking, cycling, kayaking, observation hides, etc. Thus came up the Forsyth Lodge at Madhai. The lodge used the tagline "If you have seen the tiger in Kanha and Bandhavgarh, come to Satpura." Now it is one of the most talked-about wildlife tourism destinations in the country. There are nearly a dozen lodges employing hundreds of locals now. Our local guides are being commended all over the world. This would not have happened if we had not developed a partnership with a company that had a global marketing reach. We did not want to sit and wait for visitors to discover our park accidentally. We wanted someone to reach out to tour operators across India and the globe. With the coming of new lodges, property prices in the area skyrocketed, which made some of the locals, millionaires. Some have started their own little businesses, supplying groceries, liquor, and other little things to lodges and tourists. Some even let out their fields for camping on the river bank overlooking the core area of the tiger reserve. The affluence brought to the area by wildlife tourism is now clearly on display, although much more can perhaps be done. This is a clear example of ecotourism helping the communities. Now the Madhai-Sarangpur forest is teaming with wild animals and nobody is happier than the locals.

Captain James Forsyth walked nearly 200 km from Jabalpur to Pachmarhi in 1862, to build a forest lodge. The Bison Lodge, as it was named, is now an interpretation centre of Satpura Tiger Reserve. We also decided to make a part of Forsyth's route to Pachmarhi a trekking trail. The trail was inaugurated with a one-week, heavily subsidized, trekking festival in November 2011. Fifty persons started the trek every day while another fifty finished it. The experience included two nights in tents on the way at picturesque locations. Now the trek is marketed by local lodge owners who provide all the logistics and is usually sold out.

Our people also tried to create some community-managed hospitality facilities, but these never took off, despite the popularity of the parks. The reason is simple. A tourism business cannot flourish without a strong marketing and sales capacity. Neither the government nor the communities are able to do it well. Although community-run operations sound pleasing and pious, their long-term success is always dependent on the private sector marketing the place well.

It emerges from the above that community benefits from ecotourism are significantly dependent on the success of private operators of the area. Therefore, a strong presence of the private sector is the cornerstone of any sound ecotourism programme, even where community benefits are the focus. Although efforts to build the capacities of communities to run small operations should continue, the focus should always be on real benefits rather than their cosmetic participation.

Forest Rights Act and Ecotourism

Although there are several models and levels of community involvement in ecotourism across the world, the most talked about are the ones where the entire experience, encompassing hospitality as well as wilderness, is provided by the communities. Obviously, the benefits to the communities increase as their involvement in providing services deepens. In many African countries like Namibia, Zimbabwe, Zambia, Tanzania, etc. where community-based natural resource management (CBNRM) is popular, the lodges as well as the forests are owned by the communities but the operations are managed by private operators under a contract with the owners. Communities get all the jobs and a share in the profit. In India, there are no 'communal lands', as they call the community-owned lands in Africa, except in the northeastern states. Nearly all the forest lands are owned by the government. Therefore, the communities cannot start an ecotourism programme either on their own or in partnership with private operators. At best, the communities can own a lodge or camp outside the forest while entry into the forests is controlled by the government. Communities can also not be easily given any substantive rights over the forest land as that attracts the provisions of FCA.

However, all that is likely to change, even if gradually, under the influence of the Forest Rights Act, 2006. As discussed in another chapter, more and more forests are likely to become community forest resource (CFR) over time, where local communities shall have complete management control. It will be in the interest of all stakeholders, including the government, that ecotourism, rather than timber and bamboo, becomes a major produce of these forests. This is critically important to prevent communities from destroying their forests in pursuit of quick profits. Our pundits have never considered ecotourism as a product of sustainable forest management (SFM) while it is the only non-destructive and non-consumptive use of forests. If well managed and marketed, ecotourism can generate as much income per unit area as timber production. Although it did not make sense to me in 1992, I remember someone mentioning to me, during a study tour to the USA, that the government revenue from forest recreation (ecotourism) was more than that from timber sales in many states of the US. Now I realise how profound that statement was. There is no reason why this cannot happen in India. In view of the huge Indian market and growing global interest in ecotourism, the benefits to communities can be huge. However, this cannot happen without the involvement of the private sector. This is because bureaucrats and communities just cannot run a complex business that needs heavy investments and several kinds of skills and expertise. Only private operators can do it if given a suitable legal and policy environment. Therefore, it is time we created a suitable regulatory framework for attracting the private sector into ecotourism even if our objective is to generate benefits for local communities. As ecotourism generates incomes without extraction or destruction, it can almost be a panacea for degraded forests if the communities agree to alter their extractive practices in exchange for ecotourism benefits. They will not need to worry about FCA clearances or the permission of the forest department to enter into a contract with private operators to develop and manage ecotourism programmes on their behalf. If that happens, FRA can become the boon that our politicians and civil society organisations claim it to be but conservationists are mortally worried about.

The Way Forward

The changes in the FCA rules are almost monumental. They have opened the doors for the development of ecotourism in the country. However, just removing the tag of "non-forest purpose" from ecotourism is not going to be enough if we are unable to harness the awesome power of the private sector in scaling up ecotourism. It is nobody's case that we should devastate our forests by letting in unsustainable numbers of visitors, or building massive tourism complexes and other infrastructure on forest lands. The way to go is to use the law to allow ecotourism to grow to sustainable levels, with minimal effect on land and vegetation. While the possible adverse impacts of tourism on forests and wildlife can be contained by prescribing sustainable limits and practices, its growth can be ensured only by involving the private sector. The roadmap (actions to be taken by the Central Government) for doing it can be as follows:

1. Notify a list of basic ecotourism infrastructure elements, such as toilets, washrooms, drinking water facilities, rain shelters, camping grounds, eco-resorts or eco-cottages, nature trails, dirt roads, bridges, culverts, etc. that qualify to be treated as "relating or ancillary to conservation, development, and management of forests and wildlife". No prior approval of the Central Government shall be required for these items as provided in the Explanation under Section 2 of the Act.

2. Issue detailed guidelines for the involvement of the private sector in infrastructure development, operations, and management. The guidelines should clearly specify what kind of contracts can be given to private operators without the prior approval of the Central Government. For example, no central approval should be required for private operators simply providing services like hospitality, transport, guiding, nature interpretation, etc. under a contract with FD, as it does not amount to assigning of forest land. The guidelines should also contain a generic approval to all such contracts where the assignment of limited rights on forest land is involved, subject to the limits and specifications provided in the guidelines. For example, development of a campsite or an eco-lodge, as per specified limits, or maintenance of roads, trails, or any other field infrastructure as a part of the service contract should get a deemed approval in the guidelines.

These two actions can solve many of the systemic problems related to ecotourism in one shot.

When the news that the Central Government was looking for a suitable definition of "permanent structures" in order to liberalise ecotourism came to me, I suggested the above course to them, among other things, which are no longer relevant due to the amendment of rules. In fact, I wrote the guidelines and shared them with concerned officers in the Central Government. An updated version of the draft shared with them informally is attached as **Appendix-5** at the end of this book. This basic draft can be used for consultations with states, experts, and stakeholders for arriving at a consensus on the final shape of the guidelines.

Conclusion

This chapter was originally written when the term "ecotourism" was anathema to the mandarins in Delhi while everybody else swore by it. The pressure of public opinion finally forced a change of mind in Delhi and the doors to promote ecotourism were opened. One the principal harbingers of this change was the reinterpretation of FCA. But, miles to go before we sleep.

Ecotourism is the future of India's forests and wild animals shall be the main attraction for visitors. Ecotourism is globally recognised as one of the most potent engines of conservation and rural development, especially where hunting is not morally acceptable. Ecotourism revenues are similar to milk production from domestic animals as both are produced without harming the animals and, in both cases, yield depends on how well the animals are looked after. In order to unleash the power of ecotourism, we need to have a conducive legal and policy framework. Fortunately, most of the conservation-related policies now support ecotourism as a means and motive for the conservation of natural resources. The debate about whether WLPA supports ecotourism in tiger reserves and other PAs has also been settled by the Supreme Court. The FCA rules that created hindrances in the growth of ecotourism until now have been amended. The only legal frontier to be crossed is to facilitate the participation of the private sector creating and managing the ecotourism experience.

Will the final frontier ever fall?

CHAPTER-3

Living with the Gir Lions

Asiatic lion of Gir, the pride of Gujarat, is now 674 strong, an increase of 29% over the count of 2015. (Times of India, June 10, 2020). According to the Gujarat Forest Department, lions are now occupying an area of 10500 km^2, covering five PAs (1. Gir National Park 2. Gir Sanctuary 3. Paniya Sanctuary 4. Mitiyala Sanctuary 5. Girnar Sanctuary) and four satellite areas. The actual area visited by the lions is perhaps much more than this. Out of this, the protected areas cover only 1649 km^2. The districts (Amreli, Junagarh, Gir Somnath, and Bhavnagar) in which most of the lion range lies have a combined forest area of only 1931.65 km^2. Thus, if they are occupying an area as large as 10500 km^2, this means their range is severely fragmented and dominated by human habitations. The total forest cover of Gujarat is only 14757 km^2. Most of it lies far away from the lion range, on its eastern border. The lions are confined to the eastern peninsula where they have already occupied all the sizable patches of forest (see map below). As the remaining forest patches are far from the current lion range, there is hardly any scope for the expansion of the lion range any further, except into human habitat.

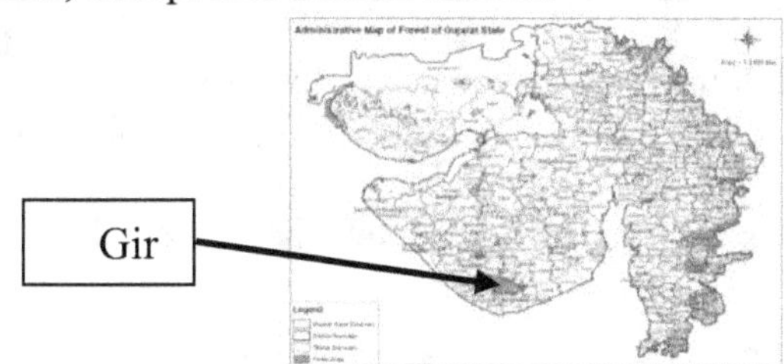

Figure 1: Distribution of Forests in Gujarat

If they disperse any further, it will certainly be into even more densely populated areas, virtually without any forests. The disgusting videos circulating in social media showing Gir lions roaming the village streets like dogs and waiting for people to throw licked-out chicken bones to them, indicate that the lions have become completely habituated to human company. The lions living outside the PAs, which made more than 40% of the population in 2015, no longer resemble the awe-inspiring predators we all imagine them to be as one sees them salivating by the side of people eating meals on cots. I had heard of people feeling disappointed at seeing rather tame looking lions in Gir. But seeing these videos makes one feel as if the lions have totally lost their pride of being the supreme predator of global folklore.

Genetic Bottleneck

Although the Gir lions are popularly believed to have recovered from a genetic bottleneck of only 20 animals in the early parts of the 20th century, the forest department of Gujarat does not seem to entirely agree with it. The historical population of the species in Gujarat as given in the departmental website is as follows:

Table 3: Lion Population: Historical Trend

Year	Population	Remarks
1884	Very few	Perhaps few dozen
1905	60-70	-
1920	50-100	Sir P.R. Gadell & J.M. Ratnagar
1936	287	First lion Census-Nawab of Junagarh
1950	219-287	Second lion census
1955	290	Third lion census
1963	285	Fourth lion census

The population seems to have remained relatively stable between 1936 and 1963. However, since the advent of modern conservation efforts in 1965, when the Gir lion sanctuary was constituted, the population has seen a steady growth to reach the current levels as shown below:

Table 4: Lion Population: Current Trend

Year	Population	Year	Population
1968	177	1995	304
1974	180	2000	327

Year	Population	Year	Population
1979	205	2005	359
1984	239	2010	411
1990	284	2015	523

The population was estimated to be 674 in 2020, although the assessment methodology seems seriously suspect (YV Jhala, quoted in *The Hindu* June 12, 2020).

Gir Lions are Not Unique

We always thought that the Asiatic lions (*Panthera leo persica*) live nowhere else except in Gir. This is no longer true. In 2017, the IUCN Cat Specialist Group revised the taxonomy of lions on the basis of a phylogeographical study. They have divided all the lions into two new sub-species, namely, *Panthera leo* (former name for all African lions) and *Panthera leo melanochaita* (Kitchener *et al.* 2017). The former occurs in India and in North, Western, and Central Africa, while *P. l. melanochaita* occurs in Southern and Eastern Africa (Bertolo *et al.* 2016). While this may dent the Gujarati pride a little, the existence of other populations of the same sub-species may also give them another excuse to refuse to collaborate in the creation of another population in Kuno National Park of Madhya Pradesh, as it no longer seems as critical as before. Or, will it trigger a change of heart? That is, why be bad boys of conservation when their monopoly of Asiatic lions is already lost? Interestingly, Johnsingh and Murali (2021) have already suggested that Kuno be populated with P. *l. leo* stock from Africa if Gujarat continues to be intransigent on the issue. They also suggest that the induction of the African *leo* lions into the Gir population may also pull them out of the inbreeding depression, the signs of which sometimes emerge in the form of the birth of blind and malformed cubs.

Meeting the King

I first saw Gir lions in 1978 as a probationer of the Indian Forest Service (IFS). Our class was in a bus following a truck that carried two buffalos as lion bait. The truck stopped at one spot and the buffalos were off-loaded. A pride of lions was waiting nearby. As soon as the buffalos came off the truck, the lions started eating them wherever they could get their teeth in. Only after several minutes, it struck a lioness that the poor bovids should be killed before eating. She found a leisurely grip on the throat and silenced the cries of pain. By then it was blood and gore all around. We came back to the camp quite confused, unsure whether to feel excited or disgusted.

The first half of the next day was spent studying the management of the sanctuary. In the afternoon, our instructor, late Mr. R.N. Mathur, happened to be passing by my door and asked me whether I would like to see more lions. After going some distance, we met a guard (used to be called *'shikari'* or hunter, back then) standing on the road. He told us that there were two lions a little off the road. We followed him into the forest on foot. He stopped a little short of the lions and stood bent over his *lathi* (stick). I stepped ahead of him a little just to take a better look but had to immediately retrace my step as one of the lions angrily protested. These adolescent lions gave me a little glimpse of the lions of our beliefs and imagination.

When we were coming out of the forest, a person was chatting with the driver of our vehicle and informed us that a female with cubs was nearby. We dashed off to see them, leaving the local guard behind, to be picked up on our way back. The man stayed back alone with two wild adolescent lions for company. Sun was already setting. When we returned after seeing the one-eyed lioness with two cubs, we found the guard sitting on the road with a fire burning in front. And, to our utter dismay, the two lions were also warming themselves on the other side of the fire!

As the lions behaved contrary to our vision of a ferocious predator, we rationalised this behaviour as one born of confidence and trust between the lions and the guards. These lions had not seen a man trying to kill them or snatching their kills. The animals perhaps also knew that the men in *khaki* were for their security. After my training, I got my posting in Kanha Tiger Reserve in 1981 and have had a fairly long association with tiger management since then. I found tigers exposed to harmless interaction with man in the tourism zones of our parks much more trusting of human presence around them in contrast to those who lived elsewhere. Back then, we also baited tigers for the tiger show. I often heard people light-heartedly commenting that the tigers they saw from the elephant back were perhaps drugged as they hardly paid any attention to the elephants carrying excited tourists. But whenever a stranger tiger turned up in the tiger show, it presented a totally different picture of a tiger — edgy, aggressive, and short-tempered. Baiting in tiger reserves was also stopped, perhaps in 1982, after Mrs. Indira Gandhi saw the gory scenes of lions eating buffalos alive in Gir. But tigers in the tourism zones of tiger reserves continued to be as trusting of men and elephants as before. The tiger show continued for nearly 40 years without baiting. Now even the tiger show has been stopped. But we continue to see tigers sitting comfortably on roads surrounded by dozens of vehicles full of noisy tourists in many parks. Or passing unconcerned through a tangle of vehicles. It does not take rocket science to conclude that these tigers do not see people in the vehicles as a threat. Certainly not as food.

Lions Living with People

The species started spreading out of the Gir forest around 1974 when about half a dozen lions were recorded in the adjoining Girnar and Mitiyala forests for the first time. Now it has spread further to Bhavnagar and Gir Somnath districts also. Lion visits have been recorded in over 1475 villages of four districts (HS Singh, 2017). In fact, the Asiatic Lion Landscape (ALL) now covers eight districts of Gujarat, including Junagadh, Amreli, Bhavnagar, Porbandar, Rajkot, Gir-Somnath, Botad, and Jamnagar, according to the 14th Lion Population Estimation Report 2015. The current lion range is not a contiguous forest. It consists of small fragments of forests connected by vast swathes of wasteland, agriculture, and habitations. Not only do the lions have to commute through villages to reach one forest patch from another, they now have become accustomed to living in and around villages as that is where most of their prey (livestock and nilgai) is. And, that is where all the videos emerge from. If their population continues to grow, the animals will depend on villages even more than now.

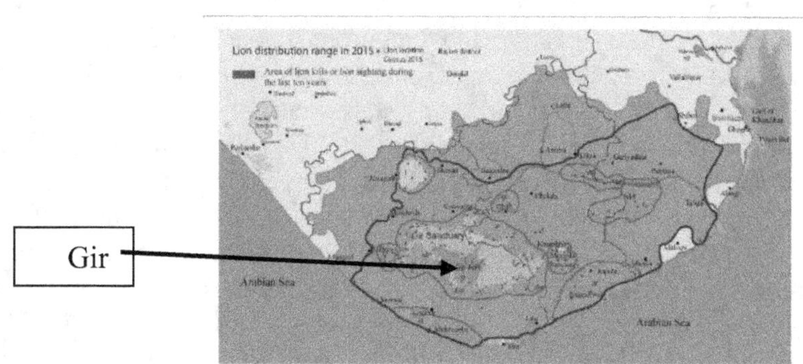

Figure 2: Lion Range in Gujarat

It seems carnivores have some special knack for living amongst human beings without conflict. Dozens of leopards live in Mumbai and Bengaluru without ever harming anybody except taking dogs and cats. Over a dozen tigers live on the outskirts of Bhopal and have injured only one forest guard in the last 10 years. Late Peter Jackson told AJT Johnsingh that one animal dealer in Nairobi lost his leopard and put traps to get it back. He caught four leopards but not his leopard. The Gir lions have been transiting through villages and agriculture for nearly half a century without ever earning the tag of 'man-eater'. Only one or two people get injured or killed in a year in mostly accidental encounters. People seem to be going about their lives without bothering about meeting a pride of lions around the corner. Videos show lions being shooed away by people with just a shout or a raised arm only. But how long shall this tenuous peace last?

Ticking Bomb

But the lions of Gujarat beat all limits of docility and conviviality. The population of lions living outside Gir, around human habitations, is perhaps much more than the official figures indicate. The 'block count' method of census used by Gujarat is prone to give gross underestimates in counting clusters of animals (prides) dispersed across vast distances. Especially, if there are not enough people to count, as was the case in 2020, due to the impact of the COVID-19 pandemic. If nothing else, the 29% increase in population since 2015 indicates that the number of villages affected by lion depredations is at least that much more than 1475 identified in 2015. With many more leopards than lions also residing around these villages, it is surprising that Gujarat has not seen any unusual intensity of man-eating. Villagers may, for now, value the presence of lions in their vicinity for keeping the more secretive and dangerous leopards at bay and also for controlling crop pests like nilgai and wild pig. But it is a ticking bomb. Lions are lions, after all. Any day one of them can turn on unsuspecting people, as one did in 2016, killing three persons and sharing the spoils with others. Even random environmental conditions can trigger such behaviour. Saberwal *et al.* (1994) found that "An average of 14.8 attacks by lions and 2.2 lion-caused deaths occurred annually between 1978 and 1991, and most attacks (82%) occurred on private lands outside the forest reserve. A drought in 1987–1988 precipitated an increase in rates of conflicts (from 7.3 to 40.0 attacks/year) ---". As there are too many prides roving the countryside, the possibility of more than one lion developing the taste for human flesh at the same time is very real. When that happens, people will forget that lions are a part of Gujarati *asmita* (Pride of Gujarat). The death of 92 lions in the first five months of 2020 alone (https://www.downtoearth.org.in/test/news/the-whole-truth-92-lions-dead-since-january-in-gir-cdv-a-cause-says-moef-cc-71721), not all due to canine distemper, clearly indicates that those who have to live with lions do not think of the lions the way the lion lovers of the world believe them to. Even if people continue to be placid about their fate in the midst of lions, no society has the right to feed its people to lions unless lions are critical to their survival or well-being. Our lions, especially in such large numbers, and the way they have become omnipresent in the countryside of Saurashtra, are obviously not.

Need to Change Tack

It is true that Gujarat has done a fantastic job of saving the species from the brink. But they should know when to stop and prevent their success from turning into a self-imposed calamity. They should know how many are too many. And, where to keep them. At least not in villages.

It is also true that we must ensure that all species continue to exist on this earth. But this cannot and must not be done at the cost of human well-being, least of all human lives. Surprisingly, that is exactly what we are doing in Gujarat. The human cost of having lions in Gujarat is going to grow as their numbers grow and they spread further and further away from Gir. The cost shall be in terms of lives and livestock lost. It can also be in the form of a deep fear that people have to live under. What kind of life is it if one does not know whether one's child is going to come back from the school in the neighbouring village or not? Or, if the lions can jump into your cattle shed in broad daylight and feast on your beloved cow? Some of that is happening now and more will happen if we do not stop the lions from proliferating and spreading. I have been asked by angry people why, after all, we are preserving dangerous animals like tigers. Gujarat officers must be facing the same question regarding lions. Lions are much more dangerous because they have started living in villages. Tigers at least live in the forests and rarely come into villages.

Incidentally, despite their growing numbers, lions are not yet out of the danger of extinction as any disease, drought or flood can kill a lot of them, as seen recently. Numbers can be a security against predation or poaching but not against forces of nature. To be safe against these forces a species has to have more than one population. The whole world thinks that's the way to go but not Gujarat. Gujarat is steadfastly blocking a national programme to create another lion population, at a safe distance from the Gir. It is heaping misery and misfortune on its people by increasing the lion population to dangerous levels rather than heeding global advice. Sooner or later, the state (and the country) has to look for an alternative path as the misery becomes too much to tolerate. I hope they will do it sooner than later.

New Path

What is that alternative path? It is a path aimed at making people, if not livestock too, safe against attacks by lions. It is also a path that makes local people think of lions as an asset rather than as a threat. Under this strategy, any human casualties shall be despite the best efforts of the state to prevent them. Moreover, a large number of people will get jobs because of the presence of lions rather than losing livelihoods as happens now. Now we are doing nothing except preaching to the people to be careful. This new lion conservation paradigm shall consist of the following components:

1. All lions living outside protected areas must be immediately removed. If they cannot be translocated to PAs or zoos, they should just be destroyed.

2. All protected areas housing lions must be expanded as far as possible and should be completely fenced. If there are points on their perimeter where an effective fence cannot be erected due to geomorphological reasons (e.g. large rivers), these points should be protected by check posts equipped with the capacity to capture or deter lions.

3. As lions are prolific breeders, their population has to be kept within the carrying capacity of their habitat by regularly removing surplus animals. The surplus animals can be used to populate new protected areas. Or, they can be sold to other states or zoos interested in creating lion populations. One Kuno will also not be enough to soak up all the surplus lions of Gujarat. If there is no demand for lions, they should be just hunted or euthanised.

4. Old and overmature male lions can be allowed to be trophy-hunted by rich tourists to raise funds for conservation. The same should apply to leopards and any other trophy animals (e.g. nilgai) that the hunting world may be interested in. One lion can easily get a crore rupees in trophy fee and another crore in the form of incidental services. Perhaps as much from saved livestock. In fact, Asiatic lions being very special, the earnings may be much more if we use some creative marketing.

It is well-known that mortality in a stable population is generally compensatory i.e. the same proportion of the population dies each year although the agents causing mortality may vary. According to a reply given in the state assembly, 313 lions (90 lionesses, 71 lions, and 152 cubs) died of various causes in two years, 2019 and 2020 (*The Hindu*, Ahmedabad 06 March 2021). Although these seem to be abnormal years, it is obvious that earning 100 crore rupees per annum from the sale of lions which are in any case going to die should not be impossible.

5. Large patches of government forests, government wastelands (unclassed forests), and community wastelands, along with adjoining unproductive croplands, can be converted into community-based lion conservancies. Conservancies should operate as tourism businesses with all the profit going to the communities and participating landowners. They should be encouraged to partner with professional ecotourism companies, which have the technical, financial, and marketing capacity to generate a world-class experience, on a profit-sharing basis. Tourism drives conservation all over the world and has saved hundreds of species from the brink, especially where local communities benefit from conservation.

Frozen Minds

Thus, this new strategy shall consist of two prongs. One, to control lion numbers and movements; second, use lions to feed people. Inexplicably, the Indian conservation intelligentsia is against both these approaches. They want wild animals to spread everywhere and do not want to control their movements through fences. On the contrary, they want long, meandering, forest corridors to connect small populations forgetting that India just does not have the land for such luxury. If the animals commuting through these corridors of conflict get killed on the way, or kill people, it is only collateral damage for them. When one suggests controlling numbers, their imagination does not go beyond expensive and unimplementable contraception rather than utilising the surplus or unproductive animals for human well-being. For them, common sense is anathema.

Wild animals can feed people only through tourism and hunting. Not to speak of hunting, our eggheads would allow even tourism only as a compromise. They think tourists disturb wild animals and it is a sin. To them, disturbance caused by visitors is almost equivalent to poaching. Who will forget that the Government of India (through

NTCA) tried its best, between 2006 and 2012, to coax states to phase out tourism from PAs until it was forced to change tack in the Supreme Court?

As for hunting, we have progressively weeded out or denatured all the provisions in WLPA which allowed hunting of animals when needed. In this process, we have completely messed up the law as now it is riddled with contradictory provisions. For example, we all believe that WLPA allows killing only if an animal or group of animals becomes dangerous to human life or property (Sections 9 and 11). Nobody notices that we can also "destroy" wildlife in PAs for "better management" {Sections 29 and 35 (6)}. Removal or destruction of surplus or unproductive (past breeding age) animals would obviously be "better management". Thus, lions can be trophy-hunted in the name of "better management" in PAs, and in the name of removing the threat to human life outside. In fact, we can use both these arguments for hunting inside PAs. The same goes for other species. However, our frozen minds are unlikely to take advantage of this legal paradox any time soon.

Conclusion

Thus, despite our debilitating conservatism regarding wildlife tourism and hunting, we can still use these tools for making the conservation of wild animals, lions in this case, sustainable and desirable. It can be done within the existing law, although the law should be amended if we have some common sense.

Gujarat forest department has to capture hundreds of lions and leopards every year as they run into conflict with people. They are either released back in the forest, to face the same fate again, or are put in cages to live a miserable life. All at huge cost to the state. Hundreds die in conflict, disease, or poaching. Having such animals hunted before they become a problem shall convert them into an asset from being a liability. This will save more lions in the long run than letting them be killed in conflict or cages.

CHAPTER-4

Living with the Forest Rights Act

Background

Wildlife conservation in India is based on the fundamental premise that wild animals and their habitat (forest land) are the property of the government and the management of wildlife is the business of the forest department. But The Scheduled Tribes and Other Traditional Forest Dwellers (Recognition of Forest Rights) Act, 2006, or the Forest Rights Act (FRA) as it is popularly known, has changed everything. Although the animals are still the property of the government, the control of the forests is now vested in the communities in the name of "community forest resource" (CFR). We do not see and feel this dramatic shift because communities have not yet taken over these lands, except in a few cases. In many places communities have not yet filed their claims while authorities are blocking their claims in others.

FRA says that every village community has a right "to protect, regenerate or conserve or manage any community forest resource". CFR is defined as the "customary common forest land within the traditional or customary boundaries of the village or seasonal use of landscape in the case of pastoral communities, including reserved forests, protected forests and protected areas such as Sanctuaries and National Parks to which the community had traditional access". The delineation of the CFR is to be done by the villagers themselves and "such delineation shall formalize and recognize the powers of the community in access, conservation and sustainable use of such community forest resources" {FRA Rule 12 (g)}. Thus, no authority has the power to change what the villagers want as their CFR. Therefore, it is reasonable to believe that virtually all the forests of India can go under community control one day. It all depends on when the communities become aware of their power to carve out their own CFRs, limited only by the claims of adjoining communities. This awareness is bound to come, even if slowly.

While the communities shall have complete control of their CFRs, any forests not claimed as CFR shall be subject to several other rights, including the right to the collection of minor forest produce (MFP) (including bamboo), and the right to the grazing of livestock. Right for "habitation or for self-cultivation" can be claimed only on lands occupied prior to 13.12.2005. However, a virtual mayhem is going on in the forests, fuelled by the hope that this date shall be revised sooner or later.

These rights can be claimed on "all forest lands", including national parks, wildlife sanctuaries, and reserve forests, as mentioned above. Although the rights recognised inside PAs can be subsequently modified and acquired by the government, this can be done only with the consent of the communities. Thus, if the communities decide to manage their CFR (and other forest lands where their usufruct rights have been recognised) their own way, PAs and reserve forests shall completely lose their meaning. After all, PAs and reserve forests were created after settling all rights.

Management of Protected Areas as Community Forest Resource

Wildlife conservation under the WLPA has two basic planks. One, that wild animals are protected everywhere i.e. they can be killed or captured only under exceptional circumstances. Two, special measures are taken to increase their populations in PAs. WLPA does not allow "sustainable use" of wildlife which is the central theme of FRA. Now that FRA empowers communities "to protect, regenerate or conserve or manage" large chunks of forests *for sustainable use*, it naturally implies sustainable use of wildlife as well. Thus, FRA has removed both these planks and wildlife conservation, as we know it, has no solid ground to stand on now. I know this interpretation will be contested by most people as FRA has not recognised "the traditional right of hunting or trapping" of wild animals {Section 3(1) (i)}. However, this exception seems to have no meaning, seen in the light of the right to sustainable use of CFR. The exception may be relevant outside CFRs but the primary objective in a CFR is the sustainable use of all that grows there. As CFR management cannot be imagined without the freedom to cut and plant trees (although the law is silent about it), similarly, it cannot be imagined without managing wildlife populations. This is because wildlife is as much a forest produce as plants. Moreover, wild animals can have a strong effect on the health and profitability of the CFRs.

Thus, the conservation of wildlife is now completely at the mercy of the communities, especially in CFRs, although the real impact is yet to come. According to a conservative estimate by the civil society organisations, 34 to 36 million hectares of forest lands qualify to finally become CFR (CFR-LA, 2018) which makes nearly 53% to 56% of India's total forests. This does not include the Jammu & Kashmir and the states of the northeast, although 56.31% of the forests in the northeast are already community property (Poffenberger *et al.*2006). More than 1.065 million ha in Maharashtra, Odisha, Kerala, Gujarat, and Karnataka had already been assigned to communities as CFR by December 2017. CFR rights have been recognised inside the core area of Simlipal Tiger Reserve of Odisha, BRT Wildlife Sanctuary of Karnataka, and Shoolpaneshwar Wildlife Sanctuary of Gujarat. Claims have been received in the core areas of Melghat and Tadoba Andhari tiger reserves of Maharashtra and are likely to be recognised sooner or later. Even relocated villages have filed CFR claims in these reserves. One day, the managers of these PAs will come to realise that their writ no longer runs and there will be calls for them to fold up and go home. This has already happened in Shoolpaneshwar and BRT sanctuaries.

Although the pace of creation of CFRs has been slow so far, it is an unstoppable process. Even if the legality of the right to sustainable use of wildlife in CFRs is questioned by the conservationists, it is anybody's guess whether wildlife will survive on lands where the owners see it as a threat. Therefore, perhaps the best bet for wildlife would be to preserve it through sustainable use under FRA rather than inflicting it on communities with the help of WLPA. In any case, the protection provided in WLPA is unlikely to be effective as forest departments will be patrolling less and less of the forests in future. As nobody in India has the expertise and experience in sustainable use of wildlife, this will also mean learning a new way of doing conservation. In fact, this will apply to the conservation of forests in general.

Role of Forest Departments in Future Forest Management

In the light of the above discussion, it is obvious that forest departments shall have to go out of the way to secure any significant role in the management of forests and wildllife as the areas under CFR grows with time. The broad contours of the ways the forest departments can stay engaged in the management of forests and wildlife under the new regime can be as follows:

1. As the right to "protect, regenerate or conserve or manage" more than half the notified forests, including PAs, is likely to be vested in local communities, forest departments can contribute to the management of these forests only if the communities welcome their support. Therefore, FDs will have to make themselves desirable to the communities.

2. Forest departments can seek engagement with communities in two ways. They can try to convince the communities to let them manage the forests as per a management plan approved by the communities and under the supervision of the communities. Alternatively, they can seek a consultative role with the communities if the communities do not want to hand over their forests back to the FD for management. The department has to be equipped and organised to provide both kinds of support to the communities.

    Management of community-owned PAs by the government is possible as in Australia. The famous Kakadu and Gurig national parks in the Northern Territories province of Australia are owned by the local aborigine tribes while they are managed by the Conservation Commission of Australia as per an agreed management plan. All the profit from these parks goes to the owners.

3. The concept of reserve forests, national parks, wildlife sanctuaries, and tiger reserves will become redundant as the communities may decide to manage their CFRs under a new approach. For example, they may decide to raise plantations in places that are now parts of national parks. They may also decide to manage areas currently outside PAs for wildlife management and tourism, depending upon potential benefits. FDs will have to demonstrate the comparative potential of various management approaches to generate sustainable benefits for the communities in order to convince them to opt for a particular management approach.

4. Owners of CFRs who decide to manage their areas as wildlife management areas, *a la* PAs of today, may form their own rules irrespective of what the WLPA ordains. They may decide to hunt

animals more liberally than we have been doing so far. As CFRs are meant to be managed for maximising benefits for communities through sustainable use of resources, it will be natural for the communities to consider wild animals as a part of the resource basket. Although they will not need WLPA to decide their management strategy, even WLPA allows exploitation, destruction, and removal of wildlife from PAs for the sake of better wildlife management (WLPA Section 29 and 35). As mentioned before, the exclusion of "the traditional right of hunting or trapping" wild animals from the list of rights recognised under FRA does not stand in the way of sustainable use of wildlife in a CFR as these are two separate rights. Foresters and wildlife biologists shall have to work closely with the communities in order to ensure that people avoid the temptation to overexploit wildlife. This will be a big challenge for FDs as they have never seen wildlife as a natural resource. They will have to train a large number of field officers in this discipline so that adequate field hands are available to work with the communities.

5. Government rules and guidelines on wildlife tourism will become irrelevant as the communities shall not be bound by them. For example, the tourism guidelines issued by the National Tiger Conservation Authority (NTCA) that limit tourism zones to 20% of the area of a PA shall not apply in a CFR. Communities may not be interested in imposing any carrying capacity limits prescribed by NTCA and may also like to build lodges or camps inside forests. Communities may develop their own tourism regulations which may vary from CFR to CFR unless a group of CFRs is under common management. In order to ensure healthy and sustainable tourism practices in CFRs, particularly in former PAs, FDs shall have to reach out to concerned communities and build their capacities to develop low-impact and high-value tourism products.

6. When sustainable incomes from forests and wildlife become the sole criteria for their preservation, tourism as an additional (even principal) source of income to the communities shall strengthen their stakes in conservation. Tourism incomes can significantly douse the temptation to cut trees and kill wild animals. Therefore, FDs must encourage communities to develop ecotourism as a major forest product, as far as possible, even outside traditional wildlife reserves. They may even be allowed to bring in animals

from outside if necessary. As community-operated tourism operations generally fail for the lack of strong marketing and quality of services, FDs must promote partnerships between communities and professional travel agents and lodge operators who can assist the communities in creating marketable tourism products.

7. Communities will need help in managing wildlife populations sustainably but Indian foresters have no expertise in this domain. Indian NGOs also do not have any exposure in this field. In order to ensure that wildlife is managed scientifically, FDs shall have to acquire this expertise at the earliest so that communities can be advised and assisted properly. Management of wildlife populations does not imply hunting alone. It may involve the capture and translocation of animals from one area to another. If a community wants to manage its area for wildlife tourism, it may need to buy or borrow animals from a richer CFR. Although sustainable use of wildlife is inherent in the concept of CFRs, killing, capture, and translocation of wild animals is regulated by WLPA. As FRA prevails over other laws, to the extent they overlap (Section 13), it is obvious that communities will not need to follow WLPA for killing or capturing wild animals in CFRs. In the context of this conflict, FDs shall have to explore ways of liberalising these activities as far as possible within the law. Perhaps the easiest way would be to declare the heads of the communities interested in wildlife management as the honorary wildlife wardens and delegate the powers of the CWLW to permit the hunting of wild animals to them as per the provisions of Section 5 of WLPA. In the long run, WLPA will have to be amended to facilitate wildlife management by communities, rather than by FDs.

8. Communities owning CFRs shall be free to go to any other organisation or individual for technical support or management contract, instead of the FD. In such a situation, FDs will have to compete with private operators. They will also have to strengthen the hands of the communities in contract negotiations with such private operators.

9. FRA has caused a five-fold spurt in forest encroachments (Pabla, 2020) and forest departments have been disempowered to evict even new encroachers (Section 5). Many PAs are also falling victim to rampant encroachments. Therefore, forest departments must assist in fast-tracking the creation of CFRs, rather than

resisting the process as of today. This is necessary because strong community stakes in forests may be the only way to stop encroachments, now that no government agency has the power to do so.

10. **Management of Human-Wildlife Conflict**: If wildlife survives or increases under the large-scale community management of forests, FDs will have the responsibility to manage human-wildlife conflict (HWC). While the destruction or capture of carnivores and elephants that become dangerous to human life will be the direct responsibility of the FDs, communities shall have to be allowed to manage the populations of herbivores living off their crops. The power of the communities to the sustainable use of resources will not be available outside CFRs. There can be two ways of dealing with this situation. The affected communities can be appointed honorary wildlife wardens under Section 4 of the WLPA and necessary powers to allow the hunting of specified animals can be delegated to it under Section 5. Alternatively, the same power can be delegated to DFOs who can permit the affected communities to cull a certain number of animals either annually or when otherwise required. The communities may hunt the specified numbers either through their own members or have them hunted commercially to generate further benefits for their members. Payment of compensation for human or livestock deaths or for crop losses where hunting is not permitted shall also be the responsibility of the DFO as at present.

11. **FD to Act as Umbilical Cord:** One important challenge in the new regime shall be to maintain a live link between the communities and the government, despite there being no authority empowered to regulate the conduct of the communities. This will be required for the transfer of financial and technical inputs from the government to the communities as well as to get feedback from the communities to inform future policy on the subject. This umbilical cord shall be required even for those communities who may not be accessing any contractual or advisory services of the FD. Most of the investments in forestry come from the central government in the form of central sector (CS) or centrally sponsored schemes (CSS). Now also from Compensatory Afforestation Fund Management Authority (CAMPA). Communities cannot protect or manage their forests and wildlife without the continuation of this support system. FDs shall have to ensure that this support continues to reach the

communities. The process for disbursing financial assistance to the communities under CS, CSS and CAMPA, as well as state-level investments in the forestry and wildlife sector, will have to be changed to fit into the new ecosystem. While FD will create suitable platforms for informing the communities about the availability, extent, and nature of government support, communities may avail this support perhaps on a first-come and first-served basis, as the resources are never going to be enough for everybody. FDs can assess the entitlement of applicants based on suitable eligibility criteria, including the record of submission of information on specified parameters. Other avenues for implementing government programmes and generating critically required management, social and financial information, may also have to be explored for supporting future policy development.

Compliance with International Obligations

An important fallout of FRA is the loss of power of the government to take action regarding issues having implications far beyond the individual communities. Communities have complete independence as to how they want to manage their CFRs. Therefore, government can only informally encourage them, through incentives and disincentives, to support government action for compliance with its international commitments and obligations on environmental issues. Government shall have to use its financial assistance programmes creatively in order to meet its international commitments and obligations. There are instances of communities opposing afforestation programmes on the ground that FD has no right to interfere in the management of their forests, although their CFR claims are still pending. If the funds are directly given to the communities, they may happily do what the government wants.

The government may also use the provisions of the Indian Forest Act 1927 (IFA) to intervene where communities are totally intransigent. It should be possible for the government to use Section 35 (Protection of forests for special purposes), Section 36 (Power to assume management of forests), Section 37 (Expropriation of forests in certain cases), and Section 38 (Protection of forests on request of owner) of IFA to control the management of community forests, if it becomes unavoidable, although it will be quite inconvenient in the current political climate.

Incidentally, the reasons for intervention under these sections do not include wildlife conservation. Therefore, these sections may have to be suitably tweaked for this purpose. Many states have already modified these sections to suit other local requirements. Although amending any forest law to increase government control on forests will also be politically difficult, it will still be easier than tinkering with FRA.

Reengineering the Forest Departments

Obviously, the paramilitary nature of the forest departments of today is going to be useless in the new context. They will have to transform themselves into service agencies to support the communities in managing their forests and wildlife sustainably. A hands-off policy as enshrined in the FRA or trying to interfere in the community control of forests in the garb of IFA or WLPA, will only lead to destruction. Although it will not be easy, a lot can still be done to preserve our natural resources, despite FRA. But this will be possible only if we reengineer the forest departments on the following lines:

1. There will be no need to continue the current territorial form of the organisation. It will have to be replaced by a functional organisation in which the number and kind of staff required at any location shall be allotted from a central pool from time to time, depending on the responsibility assigned by the CFR owners. Thus, there will be no beat or range system *per se* although in some places where FD gets a contract to implement full management, including protection, a semblance of the territorial form may remain.

2. There may be a regular forest office at the district (district forest officer) or sub-district level, as appropriate, where communities can contact for various services. This office will also have the responsibility to solicit business (conservation) opportunities with the communities like the business development activities of any corporate entity.

3. The principal job of the district forest office shall be to function as a support centre for the communities and build their capacity to manage their forests and PAs sustainably. They will have to be staffed with specialists in mass communications, forestry, wildlife biology, habitat management, tourism management and wildlife veterinary science, etc. so that they can provide technically sound services to the communities. FDs shall have to actively reach out to the communities in order to sensitise them to the new forest management regime and help them deal with the challenges they may face in managing their resources.

4. There will be no need to continue the offices of PA managers unless the organisation gets a full-service contract from all the communities owning a PA and they decide to continue it as a PA. As an existing PA may become part of the CFRs of several communities, FD will have to convince all the communities to continue managing their parts for wildlife management and to opt for a unified management contract with FD.

5. As the implementation of FRA is the responsibility of the Ministry of Tribal Affairs (MoTA), it will be logical to transfer the Forestry and Wildlife Division of the MoEF&CC to MoTA so that foresters and the officials responsible for tribal affairs can make FRA a common cause (Pabla 2020). Corresponding administrative changes will have to be instituted at the state level also. This is critically important because it is almost impossible to implement FRA expeditiously without the willing support of the FDs, as we have seen so far. On the other hand, only FDs can cushion its adverse impact on forests and wildlife. This is not happening at present as foresters see FRA as a threat not only to the forests and wildlife, but also to the very existence of forest departments. The only way this alienation can be removed is by putting the champions of tribals and forests under one roof so that coordinated policies and programmes can be devised for the benefit of both.

Harmonisation of All Forest Laws:

Above suggestions amount to what is possible within the current legal regime to minimise the adverse impact of FRA on forests and wildlife. However, it may not be adequate to save our forests and wildlife as FRA and other forest laws are pulling in different directions and FRA has precedence over other laws in critical matters. This situation is neither good for our forests, nor for the people for whom everything is being done. We must immediately examine how to stop these laws from coming in each other's way. While FRA must provide scope for the operation of other laws consistent with its overall goals, the forest laws, namely IFA 1927, WLPA 1972, and FCA 1980, should also accommodate the spirit of FRA. Most of all, we will need a government agency that has the legal authority to engage with the communities and regulate their conduct to ward off nefarious influences. Please refer to "Laws At War" by this author to see the detailed proposals for minimum amendments required in each of these laws to enable their implementation without mutual friction.

Conclusion

Forest Rights Act is now a fact of life. It does not recognise PAs and allows sustainable use of forest products by communities. Sustainable use of forests in CFRs naturally includes the sustainable use of wildlife as well. Its impact on wildlife is likely to be felt gradually as more and more PAs come under community control and the communities realise the full scope of their new rights. As forest departments have not been given any authority in the management of CFRs, the only way for them to stay relevant and ensure the conservation of wildlife is to transform themselves into service agencies and motivate the communities to manage their CFRs sustainably. The steps suggested above can help achieve this objective.

Without this approach, our forests will always be on fire and any attempts by foresters to douse these fires may in fact singe them more than the forests. There will be no escape for our wild animals from the *davanals* (mythical wildfires of our epics) likely to be unleashed by FRA.

CHAPTER-5

Living with Forest Fires

I grew up (in IFS) hating forest fires and spent my youth fighting them in the national parks of Madhya Pradesh. Every summer was like hell. A new fire would start before we had put out one, day in and day out. The Madhya Pradesh Forest Manual expects every forester to drop everything and head to a fire site the moment one hears of it. For a PA manager in India, wild fires have an even more special meaning. It is an outright catastrophe. So, we had to spend the entire summer preventing and fighting wildfires; without wireless, mobile phones, and transport.

That was 40 years ago. Now I hear fires are uncommon in most PAs. Even territorial divisions seem to have fewer summer fires. Perhaps technology and resources have made the difference.

I am not sure if what they teach about wildfires in our forestry schools has changed. We were taught that fire was a demon out to devour our forests. It killed vegetation and animals and cooked the soils. That is what everybody in India believes even today. If a forest is burnt, the public thinks it is gone forever. Once I was waiting to board a train in Delhi. I was wearing a rather fancy T-shirt with "Bandhavgarh Jungle Lodge" written in bold letters. At that time jungle lodges were very uncommon. A person hesitantly asked me if I had something to do with wildlife. When I told him that I was the director of Bandhavgarh National Park, he said, "Sir, I go to Bharatpur bird sanctuary regularly. There was a fire there this year, where can I go now?" I had to struggle to convince him that he could still go to Bharatpur as the trees and birds would be back the next year.

Interestingly, every Indian forester swears by 'General Silviculture for India' by Champion & Seth (1968). It clearly mentions that the germination of the seeds of several prominent timber trees of India, like teak, sal, and chir pine is dependent on fire. Either because it burns the leaf litter and allows the seeds to make contact with mineral soil. Or because it cracks the hard seed coat. However, nobody seemed to remember these virtues when I joined the state in 1979, after training at the Indian Forest College. The book also advocated "controlled burning" of pine forests in winter to prevent devastating summer fires. Perhaps nobody reads that part of the book. We hate fires so much that even the tradition of clearing a plantation site by burning the slash left behind in previous year's felling operations was forbidden a year or two after I entered service.

Thus, what remains of our relationship with forest fires (Americans call them wildland fires or wildfires) is that it kills all regeneration, if not all the trees.

No wonder that society expects us to put out all forest fires quickly. So much so that the High Court of Uttarakhand has laid out time-bound responsibilities of forest officers right up to the Principal Chief Conservator of Forests for dealing with fires. The order dated December 19, 2016 stated, "If the forest fire continues for more than 24 hours, the concerned divisional forest officer shall be deemed to be put under suspension and further if it continues for more than 48 hours, the conservator of forest shall be deemed to be put under suspension - --- if forest fire continues for more than 72 hours, principal chief conservator of forest shall be deemed to be put under suspension and disciplinary proceedings shall be initiated against him for not preventing/controlling forest fires." (*Times of India* 19 December, 2016). Perhaps that order still stands. Once I narrowly prevented a similar order in the Supreme Court of India regarding Madhya Pradesh. I was in the court in connection with the famous Godavarman case and a lawyer started showing to the judges pictures of a forest fire of Madhya Pradesh, which had captured headlines the previous day. The judges started mumbling angrily about the incompetence of the forest departments etc. etc. and were about to pass an order when I told our advocate that I wanted to say something about this fire event. On getting permission, I told the court that I was responsible for the protection of forests in MP and had inspected the forest in question after the fire. I was able to convince the judges that summer surface fires were a normal feature of our forests and that all life would be back to normal after a few days or months.

If we foresters also treat every forest fire as a disaster, the courts and the society will naturally consider us incompetent if a forest fire captures national headlines. But the world does not see them as we do. Many countries believe that forest fires are necessary to keep forests and wildlife healthy and diverse. Many even have laws to ensure that their forests burn at prescribed intervals.

Global Forest Fire Management Policies

After spending 15 years of my professional life in such an environment, I got a chance to go to the USA on a study tour in 1992. And to a few other countries after that. Here's what I learnt about their approach to wildfires (accounts based on my tour notes).

- Nearly one-third of the Yellowstone National Park was burnt by wildfires in 1988. Till then fires were considered a natural phenomenon and were allowed to burn out. Active fire suppression started after these fires but still, only about 25% of the fires are actively suppressed, based on roughly the following criteria:

- ✓ In general, all anthropogenic fires are suppressed but natural fires are not. Fires ignited by lightning are considered natural fires.

- ✓ Fires are actively suppressed only when fuel moisture is less than 16%, the temperature is high, and wind speed is high with no chance of rain.

- ✓ All fires that pose danger to habitation or other built-up properties are suppressed.

- The National Elk Refuge, Jackson (Wyoming) was regularly burnt to improve productivity and to recycle trampled grasses.

- In the Starkey Project experimental forest (82.96 km^2, all fenced) in the Blue Mountains of Washington state, fire suppression since 1945 had replaced the fire-hardy Ponderosa pine and larch with fire-tender fir and Douglas fir trees. Spruce budworm had since killed most of the fir trees in the previous 9 years. At the time of our visit, all fir and Douglas fir trees were being removed and a 10-15 year fire cycle was being introduced, in order to bring the original vegetation back.

- When I visited Kakadu National Park in the Northern Territories of Australia in 1993, a crew was getting ready to burn the forest by throwing incendiary devices from a helicopter. The record in my tour note says that, "Fire management is a very major operation in the Northern Territories. The basic approach is that the forests, savannas, and woodlands should be burnt the same way as the traditional inhabitants had been doing. Fires are actively suppressed only if they are a threat to human settlements or other properties. Almost everywhere the forests had either been burnt or were smouldering. The fundamental premise in fire management is that in dry tropical conditions, the forests will get burnt, whatever we do, and they should be deliberately burnt regularly at short intervals to keep the impact low. Research in Australia is focusing on the fire frequency for producing the most diverse biota." The time of our visit coincided with the cool season burning activity.

Jack Ward Thomas, who later became the Chief of US Forest Service, gifted us copies of his monumental work "Wildlife Habitats in Managed Forests" when he hosted us for a few days on our study tour. The book describes how "prescribed burning" could be used to manage "snags" and "dead and down woody material" for wildlife as a part of silviculture. I also happened to purchase another wildlife management epic, the "Game Management" by Aldo Leopold (1933) on that trip. The book elaborately describes the effects of fire on wildlife and wildlife habitats and how wildlife habitats, populations, and communities can be customised through the intelligent use of fire. Thus, by the time I returned to my state in 1996, after my 5-year stint at the Wildlife Institute of India (WII), I had started looking at wildfires a bit differently.

In the year 2000, I happened to undertake a study tour to South Africa and the USA where I visited famous protected areas such as the Kruger and Pilanesberg national parks in South Africa, Yosemite National Park in California, Welder Wildlife Refuge in Texas, and Archbold Biological Station in Texas. By this time, I had become especially interested in the wildfire management systems around the world. My tour report contains the following account of the fire management approaches of the places I visited:

"Fire management is one of the most important elements, almost the only element, in habitat management in all the sites visited, both in South Africa as well as in the USA. Instead of total fire protection, as in India, managers in these PAs recognise the role played by fires in the evolution and maintenance of ecosystems, both tropical as well as temperate, and fires are being used to achieve the objectives of park management. In short, the emphasis is to ensure that every part of the park burns according to a definite plan and interval. Burning is considered more critical to habitat than fire protection. The main consideration behind modern fire management policies is that fire has always been the most influential force in shaping terrestrial ecosystems, and all plant and animal species have evolved as a result of the historical fire regimes. As a result, altering historical fire regimes will result in the extinction or decline of many fire- dependent plant and animal species and encourage others. The exclusion of fires from any ecosystem results in the return of even more destructive fires. As a result, total fire protection is rather futile as it is impossible to keep fires out forever, in any case.

The fire management policies followed by different parks are briefly outlined below:

Kruger National Park

Kruger has had experimental burning plots since 1950, testing 12 different fire regimes. Until then, there was no system of fire management. Since then, a system of rotational burning at three-year intervals was followed until 1992. Since 1992, discussions on changes in the fire policy have been going on and the new management plan has discarded the policy of rotational burning. Now a system of burning depending upon the 'range condition' has been followed. The new policy, as enshrined in the new plan, consists of the following elements:

- All natural fires will be allowed to burn unchecked, unless they become a threat to human life and property;
- All man-made fires, both accidental and arson, shall be controlled;
- A landscape-scale management trial called the Large-Scale Herbivory-Fire Interaction Research Experiment (Lashfire) is being initiated from April 2000, for a period of 20 years. The experiment will conduct trials on three possible policies, namely Patch Mosaic System, Range-Condition System, and Lightning-Induced Burning System, on blocks as large as 75,000 ha each.

Pilanesberg National Park

This park has been following the patch-mosaic system for more than 12 years now (year 2000). The system is based on the belief that natural fires create a natural mosaic of habitats to suit the needs of most species and every patch is burned at random intervals. The management practice followed is something like this:

- The entire park is divided into a 500 m X 500 m grid.
- Total area to be burnt each year and the number of fires required is worked out by a computer programme. Approximately 1/3 of the park is burnt each year. Ecologists decide the burning programme.
- The burning programme lasts almost 8 months a year (April to October) and fires are ignited by the staff throughout the

season. Early season fires are small while the late dry season fires are larger.

- More fires are ignited in the early season. Fires are allowed to burn themselves out. All fires are 'point-ignited'. The area burnt each year is a function of the grass fuel load and the number of fires per year is a function of the percentage area to be burnt.
- The seasonality, area burnt, and fire intensity are spatially and temporally varied across the landscape.

Yosemite National Park

New fire management principles were adopted 30 years ago.

- 84% of the park is natural and fires are allowed to burn on their own. The park experiences 2-80 incidents of natural fires/year. Each burn is approximately 2,000-3,000 acres.
- Fires are not fought but are monitored. However, all man-caused fires are extinguished.
- 16% of the area has changed over time due to fire control. Out of this, 1,000 acres are burnt each year to return it to its natural fire regime.
- Fires are classified as green, orange, and black depending on their severity.
- Fire management policy for national forests is the same as for national parks.

Welder Wildlife Refuge (Texas)

This is a very small property (31.5 km^2) and there are almost no natural fires. The management decides the fire regime on the basis of fuel load in each area which is mainly determined by rainfall. But burning is a regular practice. The refuge takes measures to keep the density of brushwood low (spraying herbicides, uprooting, roller chopping, etc.) primarily to build up herbaceous fuels for burning. Fire is the main means to keep the brushwood canopy down.

Archbold Biological Station (Florida)

The station used prescribed fires for balancing the diverse goals and provide temporal and spatial heterogeneity across the landscape. The goals are: enhancing biological diversity, enhancing threatened and endangered species, mimicking natural processes, providing a diversity of research and educational opportunities, interacting with other fire management agencies, reducing fire hazards, and, conducting safe burns. A mosaic of units of various sizes, burned at various fire-return intervals is adopted. The system is built around 5-

fire return intervals, each of which is a range of years within which individual burn units are planned to re-burn. In fact, the state of Florida has a Prescribed Burning Act, 1990, and the second week of March is observed as the Prescribed Fires Awareness Week."

Minnesota Valley National Wildlife Refuge

I got an opportunity to visit this refuge in the summer of 2002. It is one of the very few, very small, urban wildlife refuges in the USA and was primarily created for protecting the natural floodplains adjoining the city of Minneapolis/St. Paul. My tour note has the following account of the fire policy of the refuge:

- All wildfires are required to be suppressed in the USA, unless an area has an approved fire management plan. This refuge has a fire management plan (FMP) and therefore follows its prescriptions.

- The refuge FMP accepted option (a) after testing the following three alternative action plans:

(a) Management ignited prescribed fires but total suppression of all wildfires;

(b) Full suppression;

(c) Management ignited prescribed fires and appropriate response to wildfires.

- The refuge management uses prescribed fires as a habitat management tool to cater to the habitat needs of all the organisms resident there. The plan is based on the belief that wildfires have been common in most ecosystems and have influenced the cycle of plants and plant communities through history. As permitting wildfires to burn on their own can be dangerous and suppressing all fires may result in even more dangerous fires, the policy adopted is an effort to burn the habitat as naturally as possible while minimizing the risks. Many species have adapted to the presence of fires while some are actually dependent on fires for seed germination and growth. The chain effect cascades down to animals as well. The prescribed fires are mainly aimed at providing natural habitats and reducing fuel build-ups. Two basic types of burns are used to reduce fuel build-ups:

- ✓ **Broadcast fires**: where fire is spread in a predefined area by experts and allowed to burn at proper intensities in a predictable manner; and

- ✓ **Pile fires**: where burnable fuels are concentrated into 'slash piles' and later burned.
- • Burning is done in all seasons depending upon the prescriptions in the plan. Burns are ignited both from the air as well as from the ground, using the following techniques:
- a) **Ping-Pong Balls**: A machine is attached to a helicopter that drops small ping-pong-like balls that are ignited by an internal chemical reaction.
- b) **Helio Torch**: A large torch is suspended beneath a helicopter, which dispenses burning gelled gasoline onto the fuels below. Ignition is controlled from the helicopter cockpit.
- c) **Drip Torch**: A hand-held fuel tank from which burning fuel is dispensed through a metal tube fitted with a drip nozzle end.
- d) **Fuses**: A solid fuel ignition device similar to a railroad flare.
- e) **Terra Torch**: A vehicle-mounted flame thrower which dispenses burning gelled gasoline onto the fuels to be burned.

Some of the above practices might have further evolved in the last 20-25 years since my visits to these places. However, the principles on which these practices were founded still rule the world, except, surprisingly, India.

Forest Fires in India

Ground evidence does not seem to support the widespread impression that fires are destroying and degraded our forests. Forest Survey of India (FSI) has been monitoring forest fires in India with the help of remote sensing satellites since 2004. According to the FSI website (https://fsi.nic.in/forest-fire-activities?pgID=forest-fire-activities), only 2.40% of our forests are exposed to a high incidence of fires and 35.71% have not been exposed to fires of any real significance so far. 54.40% of our forests experience only "occasional" fires.

According to FSI (Anon. 2019), only 9.9% of India's forests are "highly or extremely highly prone" to fires while the rest are either "moderately prone" or "less fire prone". The degree of the proneness of a forest to burning was estimated on the basis of historical fire frequency (2003 to 2016) in a 5 km X 5 km grid. The "extremely fire prone" areas experience 4 or more fires per year on an average while the least prone areas experience less than 0.5 fires per year. As these fires are mostly small {the average burn size in MP is 3 hectares according to Dogra *et al.* (2018)}, four fires in a 25 km^2 (2,500 hectare) plot again do not seem like much.

According to Reddy *et al.* (2017), an area of 48,765.45 sq. km (6.99%) of forest cover was affected by fires in 2014 while the total area of natural vegetation burnt was 57,127.75 sq. km. Most of the burnt area was in "Deccan", the highest area being in Odisha. They found fires in only 281 protected areas (out of 614) over a period of 10 years. "Just 20 districts, representing 3 percent of India's land area and 16 percent of the country's forest cover in 2000, accounted for 44 percent of all forest fire detections from 2003 to 2016. Twenty districts (not necessarily the same ones) also accounted for 48 percent of the total fire-affected area between 2003 to 2016, despite having just 12 percent of the nation's forest cover in 2000 and 7 percent of its land area" (Dogra *et al.* 2018). The former are in northeast India while the latter districts are all in central India, at the junction of Maharashtra, Chhattisgarh, and Telangana.

The figure below shows the regional distribution of forest fires, forest area burnt, and forest cover in the country. While more than half the burnt area is in the central Indian states, more than half of the fire events have been detected in the northeastern states.

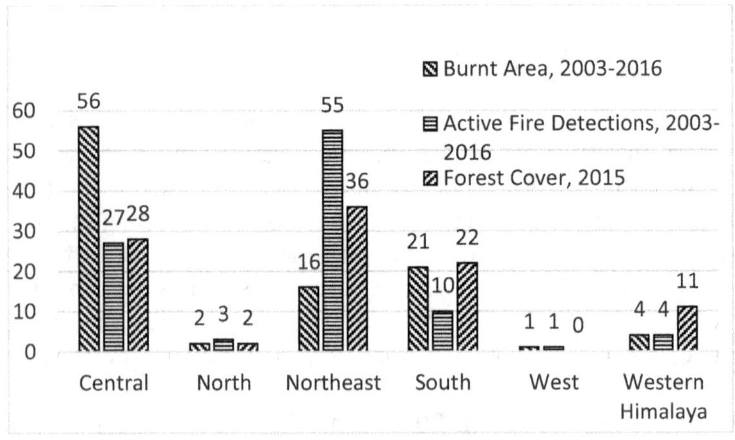

Figure 3: Forest Cover, Active Fire Detections, and Burnt Forest Area by Regions (Percentage of National Total). Source: Dogra et al. (2018).

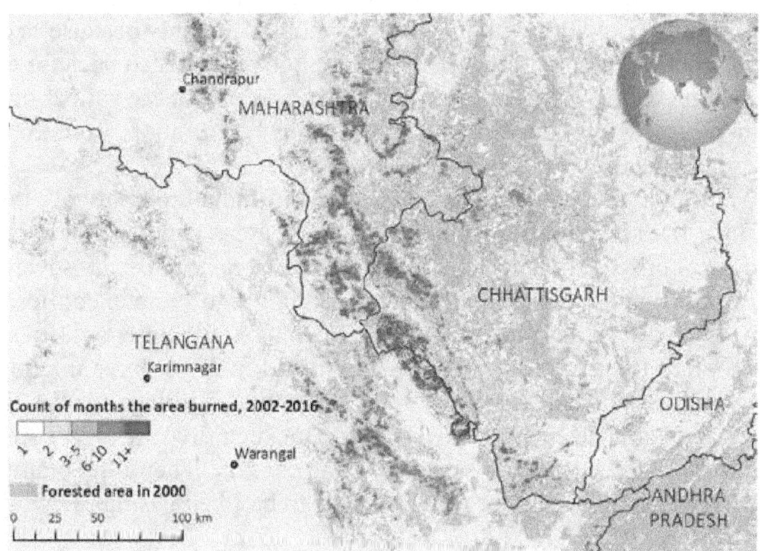

Figure 4: Forested Areas Affected by Widespread and Frequent Burning in Central India. (Dogra et al. 2018).

The number of fires recorded by FSI in 2018, 2019, and 2020 fire seasons was 37,059, 26,641, and 21,110 respectively. This clearly indicates a significant downward trend in fire incidence in the country although the trend since 2003 is not consistent at the national level. However, the number of forest compartments that were touched by fire in the years 2017, 2018, 2019, and 2020 in MP are reported to be 3031 (7.6%), 3246 (8.14%), 1581 (3.97%), and 667 (1.67%) (Departmental records). This again indicates a declining fire frequency in the state although the time period is too short for the trend to be conclusive. As mentioned before, Reddy *et al.* (2017a) report that only 281 out of 614 protected areas experienced fire incidence between 2006 and 2015, and only 8.6% area was burnt in 2014. Thus, the degradation and low productivity of our forests may be the result of a combination of factors, including fires, but not primarily due to fires. However, the declining trend in wildfire incidence and spread in India seems to be in contrast to the global trends which indicate a progressive rise in wildfires under the impact of climate change (Gera 2017). If true, reasons for this anomaly need to be examined.

Fire season in most of India extends from the middle of February to the end of May. However, it starts and ends a little early in southern

India because winters are not so cold and the monsoon arrives early. Fire season coincides with the summer months not only because of the high ambient temperature and low fuel moisture but also because this is the time when villagers tend to ignite most fires for the collection of minor forest produce (MFP), shifting cultivation, or forest encroachments.

With rare exceptions, most forest fires in India are relatively mild surface fires because they usually occur in areas of intensive human use and, consequently, low fuel loads. These areas are usually severely overgrazed and overexploited. Fires escaping into remote, coniferous forests in hilly states may sometimes get converted into crown fires as is reported to have happened in Uttarakhand in 2016. Fires in under-grazed grasslands created due to the relocation of villages in PAs are often very intense and spread very fast. But such fires are a very small proportion of the total fire scenario in the country. Therefore, blaming the fires for degrading our forests seems to be like missing the woods for the trees.

Fire Return Interval in India

Fire return interval (FRI) is a critical parameter determining the effect of fire on ecology as the time elapsed since the last fire determines the amount of fuel likely to be available to the next fire, and consequently, its severity. Although FSI has started mapping the incidence of forest fires in India, there is no analysis of the fire return intervals (FRI) so far. FSI's analysis, however, does indicate lengthening FRIs as less and less area seems to be burnt in successive years. This indicates that the future fires are likely to be more severe, unless more fuels are being extracted by man or the sources of ignition are disappearing. Whatever be the case, some sense of the trends in FRI in India can be had from the following examples.

In Bandhavgarh National Park, more than 50% area experienced FRIs of 10 years or more, as shown below, between 1984 and 1994 (Pabla, 1998).

Table 5: Fire Return Intervals in Bandhavgarh National Park (1984-1994)

Frequency of Burning	Fire Return Period (Years)	Area (km^2)	% of Total Area
Not burnt	??	106.54	23.35
Once	10	125.97	27.61

Frequency of Burning	Fire Return Period (Years)	Area (km²)	% of Total Area
Twice	5	91.67	22.09
Thrice	3.3	62.59	13.72
Four times	2.5	35.87	7.86
Five times	2	16.27	3.57
Six times	1	11.44	2.51
Seven times	1	3.14	0.69
Eight times	1	2.77	0.61

Note: The areas in this table are the sums of the areas of the affected compartments, not the actual burned areas. The compartment area was used as a proxy as there was no way to estimate the burned area precisely at that time.

In the four years between 2017 to 2020, the average fire return intervals in the forests of Madhya Pradesh were as shown in the table below.

Table 6: Average Fire Return Interval in Madhya Pradesh Forests (2017-2020)

No. of Fires in 4 Years (2017-2020)	Average Fire Return Interval (Years)	No. of Forest Compartments Affected	% Compartments.
4	1	27	0.07%
3	1.33	216	0.54%
2	2	1267	3.18%
1	4	5135	12.88%
Unburnt since 2017	??	33,220	83.33%

(Source: Departmental records)

Obviously, the FRIs for the compartments that did not burn during this period, shall be longer than 4 years.

Kodandapani *et al.* (2004) studied the FRI in the Mudumalai Wildlife Sanctuary in the Western Ghats between 1989 and 2004 and concluded that "all vegetation types had average fire-return interval of <7 years and the sanctuary as a whole had a fire-return interval of 3.3

years. This represents a threefold increase in fire frequency in the eighty years since 1909-1921." FRI for the larger Nilgiri Biosphere Reserve and the entire Western Ghats was estimated to be roughly 5 years.

In another study in the Western Ghats, Kodandapani *et al.* (2008) found "increasingly short fire-return intervals in the landscape. In the tropical dry deciduous forest, the mean fire-return interval is 6 years, in the tropical dry thorn forest mean fire-return interval is 10 years, and in the tropical moist deciduous forest mean fire-return interval is 20 years. Tropical dry deciduous forests burned more frequently and had the largest number of fires in any given year as well as the single largest fire (9900 ha). Seventy percent, 56%, and 30% of the tropical moist deciduous forests, tropical dry thorn forests, and tropical dry deciduous forests, respectively have not burned during the 7-year period of study."

However, Reddy *et al.* (2019) found that "No fires were detected in 47% of forest grid cells of India" for the 15 year period of 2003 to 2017 in a South Asia-wide study based on MODIS satellite data. They also mentioned that "The total cumulative area of 46.6% of total vegetation cover was affected by fires in Nilgiri biosphere reserve from the year 1973 to 2014. The decadal monitoring (2005–2014) has indicated a gradual decline of forest fires over the Nilgiri biosphere reserve."

The findings of Kodandapani *et al.* (2004 and 2008) are obviously in contradiction to the picture emerging from the studies based purely on satellite data. Therefore, more precise and longer-term data is required to determine the FRIs in various forest types within reasonable limits of variation. Let us hope our monitoring agencies and scientists shall pay attention to this critical requirement in the future.

What Causes Forest Fires in India

In the grandmothers' stories of our childhood, we used to hear that *davanals* (devastating forest fires) were ignited when dry bamboos rubbed against each other during storms. When I entered the forest service, I found that nobody believed in these fables, although we had extremely congested clumps of thick and tall bamboos in many areas. Even dead and dry ones. However, I started having second thoughts when I came to Bandhavgarh national park as its director in 1986. One evening in July 1986, I stopped my vehicle in a thick bamboo area just to enjoy the solitude and silence for a few minutes. It was wonderfully quiet in the cloudy evening as the tourist season had ended. Suddenly, I heard some beautiful, long, musical notes coming from one direction. The ranger accompanying me told me that the sound was coming from the rubbing of congested bamboos swaying in the wind. It did not strike me that such rubbing could ignite fires until I saw a tribal producing fire by rubbing two dry bamboo sticks over each other, next summer. I suddenly found truth in the childhood fables. I was convinced that if a puny man could produce fire by rubbing bamboos together, nature could also do it, at least occasionally, what with immense wind power at its disposal and millions of tightly packed dry bamboos swaying in all directions. Bandhavgarh was full of dead and dry bamboo after the gregarious flowering of 1984.

However, we continue to believe that there are no natural fires in India. We do not believe lightning can ignite forest fires while the only source of 'natural' fires in other countries is lightning. The USA is believed to have nearly 6000 lightning-caused wildfires annually. If it happens in the USA and Africa, why not in India? We never link lightning with wildfires perhaps because we think most of our lightning happens when our forests are drenched in rain. But we forget that nearly 30% of the lightning days in India are during the pre-monsoon period (Tyagi 2007) when the fuels are dry, humidity low, and temperatures high. While the all-India mean lightning days in a year are approximately 55, they can be as high as 100-120 days in Assam, Kerala, Jammu & Kashmir, etc. (Tyagi 2007). The total number of lightning strikes in a year may run into millions. For example, "Andhra Pradesh recorded 36,749 lightning strikes in just a 13-hour period" on 26 April 2018 (https://www.bbc.com/news/world-asia-india-43905726), "41,000 lightning strikes across India on April 16, 2019" (https://www.downtoearth.org.in/news/climate-change/what-caused-41-000-lightning-strikes-across-india-on-april-16--64068). Nearly 2,000 people die from lightning strikes in India each year (https://www.bbc.com/news/world-asia-india-53186072). If none of these strikes ignites forest fires, perhaps nothing else can! We occasionally see individual trees scorched by thunder in our forests. If the same happens in dry weather, it can potentially set off a forest fire. Perhaps, we do not know it perhaps because we usually do not try to trace the source of ignition and instinctively blame every fire on people.

Irrespective of whether we have any natural fires or not, an overwhelming majority of our forest fires are of anthropogenic origin. They may be started with the clear intention of burning the forests for stimulating a new flush of grass for livestock, as in the montane grasslands, or for stimulating a flush of tendu leaf (*Diospyros melanoxylon*) as in Central India. Communal hunting by several tribal communities also involves the use of fire to drive animals into nets, snares, or ambushes. Some of the hundreds of small fires started by people for collecting MFP like mahua (*Madhuca latifolia*) flowers or sal (*Shorea robusta*) seed often become wildfires in Central India. It is rare for an area that produces all these products to escape fire as these activities are sequential in nature. If a forest escapes being burnt by mahua collectors in March, it will be burnt by tendu leaf collectors in April or sal seed collectors in June. Some areas also burn more than once in the same season due to the late leaf fall of some species. Over half of all wildfires recorded in India are ignited for shifting cultivation in the north-eastern states (see Figure 1above). Forest encroachers in central India also burn the forest to clear it for agriculture. Accidental fires started by careless disposal of *bidis* or cigarettes in dry season or due to the escape of agricultural fires may also not be uncommon. Fires may also be started when villagers use burning sticks as torches to keep wild animals at bay when walking through the forests at night. Some tribal gods also want them to burn forests. Mr. H.S. Panwar often tells the story of a tribal youth igniting a series of fires in Kanha because he had promised some deity so if his son was cured of an ailment.

Forest Fire Management in India

Long ago, in 1947, R.C. Milward, wrote that, "Fire protection was in full swing, 115,100 km² (44,443 sq. mi.) being under protection in 1907. Despite the obvious benefits to the growing stock arising from it in the coniferous and deciduous forests of moderate rainfall, doubts were already (about 1905) being thrown upon its advisability in the wetter forests of Bengal and Burma with the insidious ousting of the more valuable deciduous by evergreen species." Another statement in the same article says that by 1939-40, "Complete fire protection went out of fashion. In inflammable and grassy forests where the valuable species are at all resistant to fire and when regeneration can be concentrated, "early burning" seems the best way out of trouble at present. It is useful in forests of chir, *Pinus longifolia*, if carefully applied. Again, fire protection in climates and under conditions favouring the development of evergreen at the expense of more valuable species has been proved wrong." (Milward 1947)

Champion and Seth (1968) wrote that the regeneration of many important timber species was dependent on fire. Every forester must have read this book. Allan Rodgers who trained an entire generation of Indian PA managers in the 1980s, wrote a beautiful paper under the title "The Role of Fires in the Management of Wildlife Habitats: A Review" in the October 1986 issue of the journal Indian Forester. He wrote that "wildlife management was more than protecting tree cover" and that "prescribed controlled burn on a patchwork basis" was required "to manage habitats".

Despite this knowledge being available to our decision-makers, there is not a word about the value of fire to our forests and wildlife in the National Forest Policy (NFP) 1988. The only thing it says about forest fires is that: "The incidence of forest fires in the country is high. Standing trees and fodder are destroyed on a large scale and natural generation annihilated by such fires. Special precautions should be taken during the fire season. Improved and modern management practices should be adopted to deal with forest fires." (Section 4.8.2).

A tremendous amount of new understanding about how fires shape our wildlands has emerged since then and most of the world has already abandoned the policy of total fire exclusion in forest management. A comprehensive study commissioned jointly by MoEF&CC and the World Bank, entitled "Strengthening Forest Fire Management in India" has already been completed (Dogra *et al.* 2018). It has recommended that "Fire has been a part of India's landscape since time immemorial and can play a vital role in healthy forests, recycling nutrients, helping tree species regenerate, removing invasive weeds and pathogens, and maintaining habitat for some wildlife. Occasional fires can also keep down fuel loads that feed larger, more destructive conflagrations ----" in the opening sentence of the Executive Summary itself.

NFP 1988 is currently under review and a new draft was circulated for public review in 2018. It seems, neither our own research nor the global winds of change have touched our policymakers. The new draft has only the following to say regarding our future approach to forest fires:

"(b) Forest fire prevention: With changes in climate and land use, fire is increasingly being viewed as a major threat to many forests and their biodiversity. The rising intensity and frequency of forest fires and their spread is resulting in substantial loss of forest functions and related ecosystem services every year. Adequate measures would be taken to safeguard ecosystems from forest fires, map the vulnerable areas, and develop and strengthen early warning systems and methods to control fire, based on remote sensing technology and community participation. Also, awareness will be created about causes and impacts of fire on forests and local livelihoods." (Section 4.1.1 Sustainable Management of Forests).

Forest fires or prescribed fires do not find any mention in the National Wildlife Action Plan (2017-2031) either, which is another important conservation policy document of the MoEF&CC.

Any person who "(b) sets fire to a reserved forest, or, in contravention of any rules made by the State Government in this behalf, kindles any fire, or leaves any fire burning, in such manner as to endanger such a forest; or who, in a reserved forest– (c) kindles, keeps or carries any fire except at such seasons as the Forest-officer may notify in this behalf," commits a criminal offence, says Section 26 of the Indian Forest Act, 1927. Interestingly, the fire protection rules mentioned ahead, were made (in 1890, and updated in 1894, 1911, and 1913) in accordance with Section 26 (b) of the Indian Forest Act, 1878, (MP Forest Manual). Nobody has reviewed these rules after that. It must be more or less the same in other states. The rules provide a list of elaborate safeguards which the public is expected to observe in the use of fires within 3 miles of reserve forests. Then the rules go on to prescribe that the state forests should be divided into three classes for the purpose of fire protection, namely:

- **Class I: Forests Completely Protected:** This class includes regeneration coupes, plantations, and any other areas needing special protection, such as grass birs, intensive lac cultivation areas, etc. These areas are to be isolated by fire lines and guidelines, and patrolled by fire watchers. Any fire occurring in these areas shall be treated as a "calamity".
- **Class II: Forests Generally Protected:** This class includes all forest areas under systematic working not covered under class I. "All areas in this class will be isolated from rest of the country by means of fire lines. No guidelines will be cut but all fire lines, roads, paths, suitable ridges, grassy maidans etc. will be burnt in successive stages as the grass dries sufficiently to be combustible and the fire allowed to burn itself out. Fire watchers may in area of this class only be employed if sanctioned by the Conservator. As a supplementary measure, the early burning of portions of this class may be sanctioned by the conservator. By early burning is meant a deliberate attempt to pass a slow fire early in the year through the whole area under such treatment."

- **Class III: Forests Protected by Law Only**: "In this class are included all forests not included in the two foregoing classes. In forests of this class, deliberate burning is prohibited, but no special measures of protection will be undertaken."

Then the manual goes into the detail as to how fire lines are to be cut, how burnt area is to be recorded and reported, and how fire reports are to be submitted, etc. It prescribes that any forest officer who sees the fire, even outside his jurisdiction, is responsible for putting it out, until he is relieved by a local official. It also talks about burning for silvicultural purposes, such as removing debris and stimulating regeneration. At the time this manual was written, there was no concept of national parks or wildlife sanctuaries although the conservator was empowered to include any areas in class I or class II for the purpose of fire protection.

MPFD does fire protection virtually on the same lines till today, except that there is no early burning, not even for silvicultural purposes. Forest areas are not formally divided into the above classes but every division prepares a fire protection plan each year where priority areas are designated. How a sensible, age-old, practice (of early burning) can be abandoned even in the face of scientific evidence to the contrary, will always remain a puzzle to me.

India flirted with "Modern Forest Fire Control" methods for over a decade since 1984, under an FAO/UNDP project, involving the use of helicopters, fixed-wing aircraft and sophisticated hand tools. However, fire-fighting in India is still done the traditional way, by beating and smothering the fire with leafy tree branches or sweeping away the litter ahead of a fire. Counter fires may sometimes be started from a nearby fire line or a hastily cleared bare patch ahead of the fire. Apart from the fire lines created specifically for fire control, all the forest demarcation lines and roads passing through the forests are also used as fire lines. Fire lines, boundary lines, and strips on both sides of roads are cut and burnt before the onset of the official fire season. Seasonal fire watchers from local communities are employed to look for signs of fire in the landscape from watchtowers or fire camps. Many PAs in MP keep squads of labourers and vehicles ready to rush to a fire site during the fire season at short notice.

As most fires are caused by the careless use of fire by people, most states try to work with local communities to reduce the chances of fires escaping into the forest. For example, MP foresters distribute nets to collect mahua flowers above the ground so that they do not have to burn the floor. Manual pruning of tendu bushes generates employment for local communities as well as prevents forest fires. Community education and awareness programmes are quite common across states.

Annual burning is done to maintain the moist grasslands in areas like Corbett, Dudhwa, Valmiki, Manas and Kaziranga tiger reserves as reported in Rawat and Adhikari (2015) and the authors recommend the continuation of the practice. Dogra *et al.* (2018) have also reviewed the fire-fighting methods in the country. According to them, early burning is practised only in Himachal Pradesh and Uttarakhand. No state is reported to manipulate forest cover, through practices such as thinning, pruning, or planting of fire-resistant species for reducing fire risk. The mechanical leaf blower used in Odisha is perhaps the only sophisticated fire-fighting tool used in India these days. Even simple fire beaters/swats and rakes are very uncommon. The recent induction of truck-mounted water tankers sometimes comes in handy to douse milder fires along the roads, as well as to keep the fire fighters hydrated. Perhaps no state uses special fire-resistant clothing, shoes, or helmets.

Fire detection has improved tremendously since the advent of satellite-based surveillance. FSI started an SMS-based forest fire alert system in 2004 and had 11,639 registered users in 2017 (Dogra *et al.* 2018). Madhya Pradesh started a similar system even before FSI. The introduction of radio communications, mobile phones, motorised transport, etc. has further reduced response time. FSI is in the process of starting an early warning system based on the perceived fire danger rating of an area based on weather forecasting and fire history. Efforts are also on to implement a burn area assessment with the help of satellite imagery. Many states like MP, Telangana, and Tamil Nadu have started zoning fire-sensitive areas based on fire history but no organised attempt has yet been made to develop a fire danger rating system for the country. Fire-fighting is considered to be a kind of lowly unskilled job and perhaps no state provides any training to their staff and labourers. Involvement of the fire department or the disaster management agencies is almost unheard of. This may be because forest fires in India rarely damage built-up property as often happens in many other countries. Death of 9 trekkers in a forest fire in the Kurangini hills of Tamil Nadu in March 2018, however, shows how devastating forest fires, sometimes, can be in India as well.

Local staff is required to file a fire report after the fire has been put out. Generally, the parameters recorded in these reports include the day and time of the fire, area burnt, financial loss due to damage to timber trees (or plantation), cause of the fire, and the cost of putting the fire out. Although it should now be possible to assess the burn area reasonably accurately with the help of a GPS, I think the area is still estimated ocularly for want of time and equipment. Underreporting of the burn area is common as ocular estimation of a large irregular shape invariably results in underestimation. Moreover, a large fire is also an adverse reflection on the responsible staff. Financial loss is usually reported as nil as only "unsaleable grasses and leaf litter" is burnt. No assessment of the ecological effects of fires is done. Generally, there are no attempts to rehabilitate the burn area either. Only Uttarakhand reports the construction of check dams and contour trenches in burn areas to prevent erosion and to improve water infiltration into the soil.

My Baptism with Fire

Although our forest fire management systems are still quite primitive, we seem to have come a long way in the last 40-50 years. My first real exposure to firefighting was in Panna National Park in 1983 when we started creating the park administration. Before that, my short stint in Kanha had not allowed me to get intimately involved. Although we had no money and very few people on the staff, the first year was rather easy as the park was heavily overgrazed and we had some midsummer showers. The next monsoon was good and we had stopped livestock grazing in almost 80% of the park by then. Panna is mostly a dry savannah land and a good monsoon without overgrazing released the pent-up energy of the grasslands. The next summer was like hell as fires raged everywhere, sometimes several burning simultaneously. We had only two vehicles (jeeps) in the park and their main use during the fire season was to ferry the labourers, their food, and drinking water. I do not know how many nights I spent fighting fires. Once, I even got caught in a thorny *Zizyphus* bush in front of an advancing fire front and almost panicked before I could extricate myself. With miles and miles of burned grassland, and no cover or food, I often wondered how the animals were coping with the situation.

Almost 30% of the park was burned in 102 fire incidences in 1984 (Pabla, 1987). Perhaps some of the blame for this near disaster can be placed on the complacency resulting from the previous year's experience and some on the weather, as it did not allow us to burn our fire lines properly. We were well prepared in the 1985 season. 130 km of new fire lines had been created and fire watchers were in place everywhere. A few makeshift fire watchtowers were created on tree tops with bicycle-borne runners ready to rush to the nearest village if the watchers saw smoke somewhere. We had seen the futility of beating the fire with brushwood and there was no bamboo to make brooms for sweeping leaf litter. So, we had designed our own fire beaters and rakes after testing several materials and designs in the previous winter. Fire beater is still popular in Panna (also with its tigers, as one cub was photographed carrying a fire beater) although it has not spread to other parks even after 35 years. In 1985, only 7% of the park was burnt in 33 incidents while some 12.5% was burnt in 1986. I was damn happy with the progress.

Figure 5: The Panna Fire Beater

I moved to Bandhavgarh in July 1986. Although Bandhavgarh had a wireless communications facility, there was only one wireless station inside the park (at Tala). So, we set up fire observation stations on top of prominent hill features and equipped them with radio sets. We also introduced the fire beaters and fire rakes for dealing with fires. All this proved very effective as only 4.4% of the park was burnt in 52 fire incidences in the 1987 fire season, despite the park being littered with dead bamboo clumps as a result of gregarious flowering a few years ago.

Although we had improved the fire detection efficiency by posting observers on hilltops, we discovered that location of a fire was still very difficult as the observer could not pinpoint the fire site accurately. He could only say that he was seeing smoke in a certain direction. Many fires were visible from the hilltops but not from the base. Our crew would often struggle to find the fire before it became a serious one. This forced us to innovate again. By the next year, we had designed a device that could describe the fire location within a few hundred metres. It consisted of a protractor (angle measuring device used by students of geometry) fixed on a drawing board, with a pin in the centre on which a 1/4" diameter aluminium pipe could rotate. The watcher would read the bearing of the fire through the pipe and communicate it to a control room. The control room would immediately pinpoint the location by triangulating the bearings from two or more towers and despatch the crew. This reduced our response time considerably. I am sure the burned area further came down but did not have a chance to collate the data due to my transfer in July 1988.

Many years later, in the year 2000, when I became in charge of forest protection in the state, I had to devise another method to improve the accuracy of fire-reporting. Although I encouraged my people to report the burned area as accurately as possible, I was sure that our estimates were gross underestimates. Measurement of every burn was impossible due to the paucity of time and expertise at the lower levels. Although global positioning systems (GPS) had made their appearance by then, they were rare and expensive. Ocular estimates were always underestimates as one could not see the entire burn from one place. Deliberate underreporting was also not uncommon for well-known reasons. So, I directed the field officers to measure the burned area on the map rather than on the ground. They were just to note the landmarks (roads, streams, etc.) nearest to the boundaries of the burn and mark them on the map of the compartment. Measuring the area between these landmarks on the map was a routine matter. I am not sure how much difference this little innovation made to the accuracy of fire reporting, but it does deserve a mention in the trajectory of the evolution of fire management in MP.

Now, when even the GPS is *passé*, and the burned areas are being measured by satellites, with fleets of vehicles, wireless sets, mobile phones, satellite alerts, and so on, we seem to be living on a different planet. But still, miles to go!

The Central Meadows of Kanha

Having thus become aware of a different perspective on forest fires, I started talking about it around the year 2000 and even made a few presentations at some national-level gatherings. As the head of the forest protection wing, I even had a departmental committee set up to examine the question of whether we needed to review our forest fire management policy, as enshrined in the MP Forest Manual (outlined before). But that committee never met for various reasons. However, the condition of the central meadows of Kanha Tiger Reserve made me desperate to do something. This meadow, formerly the cropland of the village Kanha, after which the park has been named, is the signature landmark of the tiger reserve. When I came back to the wildlife wing in 2005, the meadow was (still is) dominated by huge patches of unpalatable grasses such as *Imperata cylindrica, Desmostachya bipinnata* (Kush grass), *and Aristida adscensionis* (Needlegrass), etc. and the density of animals in the grassland seemed to be much less than what I remembered in the eighties. I had seen the grassland in alternating phases of development and regression since 1980 when I first came to Kanha for a month of training as an IFS probationer. Although I have not seen it being systematically burned since that day, it has been occasionally hit by wildfires. Although it was considered a healthy habitat back then, as it supported very high animal densities, I remember our inimitable research officer Dr. P.C. Kotwal complaining about its suitability for barasingha (Swamp deer, *Cervus duvauceli branderi*) having been impaired by fires. Mostly, it had short and medium grasses with patches of tall *kans* grass (*Saccharum spontaneum*), the preferred habitat of barasingha. Conservation of barasingha was a top priority issue for the park as this was the only population of the *branderi* sub-species in the world. At that time, the Kanha herd of barasingha used to migrate to another meadow, Somph, nearly 15 kilometres away, for fawning in the monsoon. It returned to the Kanha meadows for rutting in winter. However, the barasingha herd stopped coming to Kanha meadows altogether, perhaps sometimes in the early nineties. Although the reasons are not well understood, I used to attribute it to the overpopulation of spotted deer in the meadow. I remember dubbing the meadow a "dustbowl" with very scant tall grasses and being dominated by short annual grasses such as *Eragrostis japonica*. I also remember talking about reducing the number of waterholes in the meadows to encourage spotted deer to emigrate in order to bring tall grasses, and barasingha, back. The management started removal of dichotomous weeds and uprooting of woody plants like *Butea monosperma* (Palash), *Lagerstroemia parviflora* (Lendia), etc. from the periphery of the grassland to stem the invasion by the woodland species. The park also started the rotational closure of some parts to encourage the growth of tall grasses. More or less the same management approach continues even today, except that the closure is now supplemented with the planting of grasses like *Saccharum* and *Themeda*. However, despite this intensive management, the condition of the grassland continued to deteriorate, resulting in the invasion by coarse, unpalatable, grasses like *Imperata, Desmostachya, Aristida,* etc. Although there was no formal assessment, the game density in the meadows, particularly the spotted deer, also appeared to be much less than before. The relationship seemed straightforward: the loss of palatable grasses led to the spotted deer dispersing into more favourable areas. The restoration methodology adopted by the local management seemed to make only a minor difference as only small areas could be treated each year, due to high cost and other reasons.

This was the situation when I returned to the wildlife wing of the department in 2005. My impressions of the condition of the Kanha grasslands have been confirmed by Pandey (2015) who had studied the ecology of 38 grasslands of Kanha Tiger Reserve, including the Kanha Meadows in 1979-1981, and reassessed the status of the grasslands in the year 2003-04, after 20 years. The study revealed that *"there has been an increase in the proportion of unpalatable and fire resistant grasses, weeds, and woody species in several grasslands since 1981. In several grasslands, the perennial rhizomatous species have been replaced by the annual and ruderal species resulting in the decline in forage quality as well as quantity. Judicious use of fire and exclosures for the management of degraded grasslands and regular monitoring of grassland communities in response to management interventions are recommended."*

These meadows were our showpiece. It was the heart of Kanha and Kanha was virtually our heart too. I used to be pained to see them in such pitiable condition and wondered what good were we if we could not keep even our heart healthy. I suggested the use of fire to eliminate unpalatable grasses from the Kanha meadows to the local managers, but everybody was hesitant. In fact, nobody, including myself, knew how to use fire as a tool to tailor wildlife habitats to our needs. Nobody in India, foresters and ecologists included, had ever learnt the art and science of habitat management beyond closure, weeding, and replanting grasses. Even where fire was being used to maintain grasslands, as in the Terai and Duars area, the fire regime (i.e. fire type, frequency, intensity, and season) was not based on any scientific research. I was aware that the world was using prescribed fire as a habitat management tool. But being aware is not the same as being a practitioner. Long ago, I had interacted with the Indian Grassland and Fodder Research Institute (IGFRI) in this regard, but their expertise also seemed to be limited to the agricultural environment. I did not want to do something just out of fancy but wanted to use real science to do the job. Therefore, I started thinking about taking advice from a recognised fire ecologist or rangeland ecologist, as they are called abroad. I requested our South African friend Les Carlisle to suggest someone as South Africa was at the forefront of wildlife management in the world. On his suggestion, we invited one Mr. Francois de Wet to give us a workshop on the use of fire in grassland management in Kanha in October 2010. We also invited all the retired field directors of Kanha Tiger Reserve to this workshop, so that we could learn how they had managed this grassland and what their results had been. His (de Wet's) presentations were a revelation to us all. But he suggested that one Dr. Winston Trollope was the guru for almost all the rangeland ecologists of South Africa and it would be far more useful to have him take a look at our grasslands. I wanted nothing but the best. So, we contacted Dr. Trollope, again through our friend Les Carlisle, who readily agreed to visit us. Dr. Trollope was some 85 years old and did not travel without his wife, Lynette, who herself was a rangeland ecologist of repute. He also brought with him Chris de Bruno Austin, the CEO of the company called 'Working on Fires International' (WoFI) which he advised. Mr. Marius Renke, a very experienced ranger from Kruger National Park of South Africa also joined the group. They gave us another workshop on how to use fire to manipulate the composition and structure of grasslands with the help of prescribed fires, in November 2011. On our request, they also visited Bandhavgarh, Panna, and Pench tiger reserves and gave recommendations on the way fire could (or could not) be used to improve the condition of grasslands in these parks. Their inputs further reinforced what Francois de Wet had taught us. We had never looked at grasslands and fires the way they did. A brief summary of their teachings is given in the following pages.

How Fire Shapes Ecosystems

In order to understand how to use, or allow, fire to produce desired results in ecosystem management, it is important to understand how fire actually works. Some work has been done in India in this field as discussed later in this chapter. However, The Rocky Mountain Research Station, situated at Fort Collins, Colorado, USA, has published a 5-volume series entitled "Wildland Fires in Ecosystems" which contains a state-of-the-art account of how fires influence the evolution and maintenance of ecosystems. This series was first published on the basis of a workshop held in 1978 and has been revised many times since then. Although I intend to discuss these effects in detail in the next volume in this series, a very brief summary of these effects is as given below.

Fire is one of the primal forces of nature that drives life on earth. It does this primarily by killing and consuming life and its remains and altering the properties of soils and waterflows which sustain life. The decomposition of organic matter is the foundation of life. Fire complements biological decomposition in recycling the constituents of life, i.e. carbon, water, and other materials. The role of fire is especially significant in sustaining life in areas where biological decomposition is unable to keep pace with productivity, such as in cold regions. By killing and injuring some organisms it creates opportunities for others to colonise or prosper. The effects of individual fires on biota can be significantly different from the effects of long-term fire regimes. The effects depend as much on the adaptations of the affected species as on the characteristics of fires and fire regimes.

Effects of Fire on Soil and Water

Fire modifies the physical, chemical, and biological properties of soils by burning the organic matter and altering water flows. The effect depends on the amount of heat produced and how deep the effect travels. These influences run as follows:

- Removal of protection provided by vegetation and layers of organic matter on the surface makes it more vulnerable to erosion. It also lowers the porosity of soil and sometimes leads to the formation of water-repellent layers on or below the surface of the soil due to condensed organic matter. This reduces water infiltration and increases surface run off, leading to increased erosion. Reduced evapotranspiration, due to the loss of vegetation may also lead to increased streamflows and sub-surface water flows. Dry streams and springs have been seen to start flowing after severe fires in catchments. Changes in sediment levels and streamflows as a result of severe fires may be hundreds of times more than pre-fire levels depending on the severity of fire, topography, and post-fire precipitation.

- Combustion of soil organic matter alters the chemistry of soil and water, leading to altered availability of nutrients in soil and water bodies. Changes in water quality and water temperature can affect fish and other aquatic fauna downstream.
- Although fire destroys soil microorganisms, most microorganism communities are quite resilient and are able to recolonise the burnt sites over time, depending on fire severity.

Effects of Fire on Flora

Plants and their debris are the fuel that feeds fires. While fire kills and injures plants, it also stimulates regeneration and resprouting. Fire also affects plants indirectly by changing the soil condition and its capacity to process water. Fire effects on plants can vary significantly among fires and on different areas of the same fire. Fire behaviour, fire duration, the pattern of fuel consumption, and the amount of subsurface heating all influence injury and mortality of plants, and their subsequent recovery. Post-fire plant responses also depend upon the characteristics of the plant species on the site, their susceptibility to fire, and the means by which they recover after fire.

Most plant cells die when they are subjected to temperatures between 50 to 55°C. The higher the temperature, the quicker the cell mortality. The overall effect of fire on a plant is the sum of its effects on growing points, stem and roots. Death may actually occur several years after the fire injury and is often associated with secondary agents of disease, fungus, or insects. The resistance of plants to these agents is often lowered by injury and wound sites provide an entry point for pathogens. Plant characteristics that help woody plants to survive fires include tree height, self-pruning of lower branches, thick branches, larger buds, and the thickness and insulating properties of the bark. Tree resistance to fire generally increases with age. Most grasses usually survive wildfires as their aerial parts are already dead when fires usually occur.

Many plants recover from fire by means of the sprouting of their dormant buds. These buds may be located above or below the soil surface. When fire kills a dominant shoot, buds below the dead part start sprouting due to the loss of apical dominance. Plants may sprout soon after a fire, or not until the following spring if the fire occurs after the plants have become dormant. Burn severity or depth of burn is a function of the duration of the fire. A low severity fire has little effect on most buried plant parts and can stimulate significant amounts of post-fire sprouting. The recovery of herbaceous plants after a fire depends largely on whether their underground regenerative structures are exposed to lethal temperatures or not. Cool-season grasses that green up early in the growing season can be killed by the burning litter of associated warm-season grasses that are still dormant and more heat-resistant. Perennial grasses may also be killed if fire burns in the cured litter of annual grasses while perennials are still actively growing. Grasses in forested areas can incur more damage from fires as their rhizomes are likely to be located in the combustible litter and duff (decomposed organic matter) layers.

Post-fire seedling establishment depends on the amount of seed present and the conditions required to induce germination and support initial seedling growth. Requirements for successful germination and establishment can differ significantly among species. Seeds for recolonisation may originate onsite or may come from off-site through various seed dispersal mechanisms. Seeds stored underground by birds, squirrels, insects, etc. for feeding or buried under litter or snow, may also be a significant source for some species. Seeds may survive in underground seed banks for hundreds of years. Many adaptions such as serotiny (late seed shedding) or production of seeds above the vulnerable heights help plants regenerate after fires. The post-fire seedling establishment may also depend on factors such as seed environment (microsite on which the seed rests), fire-stimulated germination, and burn severity, etc. Fire stimulated germination of teak and the establishment of viviparous sal seeds due to removal of leaf litter by fire are two important Indian examples of fire-assisted plant regeneration.

The condition of plants at the time of the occurrence of a fire significantly influences post-fire recovery. The amount of stored carbohydrates in unburnt parts of a plant is a major factor. If a severe fire occurs at a time when most of the stored carbohydrates have already been used up (say, in flowering and fruiting), and most of the photosynthetic parts are killed, recovery will be equally difficult. Heavy post-fire grazing or browsing of perennial plants in the first growing season after a fire is likely to cause the most harm, particularly in arid and semiarid range communities. It can also alter the post-fire succession. The season of fire has a significant influence on the flowering of plants. Regardless of the season of fire, the phenological stages of the vegetation influence its flammability as well as its post fire response. The moisture content of the foliage determines its flammability and older leaves have less moisture compared to younger leaves. Seasonal differences in the moisture content of surface vegetation can determine whether the vegetation is a heat sink or is dry enough to be a heat source and thus contribute to fire spread.

Differences in seasonal weather in shrub/grass types can result in a large range in grass production, particularly annual species, which creates different fire behaviour potentials. The pattern of fire effects across the landscape varies with burning conditions. Areas of tree crown consumption, crown scorch, and little crown damage can be intermixed. Heavily burned areas of the forest floor where significant amounts of fuel were consumed and most buried plant parts were killed can be adjacent to areas where pre-fire fuel loading was low, and little subsurface heating occurred. During a dry season, especially in a drought, a much higher percentage of the forest canopy is likely to be scorched or consumed. Lethal temperatures may be driven to greater depths because of excessive surface fuels. During a wet year or early in the year before significant drying has occurred, less canopy will be killed and consumed and few buried plant parts will be killed.

Effects of Fire on Fauna

Fire regimes have been a major force in shaping landscape patterns and influencing productivity throughout the world for thousands of years. Faunal communities have evolved in the context of particular fire regimes and show patterns of response to fire itself and to the changes in vegetation composition and structure that follow fire. Animals' immediate responses to fire are influenced by fire season, intensity, severity, rate of spread, uniformity, and size. Responses may include injury, mortality, immigration, or emigration. Animals with limited mobility, such as young, are more vulnerable to injury and mortality than mature animals. Contrary to popular belief, very few adult animals actually die in a fire.

The animal species native to areas with a centuries-long history of fire can obviously persist in habitat shaped by fire. Many species actually thrive because of fire's influence. Alteration of fire regimes alters landscape patterns and the trajectory of change on the landscape. These changes affect habitat and often produce major changes in the faunal communities. Bird responses to fire are classified as invader, exploiter, resister, endurer, avoider, and vacillator. The composition of post-fire bird communities depends on the existence and abundance of these classes in the vicinity of a burn.

One important effect of fire is to create and destroy snags and deadwood, both of which are important for wildlife. Fires may kill trees immediately, or just injure them sufficiently to die later or make them vulnerable to die from insect and pathogen attacks. Fires may also slow down the decay of snags and dead wood by hardening their outer wood (case-hardening). This makes them last longer in the ecosystem.

Fire's most obvious function in landscapes is to create and maintain a mosaic of different kinds of vegetation. This includes the size, composition, and structure of patches, as well as connectivity among patches. Fire changes the proportions and arrangement of habitat patches on the landscape. When fire increases heterogeneity on the landscape, animal species have increased opportunities to select from a variety of habitat conditions and successional stages. Fires often burn with varying severity, increasing heterogeneity. Bird diversity after stand-replacing fire may be higher on patchy or small burns than on large, uniform burns because the small areas are accessible to canopy and edge species as well as species that use open areas. Excluding fire from a landscape, unless it is being intensively managed for wood production, has two major effects on animal habitat. First, it increases the abundance and continuity of late-successional stages. Second, it changes fuel quantities and fuel arrangement. These have major implications for animal communities and future fires.

Effects of fire on wildlife foods depend on several factors. In general:

- Burning often increases or improves forage for wildlife from a few years to more than 100 years, depending on vegetation type.
- Fires usually increase habitat patchiness, providing wildlife with a diversity of vegetation conditions from which to select food and cover.

- The biomass of forage plants usually increases after burning in all but dry ecosystems.
- The production of seeds by grasses and legumes is usually enhanced by annual or biennial fires. Seed production by trees is usually enhanced by a 5-year or longer burning cycle.
- Burning sometimes, but not always, increases the nutritional content and digestibility of plants. This effect is short-lived, typically lasting only one or two growing seasons.

Thus, it can be seen that the effects of fire on various components of ecosystems are very complex. The overall effect is that a fire alters the availability and distribution of food and shelter for organisms and redistributes and recomposes faunal populations and communities.

Managing Wildlife Habitats with the Help of Prescribed Fire in India

A decade or so before, burning a forest or a grassland deliberately would have been unthinkable for me as most of our forests were in any case burnt by fires set off by the *mahua* flower and *tendu* leaf collectors. No plan of prescribed burning would have been safe as uninvited fires would have messed everything up. However, with spectacular success in fire protection, particularly in PAs, which I had seen towards the end of my career, I had already started wondering how the fire-dependent species like teak and sal would regenerate in the absence of fire. I had also seen piles of dead grass blocking the next year's flush in unburnt grasslands of Supkhar (eastern Kanha) and Bhadaar in Panna Tiger Reserve. I wanted to bring a suitable fire regime back to these areas but had no idea how to go about it. It was when I was wracking my head about the issue that the idea of using foreign help came to my mind.

We, in India, have no understanding of the finer points of a prescribed fire. We have never studied fire ecology i.e. the response of the biotic and abiotic components of the ecosystem to the season, frequency, type, and intensity of fire. We may sometimes decide to burn a grassland, primarily with the objective of stimulating new flush of grasses, entirely as a personal whim or fancy. But Trollope (2007) recommended the following approach to decide whether to burn or not. And if the decision is to burn, in what season and weather to burn and at what frequency:

- The range condition burning system, based on ecological criteria, is a very practical and efficient burning system to use in wildlife areas and is strongly recommended for use in the Tiger Reserves in India. The basic rationale of the range condition burning system is that the use of fire to achieve specific management objectives must be based on the ecological status and condition of the vegetation and its known reaction to the different components of the fire regime. Therefore, before deciding whether to apply prescribed burning or not, one needs to determine the condition of the grassland in terms of its botanical composition, ecological status, and basal cover. It also involves classifying the different grass species into various ecological categories according to their reaction to a grazing gradient i.e. from high to low grazing intensities, as follows:

DECREASER SPECIES: Grass & herbaceous species which decrease when rangeland is under or overgrazed;

INCREASER I SPECIES: Grass & herbaceous species which increase when rangeland is under or selectively grazed;

INCREASER II SPECIES: Grass & herbaceous species that increase when rangeland is overgrazed.

- Secondly, the decision would depend on the grass fuel load (kg/ha) of the area under consideration. This can be determined by using the circular Disc Pasture Meter (DPM).

Figure 6: Disc Pasture Meter used for estimating grass fuel loads

The DPM is an aluminium disc. A calibrated aluminium rod runs through its centre. When the disc is dropped onto a grass sward, the height at which the disc settles gives an estimate of the fuel load in kilograms per hectare. The more grass there is, the higher off the ground the disc settles. The average of several readings, depending on the size of the area, gives the approximate fuel load of the area. This instrument has been successfully calibrated for grasslands and savannahs in southern and east Africa. Although we must test the calibrations of the instrument for Indian grass communities, Dr. Trollope found that the instrument provided very 'credible quantitative descriptions' of Indian grass communities. A separate survey technique called the "Adapted Point Centre Quarter Method" is used for assessing and monitoring the tree and shrub vegetation.

- When the grass sward is in an undergrazed condition dominated by Increaser I species, it needs to be burnt to increase the better fire-adapted and more productive and palatable Decreaser grass species. If the grass sward is in a pioneer condition dominated by Increaser II grass species caused by overgrazing, prescribed burning should not be applied. Burning is generally not recommended when rangeland is dominated by Increaser II species in order to enable it to develop to a more productive stage dominated by Decreaser grass species.

- Prescribed burning is necessary when the grass sward has become overgrown and moribund as a result of excessive self-shading. This happens when the standing crop of grass is generally >4000 kg/ha as estimated with the DPM.

- The criteria used for deciding whether to use fire to control the encroachment of undesirable plants (trees/ shrubs or unpalatable grasses) involves the same ecological criteria describing the condition of the grass sward. However, the grass fuel loads required for prescribed burning will differ depending on the encroaching plant species.

- **Type of Fire:** Fires burning with the wind either as surface head fires in grassland or a combination of surface head fires and crown fires in tree and shrub vegetation be used with prescribed burning because they cause the least damage to the grass sward but can cause maximum damage to woody vegetation if necessary.

- **Fire Intensity:** When burning to remove moribund and/or unacceptable grass material a cool fire of <1000 kJ/s/m is recommended. This can be achieved by burning when the air temperature is <20°C and the relative humidity >50%.

When burning to control undesirable plants like encroaching bush, a hot fire of >2000 kJ/s/m is necessary. This can be achieved when the grass fuel load is >4000 kg/ha, the air temperature is >25°C, and the relative humidity <30%. This will cause a significant top kill of stems and branches of bush species up to a height of 3 m. In all cases, the wind speed should not exceed 20 km/h (Trollope, 2007).

Head Fire

Back Fire

Figure 7: Examples of head fire and back fire burning with and against the wind respectively.

- **Season of Burning:** Least damage is caused to the grass sward if fire is applied when the grass is dormant. Therefore, when burning to remove moribund and/or unacceptable grass material burning should preferably be applied as soon as the curing of the grass fuels is ≥75%. This condition will be in November/December when the grass sward becomes dormant after the monsoon rains. Conversely, when burning to control encroaching plants like trees and shrubs, burning should be applied later in the dry season when the grass curing is ≥85% i.e. January/February. Burning should be avoided during the intensely hot and dry period.

- **Frequency of Burning:** The frequency of burning should depend on the local conditions and the objective of burning. If the objective is to remove moribund and/or unacceptable grass material, the frequency shall depend on the rate at which excess grass litter accumulates. The litter accumulation rate depends on the productivity of the grassland and the prevailing grazing pressure. Thus, the frequency of burning in low rainfall areas/years and/or with high ungulate densities should be low, and vice versa. When burning to control the encroachment of undesirable plants like trees and shrubs, the frequency of burning will be determined by the growth patterns of the encroaching species and must be varied accordingly. In order to ensure that there is no forage shortage for ungulates during the post-burning period, an upper limit of 50% of the target area should be considered for burning each year. In low rainfall areas (<500 mm p.a.) the upper limit should be 33% of the areas that qualify for prescribed burning. These prescriptions should be tested and modified as necessary on the basis of local experience.

- **Post-Fire Range Management:** The highly palatable and nutritious post-fire regrowth attracts ungulates, while it is important to prevent overgrazing of burnt areas. Therefore, the areas planned for burning should be sub-divided into three to four blocks that are then burnt at approximately monthly intervals commencing in November/December during the winter period. The animals will thus keep moving to newly burnt areas, resulting in spreading the impact of continuous grazing in one burnt patch.

- **Fire Danger Rating System for Prescribed Burning**: Assuming that the ecological requirements for applying a prescribed burn have been met and the reasons for burning are clearly understood, the first step in the application of a controlled burn is to assess the weather conditions in order to safely apply fires of the required intensity. Fire Danger Index (FDI) is a practical and effective Fire Danger Rating System for assessing the weather conditions relative to the potential fire behaviour that can be expected during a burn. FDI is defined as *a numerical index describing the flammability and potential fire intensity of plant fuels as influenced by air temperature, relative humidity, wind speed, and degree of curing*. The calculation of the FDI for prescribed burning involves considering the combined effects of air temperature, relative humidity, wind speed, and curing of the grass fuel on fire behaviour. Weather conditions for the calculation of FDI can be measured with the help of a Kestrel Weather Meter Model 4500.

Figure 8: Kestrel Weather Meter Model 4500.

The "Grass Curing Factor" (GCF) represents the live portion of the plant material in the grass fuel expressed as a percentage. The GCF has further been related to the "Fuel Moisture Content" of the grass which can be determined by simple drying experiments in a laboratory. The FDI is calculated by using the formula:

FDI = Burning Index [(Air Temperature/ Relative Humidity) + (Wind Correction Factor)] x (Grass Curing Factor).

Ready-made charts for determining the effect of all these factors on the burning index and FDI are available.

FDI, together with related fire intensities, can be used to provide guidelines for controlled burning for specific objectives. The following chart shows the various fire danger stages, fire intensities produced by them, and the potential effect of burning under these conditions on vegetation.

Table 7: Fire Danger Rating System using Fire Danger Indices (FDI's) as a means for selecting suitable burning conditions for prescribed burning (Meikel et al. 2011).

FIRE DANGER STAGES	FDI	FIRE DANGER	FIRE INTENSITY kJ/s/m	PRESCRIBED BURNING
BLUE	0-20	LOW	<500	Too cold, humid, or wet for prescribed burning.
GREEN	21-45	MODERATE	500-1000	Suitable for prescribed burning to: • Remove moribund and/or unpalatable grass material; • Construct burnt firebreaks.
YELLOW	46-60	DANGEROUS	1001-2000	Suitable for prescribed burning to remove moribund and/or unpalatable grass material up to a maximum FDI of 55.
ORANGE	61-75	VERY DANGEROUS	2000-3000	Suitable for prescribed burning to control and/or prevent the encroachment of undesirable plants e.g. bush encroachment.
RED	76-100	EXTREMELY DANGEROUS	>3000	Too dangerous and unsuitable for prescribed burning.

Thus, no prescribed burning should be undertaken under red danger conditions while green, yellow, and orange conditions can be used for removing moribund debris, removing unpalatable grasses, and prevention of encroachment by undesirable bushes, respectively.

• **Animal Ratios:** Range ecologists divide grazing animals into two categories, namely:

- ✓ **Bulk grazers or Coarse feeders** - large grazing animals which normally do not exercise a high degree of selective grazing.
- ✓ **Concentrate grazers or fine feeders** - generally smaller grazing animals which exercise some or other form of species or area selective grazing.
- In the Indian situation, gaur and wild buffalo would be bulk grazers while most of the deer and antelopes would be classified as concentrate grazers. The need to burn or not generally depends on the relative abundance of these categories. If there is an overall dominance of concentrate grazers at a high stocking rate this generally results in extreme overgrazing resulting in a dominance of Increaser II grass species and a low accumulation of grass fuel and no necessity for burning. Conversely, at stocking rates equal to the grazing capacity of the grass sward, an overall dominance of concentrate grazers generally results in extreme selective grazing resulting in a dominance of Increaser I and II grass species and a significant accumulation of grass fuel and the necessity for burning. It is recommended that in wildlife areas a maximum ratio of 1 animal unit (AU) bulk grazers : 1 AU concentrate grazers should be applied in high rainfall areas and a maximum ratio of 1 AU bulk grazers: ½ AU concentrate grazers in low rainfall areas. All of MP's tiger reserves would fall in the former category. {The AU rating of common Indian wild animals (average of all ages and sexes), considering 1000 pounds body weight as one AU would be approximately as follows: Gaur (1 AU), spotted deer (0.2 AU), sambar (0.54 AU), nilgai, barasingha (0.47 AU), blackbuck, chinkara (0.12 AU), barking deer (0.12 AU)}.
- Currently there is a serious deficiency of knowledge on the fire ecology and effects of burning on grassland and tree/shrub communities in the tiger reserves of Madhya Pradesh. This information is essential for the formulation of suitable fire regimes for prescribed burning in the vegetation types where fire is recommended. It is clearly apparent from the field visits (by Trollope *et. al*) that prescribed burning is a necessary and essential management practice in the grassland and grass-dominated forest communities to maintain the vegetation in a palatable and available condition for utilization by the different ungulate species in the four Reserves. This

information can be generated only through suitable field trials. It is strongly recommended that this essential information on fire ecology be generated locally rather than depend on African experience as the edaphic and climatic features are quite different. Detailed specifications of the trial project, as proposed by Dr. Trollope, are given in **Appendix-6** of this book. Until the completion of trials, prescribed fire as explained before may be used as an interim measure. An integrated fire management plan for each PA should be prepared on the basis of the results of the fire trials experiment.

- Dr. Trollope recommended prescribed fires for the grasslands and grass-dominated forests for Kanha, Panna, and Pench tiger reserves. However, prescribed fire is not recommended in Bandhavgarh because the grass fuel loads are generally <4,000 kg/ha, and the grass sward is generally dominated by Increaser II grass species resulting from the overall infertile and shallow soils in the Reserve. (The conditions in the new meadows of Bandhavgarh, resulting from recent village relocation, may have to be reassessed.)

- Where the objective is to eradicate *Lantana camara* from the habitat, consideration be given to physically removing the *L. camara* and treating the stumps with an appropriate weedicide. Following this, apply a prescribed rotational burning program involving the application of cool fires <1,000 kJ/s/m to minimise the impact of the burning on the shrub vegetation and allow it to thicken up. This will provide ideal habitat for tigers but with indigenous shrub species that do not form impenetrable thickets with a very low grazing capacity, like *L. camara*. Pench Tiger Reserve, where Lantana is especially considered important as hiding cover for tigers, should embark on a long-term program to eradicate all *L. camara* using manual means and experimenting with frequency and season of burning to formulate a fire regime for its eradication

- Regarding the prevailing practice of closing grasslands to grazing (by fencing them) for 3 months during monsoon, for their rehabilitation, in Kanha and Pench, the recommendation is that they should be closed only for one month instead of 3 months. Longer closure produces tall and thick grass sward which is generally unpalatable to deer.

- For controlling woody species in grasslands such as Palash (*Butea monosperma*), Lendia (*Lagerstroemia parviflora*), Tendu (*Diospyros melanoxylon*), and Bhirra (*Chloroxylon swietenia*), it is necessary to burn under very hot dry windy conditions in order to generate high-intensity fires. Cutting the bushes and spreading the slash around stumps before burning should be more effective.

- Although ticks can persist in frequently burnt areas, there is sufficient evidence that frequent fires reduce tick population by altering the habitat in which they thrive, i.e. moribund grasses and excessive shrub density.

- The practice of burning merely to produce an out-of-season flush of grasses is not good as it reduces grass vigour and increases surface runoff of water and soil erosion. (My own experience in Panna National park in the eighties was that the green shoots produced by early fires dry up again by peak summer and are not much help in the 'pinch period'.)

Research on Forest Fires in India

Perhaps the principal reason why the global shift in attitude towards wildfires that started more than 100 years ago has not entered Indian minds is that our research and training institutions have not paid much attention to this subject. Until about a decade ago, there was virtually no research on the effects of fire on natural ecosystems in India. Any references that were available were just anecdotal and merely portrayed wildfires as an adverse impact on ecology. Of course, Champion and Seth (1968) stressed the role of fire in the regeneration of several tree species and recommended early burning in several biomes, particularly the Himalayas. Rodgers (1986) for the first time reviewed the importance of fire in wildlife management and recommended the use of fire on a "patchwork" basis. Apart from these two references, I could not find any report taking a balanced view of forest fires in India. Although FSI started compiling information on the incidence of wild fires in the country in 2004, estimation of burned area with the help of satellite imagery is still in experimental stages, as mentioned before. Scientists of the North Eastern Space Applications Centre (NESAC) made a nationwide assessment of burned area as well as fire incidence in various protected areas and vegetation types and came up with several publications discussing the extent of forest fires in the country (Reddy *et al.* 2017 and 2019).

However, publications on forest fires started appearing at a fairly fast pace by the turn of the century, particularly in the last decade. Nearly all of them discuss the impact of fires on tree diversity and regeneration, or grassland management (mostly in PAs). I have not found even one paper discussing the impact of fire on mammals, birds, or any other class of animals. Here are a few that looked interesting to me.

Saha & Howe (2003) found that in Central India "low intensity ground fires killed seedlings (<1 year old), resulting in a 30% decrease in seedling diversity in burned relative to unburned plots. Overall fire-related mortality of seedlings was 74% for 17 root-crown resprouters, compared to 63% for six root-sprouters. --- the number of juvenile (>1 year old) stems of root-sprouters increased in burned study plots but decreased in plots protected from fire. If this process (annual burning by local people) continues in the Mendha Forest in India, >80% of its tree diversity could be lost within 100–200 years." Mendha is a village in Maharashtra.

Kodandapani *et al.* (2008) found that in the Western Ghats, "Forest fires had significant impacts on species diversity and regeneration in the tropical dry deciduous forests. Species diversity declined by 50% and 60% in the moderate and high frequency classes, respectively compared to the low fire frequency class. Sapling density declined by ca. 30% in both moderate and high frequency classes compared to low frequency class. In tropical moist deciduous ecosystems, there were substantial declines in species diversity, tree density, seedling, and sapling densities in burned forests compared to the unburned forests. In contrast forest fires in tropical dry thorn forests had a marginal positive effect on ecosystem diversity, structure, and regeneration."

Hiremath and Sundram (2010) hypothesized that the invasion of *Lantana camara*, one of the most noxious weeds of Indian forests, "may be facilitated by fire". However, Sundram *et al.* (2012), while studying the traditional ecological knowledge of Soliga tribal community in the BRT Wildlife Sanctuary, found that the Soligas believed that the proliferation of Lantana camara in the sanctuary was due to fire exclusion in the early stages of the species' spread.

Verma & Jayakumar (2012) reviewed the literature on the impact of forest fire on physical, chemical, and biological properties of soil and concluded that "The impact of fire on forest soil depends on various factors such as intensity of fire, fuel load and soil moisture.

Fire is beneficial as well as harmful for the forest soil depending on its severity and fire return interval."

Verma & Jayakumar (2014) found that "fire incidences, irrespective of time of occurrence, negatively impacted species diversity, stem density and basal area, but improved the seedling and sapling density in all burn classes" in a tropical dry deciduous forest of Western Ghats.

Verma *et al.* (2017), in a study of effects of fire on tree diversity and regeneration in Mudumalai Wildlife Sanctuary, concluded that "Tree diversity decreased in 2-year-old and 5-year-old burnt plots and was reached to the level of unburnt plots in 15 years of interval. Stems of small size classes started increasing after the fire. Seedling density increased linearly in subsequent years after fire but sapling and tree density recorded less than control in B2 but was higher in B5 and B15. The overall fire affected diversity, but regeneration showed a positive trend."

Kittur *et al.* (2014) reported that "Shrub density was maximum in zones of high fire frequency and minimum in low frequency and no-fire zones. Lower tree density after fires indicated that regeneration of seedlings was reduced by fire" in the forests of Achanakmar Tiger Reserve of Chhattisgarh.

Mondol and Sukumar (2014) found that in Mudumalai Wildlife Sanctuary, a seasonally dry tropical forest (SDTF) of South India, "Fire temperatures at the ground level varied between $79^{O}C$ and $760^{O}C$, --- . Soil temperatures varied between $<79^{O}C$ and $302^{O}C$. Results from the study imply that fuel loads in forested areas have to be reduced to ensure low intensity fires in the dry season."

Mondol & Sukumar (2015) studied the regeneration of juvenile woody plants after fire in SDTF of southern India and observed >95% juvenile survivorship in both burnt and unburnt areas. They also found that "Growth rates of juveniles ---- were distinctly higher in burnt areas compared to unburnt areas --- immediately after a fire. Rapid growth by juveniles soon after a fire may be due to lowered competition from other vegetative forms such as grasses, possibly aided by the availability of resources stored belowground."

In a study of the impact of fire frequency on tree diversity and species regeneration in the tropical dry deciduous forests of Panna Tiger Reserve (PTR), Ray *et al.* (2020) concluded that "tree species diversity was higher at moderate fire frequencies than controls, but decreased with increasing fire frequency classes. Regeneration of species was significantly different among all fire frequency classes.

Certain fire-tolerant species were increasingly dominant with increasing fire frequency classes."

Kumar *et al.* (2015) studied the effect of burning coupled with grass cutting, grass removal, and harrowing in the grasslands of Dudhwa Tiger Reserve and recommended that the existing practice of grass cutting by locals and annual burning should be continued.

Schmerbeck *et al.* (2015) studied the incidence of fire in the Palani Hills of Western Ghats for the period 2000 to 2012 and concluded that fires were keeping the grassland-forest edge (shola forests) stable. Sinha *et al.* (2015) examined the current grassland management practice of cutting and burning of grasslands in Valmiki Tiger Reserve and concluded that fires should be used cautiously in grassland management as they can cause many negative effects.

Ghosh (2015) assessed the temporal and spatial patterns of fire in Manas Tiger Reserve using MODIS satellite data. She concluded that fire was a major driver of landscape dynamics and change within the Terai grasslands.

Vasu and Singh (2015) commented that "Annual burning is being practiced for quite some time (regarding grasslands in Kaziranga Tiger Reserve) --- fire helps in the maintenance of grasslands by arresting succession from grassland to forest, increases productivity of grasses and provides high quality forage."

Shilla & Tiwari (2015) concluded that "the impact of fire and grazing on vegetation structure of grassland ecosystem at Cherrapunjee are highly variable. While grazing tends to favour the diversity of perennial grasses, fire influences the richness of annual grasses and other monocots. However, the combined effect of grazing and fire tend to increase the diversity of forbs."

As mentioned in an earlier section, some studies also tried to estimate the fire return intervals (FRI) in Indian Forests. For example, Kodandapani *et al.* (2004 and 2008) found progressively reducing FRIs in the Western Ghats ranging between 3 to 20 years. However, Reddy *et al.* (2019), found, on the basis of the analysis of satellite data, that "No fires were detected in 47% of forest grid cells of India" for the 15 year period of 2003 to 2017. They also mentioned that "The total cumulative area of 46.6% of total vegetation cover was affected by fires in Nilgiri biosphere reserve from the year 1973 to 2014. The decadal monitoring (2005–2014) has indicated a gradual decline of forest fires over the Nilgiri biosphere reserve." Obviously, there is a disconnect between the findings of ecologists and remote sensing professionals. Perhaps the difference is due to the different scales at which studies are conducted by the two classes of professionals.

When fire burns the edge of shola in Eravikulam NP the following weed species invade: *Chromalaena odorata, Eupatorium adenophorum, Pteridium aquilinum, and Strobilanthes anamallaica* (Johnsingh AJT pers. com.). Sriramamurthy *et al.* (2020) found that fire-induced adult mortality was highest in scotch broom (*Cytisus scoparius*), lowest in gorse (*Ulex europaeus*) and high and variable in wattle (*Acacia mearnsii*).

It is obvious from the above that fire has a very complex influence on ecosystems and wildlife habitats. Although Indian science has not yet begun to unravel the effects of fire on wild animals, it is obvious that these influences are equally complex too (see previous section). Therefore, a simplistic approach of total fire exclusion is clearly borne of ignorance. Perhaps Thekaekara *et al.* (2017) clinched the issue with the statement that the "blanket ban on fires in all forest ecosystems is highly misplaced, and the case for having a more nuanced policy on fire management is unequivocal." Let us hope our policymakers shall take note of this new science before they put a seal of finality on the revised National Forest Policy.

Fire in Forestry Curricula

All of the above research papers and articles, which propose a new way of looking at forest fires, are very recent. Therefore, no wonder that we still teach our foresters only the unidimensional approach to forest fires i.e. treat every fire as a calamity. For example, the "Forest Health" subject in the syllabus of the Indira Gandhi National Forest Academy (IGNFA), which trains officers of the Indian Forest Service (IFS), deals with the topic of forest fires as follows: *"General Protection: Agencies causing forest damage — fires, man, cattle, insects, pathogens, nature of damage, forest fire — damage, control and protection, monitoring by Government of India, state and division level, damage assessment with the help of remote sensing and geographical information system, forest fire management plan and budgetary provisions, ----"*. There is no mention of fire under the Forest Ecology or Silviculture subjects. Under Wildlife Management, it mentions *"role of fire, grazing and other natural calamities"* in Habitat Ecology sub-section. It is clear that fire is still clubbed with damage and no positive values are attributed to it. Although MOEF&CC ordered a revision in 2011, the emerging perspective on forest fires has not yet percolated into the curriculum of the IGNFA.

Let us hope the next curriculum revision happens soon. The same must be true of other training institutions.

Conclusion

The foregoing discussion is primarily related to the management of grasslands, savannahs, and forest communities with a significant incidence of grasses on the floor. In short, prescribed fires can be used to reduce moribund and unacceptable grass material, to change the composition and structure of a grassland, to improve the quality of forage, and, above all, to prevent unwanted fires. In even more practical terms, prescribed fires should be used only when a rangeland is dominated by the Increaser II (i.e. unpalatable) category of grasses and when the fuel load is more than 4,000 kg/ha. However, the fire regime to be applied depends on the response of local vegetation and abiotic components of our ecosystems to potential fire regimes. Although we can use Trollope's recommendations as an interim measure to kick in a culture of using prescribed fires in the management of our wildlands, we need to urgently generate local knowledge on the fire ecology of our ecosystems, as the differences in the edaphic and climatic features of Indian and African ecosystems may seriously affect the outcomes. As fire is *the* most powerful agent that shapes terrestrial ecosystems, we are ignoring this science at great peril to our ecological well-being. Natural and man-caused fires have determined the composition of our forests for thousands of years. If we want the current biota to stay with us, we have to try to mimic the fire environment in our forests to which various species of plants and animals are adapted, rather than putting them in an alien fire environment conceived by man.

Phillips (1965) described fire as "a bad master but a good servant". I hope this chapter will give the reader some sense of how to master this wily servant and make it do what we want, instead of trying to bottle it like the proverbial genie.

CHAPTER-6

Wildlife Corridors: Necessity or Luxury?

I first heard of wildlife corridors in Sri Lanka, in 1998, while preparing management plans for their PAs under a UNDP-funded project. I had grown up (in service) hearing of the need to have more and more PAs in India but nobody was asking for linking the PAs through forest corridors till then. Sri Lanka loved her elephants but did not have enough space for a populaiton of nearly 2000. Elephants migrated from forest to forest, causing havoc on the way. The country thought they should move through forest corridors rather than traversing through villages and croplands. It did not make sense to me. I could not imagine elephants voluntarily staying in these corridors while luscious crops invited them all around. Once out, there was virtually no way of putting them back in a fenced corridor. However, our client, the Department of Wildlife Conservation, expected us (the consultants) to propose a nationwide network of elephant corridors. Despite having our reservations, and only a fuzzy idea of what an elephant corridor was, we proposed a few fenced corridors (power fences on farm boundaries) between neighbouring PAs. It will be interesting to check out how our recommendations helped the country, if at all someone cared to read them. By the way, the current elephant population of Sri Lanka is reported to be around 7500! Many more people and elephants die each year in conflict now than at that time.

So, when India started talking of wildlife corridors in the context of the tiger crisis of 2005-2006, I was still not sure the idea really suited us, with socioeconomic and ecological conditions similar to Sri Lanka's. But the idea has since become so attractive that almost every conservationist thinks that India's wildlife has no future without extensive wildlife corridors. This is despite the fact that extensive wildlife corridors are neither a pure blessing for wildlife or people, nor can India afford them in terms of financial and land costs.

Corridors, What?

A wildlife corridor is a relatively narrow patch of forest that joins two or more larger forests i.e. wildlife habitats, generally PAs. Wildlife corridors are meant to allow wild animals to cross human-dominated areas or linear infrastructure (highways, rail tracks, canals, etc.) safely and harmlessly. Corridors are considered critical for the maintenance of ecological processes including allowing for the movement of animals and the continuation of viable populations. They facilitate animal migration, colonisation, and interbreeding between populations which would have been otherwise isolated. The corridors facilitate the development of metapopulations out of small fragments by allowing the mixing of animals (i.e. genes) across landscapes. Forest corridors not only help in enlarging the gene pools, they also help in optimum utilisation of the available habitat, as animals can migrate across habitat corridors to deal with periods of plenty and scarcity. Niche vacancies, created by localised mortality of territorial species, can be filled by migrations through corridors. Although initially, the corridors became the darling of the scientists in the context of classical conservation biology, their importance has increased further as they can also assist species to cope with the impacts of climate change through migration to more hospitable climes. Now corridors are considered as important for plants as animals.

Although quite often we talk of species-specific corridors, such as tiger corridors and elephant corridors, a forest corridor is for all species, unless there are barriers which some species can cross and others cannot. The need for effective corridors is much more where protected areas, and wildlife populations, are small and, consequently, are more vulnerable to the ill effects of inbreeding and stochastic climatic extremes, or epidemics. The corridors may, however, also help to spread localised diseases to the rest of the landscape.

Thus, it seems that wildlife corridors must naturally be an integral part of the land use planning and wildlife conservation planning process of a nation. Accordingly, India is also trying to preserve or strengthen whatever is left of the wildlife corridors in different parts of the country.

Legal Framework for Wildlife Corridors

Despite its appeal to conservationists and ecologists, the term "corridor" finds only a passing mention in the WLPA 1972. It has neither been defined nor is there a provision to notify wildlife corridors like PAs. However, some provisions in the Act seem to be meant only to protect wildlife corridors. Moreover, provisions in several other laws can also be used to create a network of corridors if the country so wants.

India has nearly 700 PAs scattered over its length and breadth. Any forest land lying between two or more PAs is technically a wildlife corridor and the law empowers the authorities to protect such lands. The Wildlife (Protection) (Amendment) Act, 2006 has empowered NTCA and National Board for Wild Life (NBWL) to "ensure that – areas linking one protected area ---- with another protected area --- are not diverted for ecologically unsustainable land uses {Section 38-O (g)}. As a result, these bodies can now intervene in any development project, anywhere in the country (even outside notified forests), to ensure that wildlife corridors are not disrupted. Section 38-V of the WLPA further provides that the tiger conservation plan of every tiger reserve must ensure "ecologically compatible land uses in the --- areas linking one protected area ---- with another ---- so as to provide dispersal habitats and corridor for spill over population of wild animals---" {sub-Section (3) (b)} and that "the forestry operations of regular forest divisions --- adjoining tiger reserves are not incompatible with the needs of tiger conservation" {Sub-Section (3) (c)}. There are 52 tiger reserves in the country, as of now, each consisting of one or more PAs, scattered all across the country except the inner Himalayas. They are surrounded by hundreds of forest divisions who, strangely, are now obliged to manage their forests for wildlife conservation. Thus, the country has virtually designated all her forests in the peninsular and north-eastern India as tiger corridors protected by law. In fact, NTCA and NBWL can also intervene in non-tiger landscapes, as mentioned before, to ensure that wildlife corridors are protected {Section 38-O (g)}. As "every person, officer or authority" is "bound to comply with the directions" of the NTCA {Section 38-O (2)}, WLPA seems to have gone all out for preserving wildlife corridors in the country.

Corridors in the immediate vicinity of the tiger reserves are especially protected as they fall within the buffer zones and mandatory eco-sensitive areas (ESA) which may be as much as 10 km wide if not specified otherwise. The ESA provision is applicable to other PAs also.

The Forest (Conservation) Act, 1980 further strengthens the legal bulwark in support of wildlife corridors by making the diversion of forest land for non-forest purposes difficult. GoI guidelines for the implementation of FCA mention wildlife corridors almost in the same breath as PAs, without explaining what a corridor is. Every application for the diversion of forest land for a non-forest purpose has to specify whether the land in question is a part of a wildlife corridor or not. If it is, the authorities have one more reason to disallow that application. Every diversion under FCA is also subject to the payment of net present value (NPV) as per the orders of the Supreme Court of India dated 23.08.2008. Even government agencies have to pay this money to the forest department if they have to use forest land for any project. Obligation to pay NPV, in addition to the cost of compensatory afforestation, acts as a strong deterrent against any frivolous demands for forest lands, i.e. wildlife corridors, for development projects. Thus, there is a very, very, strong legal and administrative backing for wildlife corridors in India now.

Wildlife Corridors of India

Although most forest corridors connecting protected areas in any landscape are fragmented by a dense network of crisscrossing highways, canals, railway lines, etc. and intrusion of habitations, agriculture, and industry, large animals are still able to move, occasionally, over long distances. Tigers have been recorded to have moved between Pench Tiger Reserves of MP and Nagarjunsagar-Srisailam Tiger Reserve of Andhra Pradesh/Telangana, a distance of nearly 500 km. The Kanha-Pench corridor in Madhya Pradesh, made famous by the controversy about the widening of the National Highway number 7 (NH-7), does see tigers moving from one park to the other, off and on. A Panna tiger has recently been recorded in Bandhavgarh, travelling nearly 200 km in a landscape where there is no apparent forest corridor connecting the two parks. Tigers born in Ranthambhore in Rajasthan regularly wander deep into western Madhya Pradesh and occasionally settle down there. The cake perhaps goes to the radio-collared tiger TWLS-T1-C1 from Tipeshwar Wildlife Sanctuary of Maharashtra who travelled nearly 1,500 km over a period of nearly180 days between Telangana and Maharashtra. Even if the forest connectivity in the corridors is not complete, animals like tigers can use crops like sugar cane, maize, castor (*Ricinus communis*), and orchards, etc. as cover to commute between PAs, particularly in the rainy season. These crops can perhaps be called "corridor crops".

While Madhya Pradesh and Chhattisgarh had no elephant populations until recently, Chhattisgarh has already become one of the elephant states of the country with nearly 200 resident elephants in most of its northern parts. 10-15 elephants regularly migrate deep into eastern Madhya Pradesh from Jharkhand and Chhattisgarh. Now a herd of some 40 elephants has become resident in Bandhavgarh Tiger Reserve, deep inside MP. Two tuskers were also seen in Kanha meadow. Similarly, Maharashtra and Andhra Pradesh also have almost resident elephant populations in some parts now, while traditionally they had none. Elephants are believed to be moving into new territories due to the disturbance and depletion of their native habitats because of mining and other activities. Dispersing elephants often cause much havoc along their movement routes into new areas, especially where corridors are narrow or broken, as the species and people take time to learn to live with each other. Wildlife Trust of India (WTI) has identified 101 elephant corridors that need to be strengthened and secured by reducing human dependence on them (Map). WTI claims to have already secured six of them and work is in progress in six more.

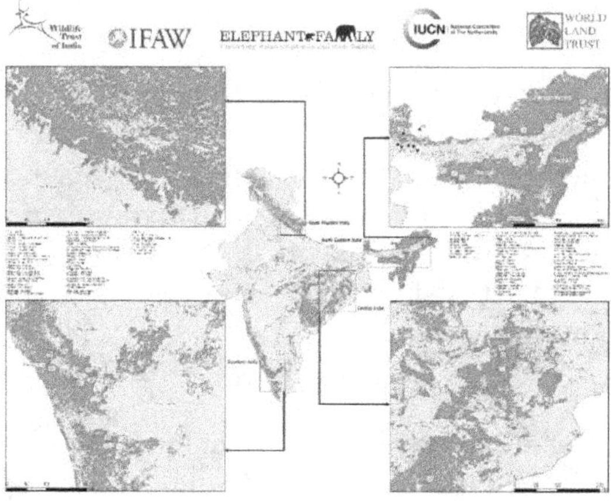

Figure 9: Elephant Corridors in India.

The unprecedented growth of the tiger population in the country also shows the occupation of the territories devoid of tigers for long. Stray tigers are being recorded even in Goa and Gujarat. Western MP is showing tiger presence after nearly a century. Obviously, tigers use some forest corridors and some artificial cover to discover new habitats. NTCA and WII have identified 32 tiger corridors in the country which they are trying to secure with the help of tiger conservation plans of local tiger reserves (Qureshi *et al.* 2014).

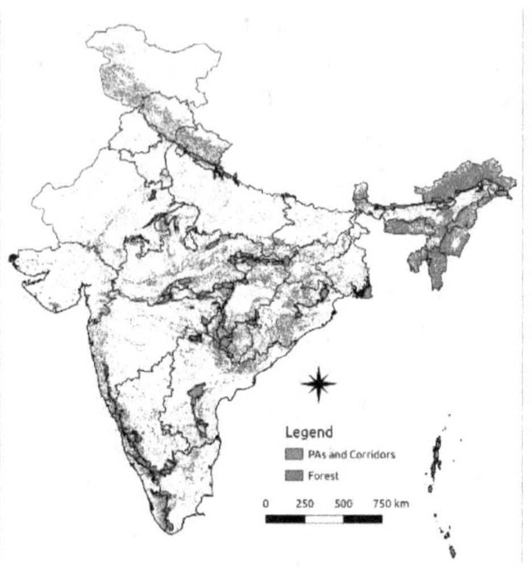

Figure 10: Tiger Corridors in India.

Although there are innumerable reasons why we should preserve our forests, their being corridors between PAs gives us one more reason to protect them against the marauding development juggernaut. As the impression that habitat corridors help preserve wildlife better has gained widespread acceptance, the policymakers listen when a development project is shown as a threat to some wildlife corridor, real or imaginary.

Corridors No Panacea

However, wildlife corridors are not an absolute win-win for wildlife. This is because the decline of wildlife in India is as much, if not more, due to poaching (killing animals for profit) and human-wildlife conflict as due to the loss of habitat and habitat connectivity. Both poaching and conflict are facilitated by wildlife corridors. The effectiveness of corridors requires PAs with porous boundaries so that animals can move from PAs to corridors, and vice versa. As corridors are inherently less protected than the PAs they connect, animals living in or transiting through the corridors are highly vulnerable to poaching. Animals go out of PAs either due to their territorial or wandering nature, or because of being attracted by luscious crops in the villages. Unfenced boundaries also make PAs vulnerable to poaching as poachers can infiltrate and hide in the virtually opaque habitat, without fearing detection.

It is important to note that wild animals are legally protected everywhere, *even inside our homes*. There is no difference between a PA and other forests, or non-forest, as far as legal protection is concerned. Therefore, the only way a *protected area* can be protected better than other forests is by having better ground control through fencing. That is the only way the rangers can have better ground control as nobody can get in without permission. However, we have to keep PA boundaries unfenced, as much in view of the conservation model we are following as due to the cost of fencing. Our current conservation model consists of a network of PAs populating the surrounding forests through spill-over of animals. This model is so deeply imprinted on the minds of foresters and scientists that they are unable to think of an alternative paradigm. We want the surplus animals from a protected area to spill into the adjoining habitats and create a larger population merging with the populations of other PAs of the region, through habitat corridors. While this may be a great idea in an ideal and safe world, we often ignore the fact that, with rare exceptions, any animals spilling out of the PAs are unlikely to stay alive for long or reach other PAs. For one occasional success, dozens or scores will perish. This is obvious from the fact that our famous tiger reserves must have sent out thousands of tigers since their inception, but their surrounds are still bereft of any significant tiger populations. This is because they run into serious conflict with people and often have to be eliminated. We regularly see it around Tadoba, Corbett, and Dudhwa tiger reserves. As a result, our so-called wildlife corridors have been the veritable sink for the animals produced at considerable cost to the taxpayer.

For example, the tiger population of Kanha National Park has always been 60-80 animals, since the early seventies. These 60 tigers of Kanha would have grown to an unbelievable 7,043 in the last fifty years, at a modest growth rate of 10% per annum, if there had been no poaching or emigration. In contrast, the entire Kanha landscape, which includes the buffer and surrounding forests, has just about 150 tigers today. In fact, the growth rate of tigers can be much higher in the absence of heavy poaching and emigration, as Panna's tiger reintroduction experience tells us.

Wildlife corridors are no blessings for people either. Wild animals kill nearly 1,000 persons each year and maim many more thousands. They kill 8,000-10,000 heads of cattle, and destroy millions of acres of crops each year. People live in constant fear and discomfort if they have wild animals around. All this happens along the so-called corridor forests. We can perhaps justify our infatuation with dangerous animals in the name of the pleasure they give to visitors in national parks and the jobs they can create through tourism. However, the same cannot be said of the animals that spill into the buffer forests and corridors where they only cause pain. The animals outside PAs are a pure and simple menace that brews in the PAs and causes trouble far and wide. No wonder these animals invite people's wrath and poachers' salivation!

Although it can be argued that corridors should be as well protected as the PAs, it is unlikely to happen. The very concept of PAs is rooted in our admitted inability to protect *all* wildlife habitats equally effectively. This is not only due to the shortage of resources, but also because rural communities are heavily dependent on most forests outside PAs and have to be allowed access for subsistence purposes.

Thus, wildlife corridors have as much going against them as for them. In short, forest corridors may improve the genetic vigour of wildlife populations of adjacent PAs but they also make PAs ineffective and vulnerable. Open PA boundaries and corridors also ensure that wildlife and local people always live in conflict and only at each other's cost.

Global Conservation Models

While India breaks her head over how to preserve habitat corridors between PAs, knowing fully well that that is where most of the animals coming out of the PAs will perish, the rest of the world has adopted a more logical approach to deal with this conundrum.

For example, all parks in South Africa and some other countries have to be fenced and any dangerous animals coming out of them have to be destroyed forthwith. However, being aware that fences cause habitat and population fragmentation, there is a strong move to drop fences between adjoining parks. For example, 19,485 km^2 area of the world-famous Kruger National Park was fully fenced until recently. But it has now dropped 50 km of its fence with the Sabi Sands Private Game Reserve (which itself is an amalgam of 17 private game reserves), adding 650 km^2 of prime wilderness, on its western flank, to its already huge area. The new entity is called the Greater Kruger

National Park. Not only this, Kruger National Park has also dropped another 50 km of its fence with the adjoining Limpopo National Park of Mozambique, in the east. South Africa, Mozambique, and Zimbabwe have also agreed to create, ultimately, a 1,00,000 km^2 transfrontier peace park, straddling their borders, dropping fences between the intervening public and private game parks, including hunting areas. But the combined perimeter of all these units is going to remain fenced so that poaching and conflict with communities can be controlled.

On the contrary, countries like Namibia, Botswana, Tanzania, Zimbabwe, Zambia, etc. have parks without fences and animals can move between the parks and the adjoining wilderness, where they can be hunted. Most of these countries have converted the surrounds of famous national parks (e.g. Serengeti) into community conservancies or game management areas (GMAs). Conservancies and GMAs are managed by federations of local communities in partnerships with government agencies, NGOs and private tourism and hunting operators. Here animals are hunted both for trophies as well as for food, but all for generating economic benefits for the communities. In these community conservancies and GMAs, animals are seen more as an asset than a liability. Neighbouring national parks ensure an inexhaustible supply of these benefits as long as the conservancies are sustainably managed. As the parks are surrounded by communities that benefit from the parks in their neighbourhood, the pressure of poaching, at least for the common food animals, is automatically controlled. Communities also tolerate wildlife damage more magnanimously because the same animals generate incomes for them. Wildlife populations in most of these conservancies or GMAs have seen tremendous growth over time.

Of course, migratory species cannot be fenced off in small PAs. These PAs have to be sufficiently large to fit the seasonal ranges within them, as in the case of Serengeti-Masai Mara complex of Tanzania and Kenya. The USA discourages fences in the migration route of elk but allows regulated hunting of elk herds when they transit between their summer and winter ranges. Smaller PAs in America are also fenced.

Our model seems to be a halfway variant of the latter where we allow animals to come out of our PAs but have no arrangements for their utilisation when they come out. We let the animals and the people loose on each other but expect them not to harm each other. Obviously, this is unsustainable as we see casualties on both sides.

No Land for Wildlife Corridors

However, presuming that wildlife corridors are desirable, despite their equivocal benefits to overall wildlife conservation, it is important to examine the question of whether India can afford to dedicate a reasonable amount of land to these corridors. A comparison of the availability of land in India with the rest of the world given below illustrates the situation:

Table 8: Availability of total land and forest land for wildlife corridors.

Country	Population* Density (km^{-2})	Per Capita Surface Area (Ha)	Per capita Forest Area (Ha)
India	410.3	0.24	0.06
China	147.4	0.68	0.15
USA	33.96	2.94	0.95
Australia	3.13	32.00	6.13
Africa	42.93	2.33	0.50
Europe	74.95	1.33	0.22
Asia minus India	102.14	1.29	0.16
World minus India	143.4	2.31	0.59

(*Based on http://worldpopulationreview.com)

As can be seen from the table above, India has by far the lowest per capita availability of geographical and forest area among large countries in the world. The per capita availability of land in India is only 2,400 square meters (60 m X 40 m), in which the country has to meet all the requirements for habitation, agriculture, infrastructure, industry, forests, wetlands, mountains, glaciers, etc. It is only 35% of China's and 10% of global land availability, per capita. Virtually the same goes for our forest lands, where the per capita availability of forest land is just 600 square metres, i.e. 30 metres X 20 metres. Most of these forests are already highly fragmented and degraded while habitat corridors require continuity of forests, of reasonable quality and width, across miles and miles separating adjoining PAs. These habitat fragments are not only separated by human habitations; the remaining patches are further sub-divided by roads, railways, canals, power lines, etc. and more such dividers are being created as the country develops economically. As per the latest estimates by the Forest Survey of India (Anon. 2018), only about half (57%) of the forest area of the country has any reasonable canopy density (40% or more). Nearly half of these denser forests are situated in the wildlife sanctuaries, national parks, and tiger reserves. Thus, most of the forests outside protected areas, which function as the wildlife corridors between PAs, are in the category of open forests (less than 40% canopy density) or scrub forests. They are heavily burdened with subsistence use by local communities and logging and planting operations of the forest departments. Forest areas under working (e.g. plantations) are often fenced by the FDs, fragmenting them further. Although successive forest assessments have shown a gradual increase in forest and tree cover in the country, the average density of forests has shown a sharp decline over time. Thus, the available corridors are degraded, often too narrow, and too fragmented to be effective for sustaining any significant wildlife populations, resident or transient. Because of the scarce land resources, competition for land is going to continue to intensify over time. More critical and immediate human needs are going to take precedence over the long term or more generalised societal needs. Thus, the condition of our wildlife corridors is likely to continue to worsen despite our efforts to preserve them.

Wildlife Corridors Misfit for India

In fact, the concept of long, winding, wildlife corridors does not really fit a country with such land scarcity and socioeconomic conditions. It presumes low human and wildlife densities where the cost of coexistence is low and occasional, and can be easily compensated either by the state or by wildlife utilisation by the people. The human densities in India are so high, even in remote areas, that the frequency of conflict with even low-density wildlife of the neighbourhood is quite high. By contrast, animals have 16 times more forest land in the USA and 8 times more in Africa, and far fewer people. Thus, animals and people do not need to come in each other's way as often. We, in India, believe that corridors are critical because our PAs are relatively small (average size <300 km^2) and cannot support genetically viable populations on their own. But the concept of habitat corridors is equally popular in Africa, the USA, and other countries where PAs are usually much larger and often contain more or less viable wildlife populations.

Therefore, the emphasis on habitat corridors is, perhaps, not entirely for ecological reasons but something else is ruling our mindsets. That *something* is the capital cost of fencing large areas and aesthetics. Wildlife-proof fences can cost USD 10,000-1,00,000 per km, depending on country, design, height, and topography. Not many conservation agencies can afford them unless the PAs are earning entities. Fences also look ugly to wilderness lovers, although it may be more beautiful once you are inside. Despite this, many African countries like South Africa, Namibia, and Botswana have made fences mandatory for PAs and private ranches. But wildlife fences are rare in western, central, and eastern Africa. By allowing the animals to range freely, these countries save the cost of fencing but inflict serious costs on the communities living along the open forest boundaries. Wildlife populations are declining in many of these countries. Although the USA does not have communities living within the wilderness, as in India and Africa, still the extent of damage caused by wildlife to the American economy is estimated to be more than USD 3.27 billion per annum, just because most forest areas in the USA are unfenced.

After studying the status of lion conservation in 42 sites in 11 countries, in Africa, a group of 39 scientists (C. Packer *et al.* 2013) says that *"Conservationists have long recognised that large carnivores should be kept apart from humans. However, fencing has so far only been widely employed in a few African countries because of aesthetic objections, financial costs and the impracticality of enclosing large scale migratory ungulate populations. -------- However, our analysis suggests that human-lion co-existence should only be considered in areas where large-scale megafaunal (and pastoralist) migration precludes any form of fencing."*

In another place the authors conclude that *"Conservationists have traditionally sought to protect endangered species by establishing wildlife refuges where even the most dangerous animals are exempt from retribution by local people. However, numerous efforts have sought to maintain dispersal corridors between reserves and attempted to promote human-wildlife co-existence in sparsely populated rural areas, either by initiating conflict-mitigation projects in buffer zones or by providing economic incentives for local people to tolerate the costs of living with wildlife. Thus, any attempt to achieve "co-existence" essentially involves an extension of conservation management over a far broader area than the wildlife refuges themselves. However, this goal will only be feasible if inclusion of the human-occupied areas provides substantial conservation returns on investment."*

The "returns on investment" in promoting "co-existence" in terms of animals saved from retribution, poaching, and accidents (e.g. road hits) in areas outside PAs (refuges), are very low in India which is not *"sparsely populated"* by any means. Therefore, prudence demands that we should look for a conservation model with better "returns on investment". Our current conservation paradigm, consisting of a network of PAs connected by habitat corridors, does not seem to pass that test. While Africa and America can, perhaps, still live with the losses of wildlife incurred in pursuit of open PAs and corridors, most species outside PAs, in India, have already been wiped out. If the corridors continue to make our PAs also ineffective and inefficient, by sucking animals out of them, it won't be a good use of taxpayers' money in a poor country.

Wildlife Corridors Block Development

Due to the scarcity of land in the country, land uses have to compete with each other for priority. We also need to find ways of accommodating competing land uses on the same pieces of land, although contending protagonists rarely show any sensitivity towards each other's concerns. Although the development agencies *are* becoming increasingly sensitive to ecological concerns of late, they still prefer to cut financial costs over environmental costs, if left to themselves. On the other hand, environmentalists often demand such over-the-top modifications to development projects, in the name of mitigating their impact on ecology, as to render them financially unviable. It often takes decades to resolve such impasses. In most cases, wildlife corridors are the bones of contention and the battles are fought in the corridors of regulatory authorities such as the SBWL, NBWL, NTCA, FAC, CEC, high courts, National Green Tribunal (NGT), and finally the Supreme Court of India.

A glaring example of the impact of this ecology versus development fight is the case of the upgradation of the National Highway 7 (NH-7) which connects Varanasi to Kanyakumari. The National Highways Authority of India (NHAI) started planning the upgradation of this important north-south route around the year 2000 but the work remained held up until 2020 where it passes through the forests on the border of Madhya Pradesh and Maharashtra. Here, the highway passes along the eastern boundary of the Pench Moguli wildlife sanctuary, which is a part of the core area of the Pench Tiger Reserve in MP. This forest (Kanha-Pench corridor) extends east up to the Kanha Tiger Reserve, some 200 km away, and beyond. Although the total width of the corridor at this point is nearly 30 km, the road follows the boundary of the tiger reserve for about 9 km.

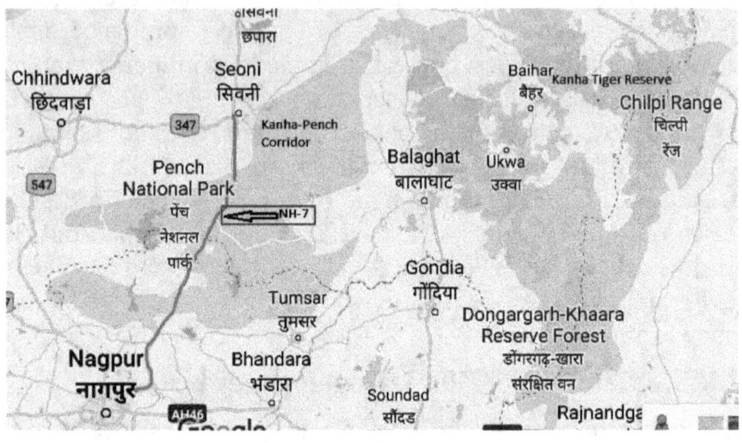

Figure 11: Kanha-Pench Corridor

When the proposal first came to the forest department for vetting, perhaps in 2006, the road was already like a wall in the middle of this forest. No animal could safely cross the road due to heavy traffic. Deaths of wild animals in road accidents were a daily occurrence. We badly needed animal underpasses (AUPs) which could be built only if NHAI was allowed to widen the road. Our field officers suggested that NHAI should be asked to construct a flyover all along the 9 km length, in order to preserve the wildlife corridor between the two tiger reserves. This would have cost NHAI an additional sum of Rs. 500-600 crores, perhaps more. Believing this to be an outlandish proposal, which nobody was likely to agree to, the then CWLW, Mr. P.B. Gangopadhyay, personally inspected the entire road length, along with the NHAI authorities, and suggested site-specific underpasses which would have allowed most large animals to cross the road almost every 250 meters. There were numerous other smaller culverts that would have provided smaller animals with additional crossing opportunities. We also demanded fences on both sides of the road in order to reduce road kills, as well as to force animals to use the underpasses. NHAI readily agreed to this proposal, although our field officers were not happy. But the proposal was rejected by the standing committee of the NBWL. We thought the matter had ended there but a public interest litigation (PIL) filed by WTI in the Central Empowered Committee (CEC) of the Supreme Court reopened the case. During hearings in the CEC, NHAI even agreed to construct the flyover, as had been proposed by our field officers, but later backed out. The CEC order of 2009, recommended that an alternative north-south route, connecting Nagpur to north India through Chhindwara (NH-547), may be developed while keeping the NH-7 stretch passing through the critical forests as it is, but closed to traffic at night (see map above). This triggered a series of public protests in view of the potential adverse economic impact on the people living along NH-7. Numerous courts, regulatory bodies, advisory institutions, NGOs, and committees merrily played football with the case for nearly a decade before finally allowing the road to be built. Now there are 14 animal AUPs and 28 other smaller culverts over a stretch of 28.5 km, with acoustic walls on both sides. Everybody sees it as a victory for conservation as pictures of animals crossing the AUPs regularly appear on social media. However, what we finally got is much less than what we could have gotten 15 years before, without killing thousands of animals since then (approximately one in two days, as per a WII study). Obviously, our friends-in-conservation would not let go of an opportunity for a good fight, for obvious reasons!

The cost of preserving this wildlife corridor is claimed to be Rs. 1,300 crore. This will perhaps be the last structure of its kind, as this "poor country" is unlikely to be able to afford similar structures at hundreds of places that need safe passage for wildlife across highways. This was indicated by the union minister for road transport, Mr. Nitin Gadkari in parliament (*The Hindu* 18-19 July, 2019). Although such costs are perhaps unavoidable, the delays caused by extreme stands can certainly be reduced through mutual appreciation by contending parties.

Wildlife Corridors can Block Conservation!

Our infatuation with wildlife corridors sometimes reaches such ridiculous levels that it starts looking like a vested and motivated exercise. A good example of this attitude is provided by how our Bandhavgarh gaur reintroduction project unfolded.

As I have indicated in my previous works there was not much love lost between MoEF&CC/NTCA and MP CWLW office due to their differences over how conservation should be done in the state. So, when we received the GoI permission to reintroduce gaur in Bandhavgarh through translocation from Kanha, one of the conditions of the permission was to rejuvenate a 200 km long (imaginary) corridor between the two parks (See "Wardens in Shackles" by this author). It was clearly a ruse to block the project, without having to say so. However, quite naively, we thought it was only an ornamental condition and sent them a sham corridor development plan costing some 350 crore rupees. Money for such projects is ordinarily provided by GoI. GoI never gave us the money but withdrew our permission barely a few days before the D-day on the ground that the corridor had not been revived. By then, a crore of rupees had been spent on preparations for the translocation of animals. Although the permission was restored a year later, on the intervention of the minister, the action showed how conservation agencies can sometimes use their self-assumed righteousness to harass the public.

As mentioned before, all forests outside PAs are wildlife corridors. So, all the forest patches between Kanha and Bandhavgarh national parks can be imagined as a part of the corridor although there is no connectivity between many patches. Madhya Pradesh State Forest Development Corporation (MPSFDC) has been allotted land about 100 km from each end of this imaginary corridor to raise commercial plantations of teak (Kundam Project). The operations have been going on since the seventies. When plantation in this patch came up for felling, sometime in 2010 or 2011, someone blocked this operation through a court injunction, claiming this patch to be a part of the Kanha-Bandhavgarh corridor. I, as the CWLW of the state, had no objection to the activities of the MPSDFC in their area, but the matter had not been resolved when I retired in 2012. Most likely, millions spent on this plantation have gone down the drain.

Even non-forest lands, lying on the imaginary wildlife corridors, are subject to our restrictions, as per the law. As mentioned before, NTCA and NBWL are mandated to ensure that the "areas" interlinking PAs "are not diverted for ecologically unsustainable uses" {WLPA sec. 38-O (g)}. The law does not say that this provision relates only to forest lands. On this ground, the development of an underground coal mine (perhaps called Mandla South block), outside the forest area, in Chhindwara district, far away from any PA, was blocked because it was situated in an imaginary forest corridor between Pench and Satpura Tiger reserves. Until then, no forest corridors had been formally identified or designated. Soon after WWF-India was assigned the job of identifying tiger corridors across the state, who identified this stretch as a possible tiger corridor. I am not sure whether the mine was allowed to go through, or not, in the end. Perhaps not.

NTCA may have the right to interfere beyond the forest boundaries but I think such highhandedness is not in the interest of long-term conservation of wildlife, as the society may react violently. Mining may be a dirty word for the conservation community, but there can be no civilisation without mining the planet. We have to learn to live with it, at least where it does not really hurt too much!

When the Central Government set up a high-level committee, chaired by Mr. T.S.R. Subramanian, in 2014, to review all the environmental laws in the country, in the context of their alleged impediment to development, I was not surprised at all. I had been fearing a public backlash against our conservation extremism all along, and here it was in full manifestation! The committee did not recommend any significant changes in the forest laws, perhaps because it was given just three months to do the job. However, the creation of the committee itself rings the alarm bells that our conservation framework is under attack. Part of the reason may be the arbitrariness with which the existing regulations are often applied to projects of public importance.

Reconnecting Habitat Fragments

Whereas the conservation lobbies need to be pragmatic in their approach to conflicts with development programmes, the development agencies also need to look at their track record and rectify past mistakes, or where the environmental impact of their originally benign creations is now coming to light, and is growing.

For example, NHAI has built numerous highways, cutting across forest blocks, without any concern for what happens to resident wildlife. These roads were built without any underpasses for wildlife, big or small, except the usual bridges and culverts which may be too far apart to be used by small animals or too small and/or dark to be used by large animals. The bigger forest blocks get divided into smaller fragments of different sizes. Most fragments are often too small to support viable populations of most species individually. The smaller blocks die a sudden and certain ecological death as the already small wildlife populations get further sub-divided into unviable fragments. One can imagine the future of a relict population of a slow-moving reptile, amphibian, or invertebrate species where the only male or female is trapped on the other side of an impenetrable highway. These highways are so wide, often with impenetrable dividers at the centre, that few animals can cross them safely. We see dead snakes, frogs, lizards, etc. on these highways every day. Most of these highways have been built on the basis of a very cursory environmental impact assessment. Even the forest departments never demand underpasses on these roads as they often report the absence of wildlife in isolated forest patches on the routes of these highways. We take notice of the potential damage to ecology only when a highway passes through or near a PA, or through a big forest. We hardly ever raise any objection when an equally damaging road passes through a small forest patch, further endangering the precarious existence of the remaining biodiversity of that patch, as mentioned above. The impact of fragmentation is much more severe on small fragments of forests than on larger patches. Once travelling from Bhopal to Pench, I was appalled to see that NH-26 passed through dozens of such patches in a short distance of some 56 km. There were several small fragments of forest clipped from the main block by the road, which could provide shelter to no species. The road had seriously eclipsed the capacity of the forest for supporting wildlife but nobody had taken note of it. On my return, we convened a meeting with NHAI to discuss the scope for retrofitting existing highways, with animal passes, where they passed through forests other than PAs. NHAI summarily rejected the proposal, despite our suggestion to consider it as a good PR move on their part. Perhaps we should have persisted with our demand, but more pressing things might have taken my focus away from this issue. I hope someone will still pick up the thread someday.

Fragmented PAs

As mentioned before, PAs are also mutilated by the presence of a large number of tarred public roads. In MP, the estimated length of such tarred public roads is more than 600 km. Major sanctuaries with important roads are shown in the table below:

Table 8: Major Roads Passing Through PAs of Madhya Pradesh.

Protected Area	Highways and Railway Lines
Ratapani WLS	NH12, NH 69, and a Railway Line (Itarsi-Bhopal)
Madhav National Park	NH 3 (Agra-Bombay Road), NH-25 (Lucknow-Shivpuri-Jhansi Road)
Satpura Tiger Reserve	SH-22 and SH-19A (Hoshangabad-Pachmarhi Road)
Orchha WLS	Jhansi-Tikamgarh Road
Noradehi WLS	NH-12 (Jaipur-Jabalpur Road), NH-26 (Sagar-Narsinghpur Road)

Protected Area	Highways and Railway Lines
Panna National Park	NH-75, (Panna-Chhatarpur Road).
Sanjay TR	Katni-Singrauli Railway Line.
Narsinghgarh WLS	NH-12 (Jaipur-Jabalpur Road)
Bandhavgarh TR	Umaria-Satna Road

Most of these roads initially had low traffic volumes. But, over time, the traffic density and speed have become incompatible with the movement of wildlife across them. Some of the roads are, of course, important national highways and their impact has all along been severe. Many others have also been upgraded to the level of national or state highways now. For example, the 165 km^2 Madhav National Park (main block) is divided into three fragments, by NH-3 (Agra-Bombay Road) and NH-25 (Lucknow-Jhansi-Shivpuri road) which are fenced along the roadsides. As a result, all wildlife populations, except those which can jump the fence (e.g. primates), are divided into three fragments. Similarly, the Ratapani sanctuary is divided by three very popular roads. Out of these, the Bhopal-Nagpur Road (NH-69) has a very high traffic density and animals hardly ever get a chance to cross the road, without risking their lives. At least two tigers were reported to be killed on the railway tracks in 2018. NH-12, connecting Jaipur with Jabalpur, also passes through a small wildlife sanctuary called Narsinghgarh sanctuary (57.1 km^2) before touching Bhopal, separating some 100 odd hectares from the main body of the sanctuary. Both sides of the road are fenced with a wire mesh. Although wildlife passes may not have been a part of the original design of these roads, it is imperative that impact mitigation steps be urgently taken in such cases now. Reconnecting, effectively, the fragments of these PAs, by providing suitable animal passes, or shifting the road outside the PA, if it is running close to the boundary, is even more important than safeguarding the corridors outside PAs. This is because the threats of mortality or fragmentation of wildlife populations in PAs is much higher. Although the forest departments have not seriously agitated this point so far, occasional moves have been rejected, both by the political establishment as well as the concerned agencies outright.

When the proposal for the upgradation of the NH-12, passing through the Narsinghgarh sanctuary, came up for discussion at a meeting of the SBWL, I as the CWLW suggested that we should recommend shifting it outside the sanctuary, both to help conservation as well as to avoid having to go to the Supreme Court every time the road needed repairs (a Supreme Court order banned the repairs of tar roads passing through PAs). The Chief Minister gave me a long lecture on not becoming an obstruction to the development of a poor state, and also lose public support for the conservation of wildlife. Similarly, the Board, chaired by the CM, refused to discuss the possible realignment of NH-3 (Agra-Bombay road) out of the Madhav National Park, terming it as a preposterous idea.

Fortunately, things have changed significantly over the last few decades. Development projects have, at least, started feigning conservation concerns, if nothing more. NHAI has itself assisted WII to produce guidelines for mitigating the impact of highways on wildlife (Anon. 2016). However, the day when we will willingly go an extra mile to save our wilderness is certainly far away!

What the Future Portends

In the light of the above discussion, we can construct a reasonably accurate picture of the future of our wildlife corridors. Under pressure from a rising population and prosperity and, consequently, rising demand for more land for habitation, agriculture, livestock husbandry, timber and firewood harvesting, industry, mining, hydroelectric projects, power lines, highways, railway lines, irrigation channels, and whatnot, the existing forest corridors are going to shrink, break up, degrade, denude, and fragment further. As these forests are subject to regular forestry operations of exploitation and plantations, they will also be internally compartmentalised due to regeneration and plantation fences. Overuse by neighbouring communities through livestock grazing, tree felling, mining, grass cutting, burning, etc. shall further reduce the effectiveness of many existing corridors. The encouragement to forest encroachments provided by FRA also does not bode well for the future of wildlife corridors. If the FDs are kicked out of the lands that become community forest resource (CFR) or PTG habitats under the FRA, or become ineffective, as many civil society organisations (CSOs) are agitating for, communities are unlikely to invite trouble by promoting wildlife interests in their forests.

Future infrastructure will certainly be greener than the existing linear structures as the pressure from the greens on their protagonists is going to increase. However, the traffic on existing roads and railway lines is going to go up exponentially. It is unlikely that we will be able to force a retrofitting programme, at any significant scale, for the existing structures that do not meet future environmental norms. The animal passes that may be constructed on future highways, railway lines and irrigation channels may or may not be equally effective or sufficient (in numbers) for all species. The underpasses will also raise the risk of poaching as criminals would know where to look for animals. Acquisition of land to plug the gaps and remove the bottlenecks in corridors is going to be expensive and difficult. Therefore, these weak points are going to become weaker over time, as more and more land is chipped away by neighbours. Due to the presence of, and increase in, bottlenecks and breaks, crop damage (and property damage in case of elephants) will go up. More animals shall die in conflict with people than ever before. The number of animals killed in road/rail hits will go up, too. More and more species shall experience disrupted breeding due to the separation of mates by the linear infrastructure. As the resilience of our forests goes down due to soil erosion, weed proliferation, and lack of regeneration, the rate of deforestation and degradation of corridors will continue to accelerate.

As a result of all these factors, the suitability of the corridor habitats for any resident populations will decline at an ever-accelerating rate. The frequency of animals successfully transiting between neighbouring PAs shall also be similarly affected. That is, more and more animals shall perish trying to negotiate unsafe corridors, with only occasional successes. As all these animals shall be spilling out of the PAs, the corridors shall become virtual drains on the PAs. As the functioning of the connecting corridors requires PAs with unfenced boundaries, the risk of poaching inside PAs will also go up as the availability of animals, for poaching, in the corridors progressively declines. Thus, the cost of having a few animals migrating from one PA to another, in terms of animals lost on the way, shall be much more than the expected benefits from a larger gene pool facilitated by the corridors. Clearly, the future of wildlife corridors in India is anything but glorious.

A chilling reminder of the future of wildlife corridors came to light in Lok Sabha recently. Union Transport Minister Nitin Gadkari remarked "'a poor country' must decide how far it can go in spending public money to protect the environment and balance out development needs. His reply came in response to a question from Congress MP K. Suresh who asked if the Minister would consider building underpasses on the National Highway between Mysuru and Wayanad to protect tigers in the Bandipur wildlife sanctuary on the lines of the Pench

Tiger Reserve in Madhya Pradesh. 'We are spending ₹1300 crore to build 9 kilometres there [in Pench]---This is public money. It is up to you to decide whether it is correct or not,' said Mr. Gadkari". (*The Hindu*, 18-19 July, 2019).

Roadmap for the Future

In the backdrop of this dismal scenario, we obviously need to carve out a strategy for wildlife conservation that is not overly dependent on wildlife corridors. Such a strategy can consist of the following broad elements:

1. **Fence the PAs:** Only a handful out of nearly 700 PAs in the country can boast of good wildlife densities today, despite 40 to 50 years of their existence. It is obvious that our current conservation model, with unfenced PAs, is wasteful as a lot of animals leak into the unsafe corridors, and perish. A documented case of this happening is the extinction of Panna's tigers. Two expert committees concluded that the extinction occurred when the last few males wandered out of the park in search of females (the park had no females towards the end) and never returned. It is not that only the animals go in and out of PAs through open boundaries. Poachers exploit this facility as much as the animals. If that were not so, our parks would have been full of animals long ago.

   In the landmark study mentioned before, C. Packer *et al.* *(2013)* conclude that, "*Lion populations in fenced reserves are significantly closer to their estimated carrying capacities than unfenced populations. Whereas fenced reserves can maintain lions at 80% of their potential densities on annual management budgets of $500 km^{-2}, unfenced populations require budgets in excess of $2000 km^{-2} to attain half their potential densities. ------ Nearly half the unfenced lion populations may decline to near extinction over the next 20–40 years.*"

   Thus, it does not require rocket science to reach the conclusion that we need to fence our parks for making wildlife conservation a success, and reduce costs. The initial costs of fences will be high, but it will be cheaper to have fenced PAs in the long run. Although determined poachers can breach any fences, as the rhino poachers in

South Africa show us, the loss of animals will be much less if the parks are fenced. We can exchange a few breeding animals between PAs periodically to improve the genetic vigour of the fenced populations. Excess animals can be used to create new populations if need be. If we have still more, we can consider promoting a hunting industry like most of the world.

Fences can be designed to selectively allow or block the movement of different species. For example, small mammals, reptiles, and amphibians can be allowed to go through the fences by increasing the mesh size closer to the ground. A combination of woven wire and power fences, designed to fit site-specific needs, can keep most animals in and poachers out of the PAs. Fences may not look great to a lover of the wilds, but they can save wild animals and the cost we incur on producing wildlife.

2. In order to be able to bring about this cultural change in conservation, we will need a fencing industry that can provide customised solutions for every situation. In India, a lot many animals get hurt after hitting the fences running. However, Bonnox fences, popular across Africa, are so flexible that they absorb most of the impact and the animals can learn not to hit the fence without getting injured.

3. We will also need an animal capture and transportation industry that can support the conservation agencies by taking responsibility for the movement of animals from PA to PA. PA managers will also have to resort to active management of populations to maintain healthy interspecific proportions as well as habitat productivity.

4. **Enlarge PAs:** If we think our PAs are too small to support viable populations if fenced, let us enlarge them wherever possible. As most states are no longer working their forests for timber production, the revenue loss from the expansion of PAs may not be much. If it reduces human-wildlife conflict, and a park next door creates jobs for them, local people should be happy to support such a move although it will cause them inconvenience in many other ways.

5. **Management Wildlife in Corridors for Community Benefits:** It is unlikely that we will ever be able to fence all

the PAs due to cost and other factors. Some places may not be suitable for fencing due to terrain and topography. At some places, the contiguous forests may be large with low human presence. Let us treat these forests as independent wildlife habitat units, rather than just corridors between PAs, and use them to produce benefits for the surrounding communities. They can be managed for tourism or sustainable use rather than having wild animals just for the heck of it. Adjoining farms, suffering from wildlife depredations, may be encouraged to convert into wildlife habitats on the lines of the Maharashtra initiative. Forests adjoining the conservancies can be assigned to the communities for protection and tourism. We may consider allowing hunting in these forests under suitable regulations, with proceeds going to the communities. The tourism/hunting operations can be run by professional companies on behalf of the communities, under a benefit sharing arrangement. Such forests will continue to function as corridors between neighbouring PAs (with unfenced boundaries) but people will be happy to see animals in them, rather than fear them. A PA fence can also be dropped if the area abuts on a conservancy land, to create a corridor. These corridors shall compliment PAs rather than compromise them as at present. If one can link the improvement in the condition of forests with carbon markets, it can strongly incentivise conservation for communities. After a long slump, carbon prices are again looking up, as they touched Euros 26 per ton on 25 September 2019 (https://carbon-pulse.com/category/eu-ets/).

In any case, communities are going to control most of the forests of India as the hold of the Forest Rights Act 2006 expands. Government has no power to interfere in the management of community-controlled forests. In order to ensure that these forests continue to survive and support biodiversity, communities will have to be encouraged to generate benefits as much from animals (through tourism if not hunting) as from trees.

A beautiful example of corridors functioning as independent wildlife production units is the constitution of the Greater Limpopo Transfrontier Park (GLTP) and Conservation Area, mentioned earlier. GLTP straddles the borders of three countries, namely, South Africa, Mozambique and Zimbabwe covering an area of about 100,000 km^2. It will integrate 5 existing national parks, including the iconic Kruger National Park into a single conservation entity with the intervening private game reserves and community conservancies acting as corridors. All the intervening fences are being dropped to allow free movement of animals although the fence around the larger entity will stay.

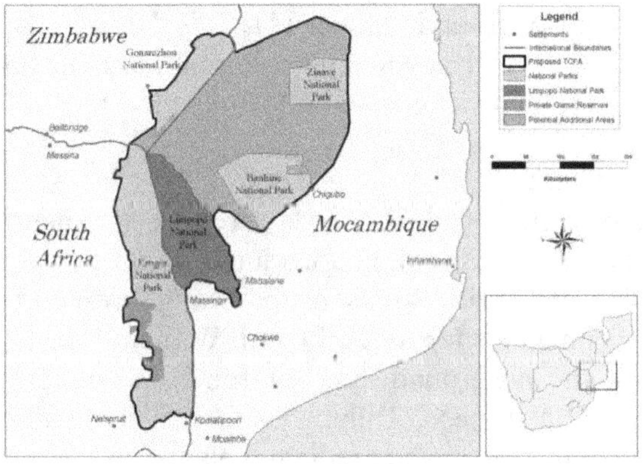

Figure 12: Greater Limpopo Transfrontier Park

6. We must continue to fight for making the linear infrastructure greener and smarter. Road crossings are more important for smaller animals than for the big ones. While we can attempt to keep the big mammals in fenced PAs, the smaller ones have to occupy all available niches which can be fragmented by roads and highways. As I have said elsewhere, these animals are more important for ecology than the megafauna as man can do most of the things the big ones do. Man cannot replicate the work of pollinators, seed dispersers, decomposers and soil workers. We need to find stronger arguments and communication strategies to protect smaller life forms despite the growing human encroachment of their habitat.

7. The most important thing that will have to change, for all this to happen, is WLPA. We need a law that ensures that managers do not have to take scores of permissions before touching an animal, and businesses are able to buy and sell wild animals for creating private or community-based wildlife reserves. Hunting of wild animals, for better management of wildlife, shall have to be allowed outside PAs as well. People will have to be allowed to defend themselves freely if dangerous animals spill into their homes and fields from neighbouring forests. At present, they can't even shoo them away without a permit.

But, not much can happen without the Wildlife Institute of India (WII) taking the lead as it is the only institution in the country with the mandate to train the field staff in making the right decisions and implement them.

Conclusion

In short, wildlife corridors of today are like an expensive antibiotic with serious side-effects and no guarantee of cure.

There are several critical reasons for saving forest corridors. Saving tigers and elephants is just one of them. Without forests, there would be no rivers and no groundwater. No birds, no butterflies. And the earth would be a furnace. Talking of forests as a source of timber, fuelwood, fodder, foods, and medicinal plants is almost old-fashioned now. Whether it is good to have more wild animals around is debatable unless they are of some use, but the need to have flowing rivers and a habitable climate regime is beyond debates. So, let us clinch this debate, once for all. Let us save our forest corridors for saving human beings, not just tigers. Tigers can perhaps be saved without forest corridors. There is no other way of saving humanity.

CHAPTER-7

Linking Ken and Betwa: Bane or Boon?

Background

Ken and Betwa are the tributaries of the river Yamuna and are, together, the lifeline for a large part of the parched Bundelkhand region of Madhya Pradesh (MP) and Uttar Pradesh (UP). Several dams and weirs constructed on them and their tributaries irrigate the region. Ken river runs for almost 55 km through Panna National Park, which forms the core of Panna Tiger Reserve. Another 20-25 km stretch of the river, downstream of the national park, forms the Ken Gharial Sanctuary, although the gharial population there is negligible, despite repeated supplementations. Betwa runs about 200 km northwest of Ken, for some distance also on the boundary of Orchha wildlife sanctuary of MP. The Government of India wants to divert 2,800 million cubic metres (MCM) water from Ken to Betwa basin by constructing a 73.8 metre high dam, primarily to irrigate nearly half a million hectares of cropland in both the states. The project will also provide drinking water to the countryside. The conservation community is opposing this project because the dam is being built at the heart of the Panna National Park, at a place called Dhaudhan, with a severe impact on the integrity of the park. Many hydrology and water resources experts also claim that Ken river just does not have the quantum of water proposed to be diverted and that there is no way the projected benefits of the project can be realised. Despite this controversy, all the governments (Centre, MP, and UP) are hell-bent on going ahead with the project. So far, the project was held up due to the states' haggling over water sharing. Even that hurdle has been cleared with the signing of the water-sharing agreement on 22nd March, 2021. Madhya Pradesh will get 1,834 MCM water for rabi (winter) crops and 2,350 MCM (million cubic meters) for kharif (summer) crops. Uttar Pradesh has settled for 750 MCM in rabi and 950 MCM in kharif season (*Times of India* 22 March 2021). Although no authority in the country has the legal power to allow the construction of a dam inside a national park, NBWL has already cleared it under pressure from the government. The Supreme Court has already made it clear that it loves river linking projects through its order dated 27 February, 2012, in Writ Petition (civil) 668 of 2002. Thus, there seems no way to stop it now, although I have no doubt that wranglings in various courts and committees will delay it further.

History

This dam has been coming for more than 40 years. The delay has, perhaps, been primarily due to the inability of the project proponents to garner enough resources and national priority for the project. However, they would like to blame the conservation lobbies and the forest department of MP for the delay. I first heard of the proposal in 1984 when the newspapers reported that the Prime Minister, Mrs. Indira Gandhi, was coming to lay the foundation stone of something called the Greater Gangau Project. Also known as the Ken Multipurpose Project, the dam was proposed upstream of the existing Gangau weir, within Panna National Park. Incidentally, all the bigwigs of the forest department in the State and the Centre were attending a seminar in Kanha when the news broke. None of them had any information about the proposal to build a major hydroelectric dam inside the national park. So, there was some hectic activity to ascertain the veracity of the news, and we learnt that the PM's programme had been postponed.

I was the director of Panna National Park at that time. On my return to Panna from the seminar, I found out that the irrigation department {the Water Resources Department of today} had made a lot of preparations for the event, without informing us. The point where the foundation stone was to be laid had been marked and an approach path had been cleared in the forest. Work on the construction of the staff colony had already started near a village called Ganj on the Panna Chhatarpur road outside the park. Ruins of this colony are perhaps still there to be seen. I impressed on the local authorities and politicians that building a dam in the forest area, without the clearance under the FCA and IFA, was illegal (there was no system of wildlife clearances back then) and that they would be prosecuted if they violated the law. Not many had heard of FCA back then although it had already been in existence since 1980. I was very sure that, going by her reputation, Mrs. Gandhi would never approve of a dam in the middle of an upcoming national park. I wrote to my department that one-third of the park would be either submerged or cut off, and the remaining park will be too small to be of any use for wildlife conservation, if the dam was built. So, the state had to make a choice, whether to have a park or the dam. As 1984 was the election year, everybody except the forest department wanted the dam. Caught in a bind, the forest minister, the inimitable Col. Ajay Narayan Mushran, called me to Bhopal, gave me a good dressing down, and mockingly asked me, "Why do you think we will sacrifice the dam for the sake of your rotten national park in an election year?" However, being the forest minister, he had no choice but to oppose the dam. So, he sent a note to the Chief Minister saying that the PM may be informed that the dam was going to be built in a national park. Sometime later, the newspapers reported that the PM's programme had been permanently cancelled. Understandably, many politicians were angry with the young DFO who could stop the PM from coming to their constituencies. I was even warned of the risk of bodily harm by some of them. Therefore, I had to take precautions about my safety, especially during the sad events following the assassination of Mrs. Gandhi, the same year.

The Reincarnation

The project again reared its head sometime in 2005 under its current name, the Ken-Betwa Link Project, about the time I returned to the wildlife wing after a gap of over 17 years. The CWLW office was asked to comment on the proposed tripartite memorandum of understanding (MoU) between the Centre, MP, and UP. We reiterated the same old objections stating it clearly that we could either have the park or the dam, not both. However, the parties went ahead with the signing of the MoU, in August, 2005, to start work on a detailed project report (DPR). Now the writing was on the wall and we, as the servants of the government which had decided to build the dam inside the national park, had no option but to fall in line. The DPR was still under development when I retired from service in 2012. Still I had to deal with it, though in a minor way, as a member of the SBWL. The proposal was cleared by the SBWL and NBWL despite the opposition of the non-official members of both the Boards. It has since received the stage-I approval of the Forest Advisory Committee (FAC) under the FCA 1980. However, FAC has imposed 47 mandatory conditions related to the payment of NPV, compensatory afforestation, relocation of villages, etc. which will have to be complied with before the permission to start work is given. All that is also subject to clearance by the Supreme Court as it has forbidden any construction work in a sanctuary or national park, without its permission, except a few items which are ancillary to conservation (Order dated 14.02.2000 and 14.09.2007 in I.A. No. 548 in WP No. 202/1995). Of course, the project will have to contend with all the public interest litigations (PIL) to stop it. In fact, the first PIL has already been filed. The latest cost estimate is reported to be nearly Rs. 18,000 crores, in addition to the cost of the implementation of environmental, forest, and wildlife action plans which may cost another Rs. 10,000 crores. Newspapers say that the cost will be Rs. 33,000 crores. I am sure, the project proponents will be able to juggle the numbers to justify the cost although it is a preposterous idea for a conservationist. However, believing that the dam is going to be built sooner or later, perhaps decades later, I have been wondering what the best deal for the park would be, in case the dam does finally come up.

The Project and the Law

As the dam is going to be built inside a national park, it has to contend with all the forest laws. While it is possible to get permission under the Indian Forest Act, 1927 and the Forest (Conservation) Act 1980, the WLPA specifically prohibits the destruction of wildlife or its habitat in a sanctuary or a national park unless it is "necessary for the improvement and better management of wildlife therein" {Sections 29 and 35 (6)}. As no authority has the power to make an exception to this provision, the wildlife clearance given by the SBWL of MP and the NBWL is clearly illegal and has rightly been challenged in the Supreme Court. However, the matter is more complex than that. The government is likely to exploit the loopholes in its own laws to be able to get a go-ahead from the court. It may argue that Section 35 (6) of WLPA does not apply to this case as the final notification of Panna National Park has not yet been issued. It is only a proposed national park at present. I hope someone will point out that the dam site continues to be a part of the Gangau sanctuary notified in 1974. Therefore, Section 29, which has exactly the same language as Section 35 (6), shall come into play. However, the most dangerous provision in WLPA, which allows the government to get away with even murder of ecology, is Section 38 O (g) related to the powers of NTCA. This provision empowers NTCA to "ensure that the tiger reserves ---- are not diverted for ecologically unsustainable uses, *except in public interest* and with the approval of the National Board for Wild Life--." As the government, rightly or wrongly, considers itself the final arbiter of public interest, it can force NTCA and NBWL to act under this section to allow the diversion of the land in question in public interest, even if it is for ecologically unsustainable uses. Thus, the only thing that can stop the project now is a determination by the Supreme Court that the project is not in public interest. As the court has already made its mind clear on the issue of river linking projects, there is not much hope there either. Unless, of course, the judges change their minds. Even if the judges decide that tigers and ecology are dispensable, I hope they will critically examine the claims of the project proponents regarding its economic benefits before passing a judgment.

Habitat Loss and Mitigation Measures

The following figures, though tentative at present, need consideration in this regard:

The dam and the canal are likely to submerge nearly 110 km^2 of land, out of which 60.17 km^2 will be forest land. Nearly 42.06 km^2 forest loss shall be in the core zone of Panna Tiger Reserve. In addition, nearly 100.0 km^2 shall be virtually cut off from the main body of the park, due to the creation of a large water body in the middle, unless steps are taken to reconnect the two parts around the lake. Approximately 17.16 lakh trees shall have to be cut. The full reservoir level (FRL) of the dam shall be 288 metres above MSL. It will submerge the nesting sites of 35-40 endangered vultures on the ledges of the river banks for some period, if the water level does reach the FRL level. The nests are at approximately 285 metres above MSL.

As against these losses, the FAC has ordered the project to pay for the relocation of as many villages around the reservoir as would create 6,017 ha of new wildlife habitat to compensate for the loss of forest land. The FAC order dated 15th May, 2017 says that "merely adding forest area of adjoining forest division to the core/buffer area of the tiger reserve will not be sufficient to compensate for the loss of forest areas as these areas are as such available for use by the tiger and other wild animals of the PTR." MPFD has identified some 27 villages for this relocation. Relocation of these villages will also develop connectivity between the forests on both sides of the water body. The park will get approximately Rs. 5,000 crores as the net present value (NPV) of the land and another Rs. 1,200 crores for compensatory afforestation and catchment treatment. Another 400-500 crore rupees will accrue to the park, being 5% of the project cost as a special compensation ordered by the FAC. The forest department will also get the resources for any additional impact mitigation actions that may be suggested by the WII study for developing a landscape management plan, which again has been financed by the project. Nearby wildlife sanctuaries Noradehi and Rani Durgawati in MP and Ranipur sanctuary in UP shall also get more resources. The project will also release 7 million cubic metres (MCM) water per month downstream, as ecological flow, to meet the water requirement of the Ken Gharial Sanctuary. The sanctuary gets virtually no water in the lean season at present, due to the presence of Gangau and Bariarpur weirs upstream. It is also reported that the funds due to the forest department are likely to be kept with Madhya Pradesh Tiger Foundation (MPTF), instead of CAMPA, to facilitate easy access and utilisation. MPTF, by the way, is a society created by MPFD to receive tax-free donations for the conservation of wildlife in MP. If all this money is used or invested wisely, it can meet virtually all the needs of the wildlife wing of the state, out of interest earnings alone, for a long time.

Life Comes Full Circle

Although cynics may still say that these are empty promises and hardly any project ever fulfils the conditions imposed by the regulatory authorities, or fulfils its claimed economic potential, to me it seems a good deal for the tiger reserve. The park expands, gets adequate money to meet its needs for a long time, and the benefit of a large water body. The part likely to be disconnected by the reservoir shall be reconnected by adding more areas to the park, around the lake. Several sanctuaries in the landscape get significant additional resources. And if the project irrigates half a million hectares of crops as well as provides drinking water to several million people, besides generating some power, who, in his right mind, would like to oppose it? True, the free-flowing river would be gone and my beloved Gheri Ghat would now be underwater, at least for a few weeks a year. It will also be a complete mess during decades of construction activity. I am sure, the damage to the park is going to be much more than what the documents say. And the economic benefits will not be even half of what is being projected. Left to me, I would love to keep the park as it is today, wild and untamed. But there are other, more powerful, stakeholders, who see it differently and who can have their way despite my opposition. They can even change the law if it comes in the way. Therefore, the best way for us now is, perhaps, to let them build the dam but without destroying the park. Even make it bigger

and better, as proposed. While this will end half a century of stalemate, the case will also set the template for all future projects, so that the country can make the right choices without wasting time.
It seems life has come the proverbial full circle for me.

Dear Reader, if you have enjoyed the book and found it useful, would you care leaving a brief review at your retailer's website and at your social media pages?

APPENDIX-1

Rules for Hunting Crop Raiders

Government of ------ (State)
Forest Department

Notification No.------------------ Dated --------------------In exercise of the powers conferred by Section 64 of the Wild Life (Protection) Act, 1972 (53 of 1972), the State Government hereby makes the following rules to regulate the hunting of wild animals which have become dangerous to standing crops, namely: -

1.   These rules shall be called The ------ (name of the state) Crop-Raiding Wild Animals (Hunting) Rules, 2021. They shall be applicable to the whole of the state.

2.   In these rules:-

   (1)   "Act" means the Wild Life (Protection) Act, 1972.

   (2)   "Bag Limit" means the number of animals of notified species specified in a hunting permit.

   (3)   "First/Sole Hunter" means the person who applies for a hunting permit and who is mentioned in a hunting permit as "First/Sole Hunter".

   (4)   "Gram Sabha" means the gram sabha as defined in Section 4 (c) of the Panchayats (Extension to Scheduled Areas) Act, 1996 (No. 40 of 1996).

   (5)   "Hunting" has the same meaning as in the Act, but its scope here is limited to killing with the help of firearms.

   (6)   "Hunt Coordinator" means a person appointed by the authorised officer to coordinate and facilitate the hunting activities in a hunting block.

   (7)   "Hunter" means a person who holds a hunting permit issued under these rules in his name.

   (8)   "Hunting Block" or "Block" means the agricultural land and other fallow land of a village or villages constituted as a hunting block and in which hunting of wild animals is permitted under these rules.

   (9)   "Hunting Party" means the hunters specified in the hunting permit and their helpers and observers in respect of whom the permit fee levied under these rules is payable.

(10) "Hunting Permit" or "Permit" means a permit issued under rule 8, authorising its bearer to hunt animals belonging to notified species in the specified hunting block.

(11) "Notified Species" means a species specified in schedule II of the Wild Life (Protection) Act 1972, which has become dangerous to standing crops in any part of the state and has been notified as such under rule 4.

(12) "Hunting Quota" means the number of animals of various species that can be hunted in a hunting block in a calendar year.

(13) "Shooting" means discharging a firearm at an animal with the intention to kill it.

(14) Any terms not defined here shall have the same meaning as in the Act.

3. As provided under Section 11(1) (b) of the Act, if the Chief Wild Life Warden is satisfied that certain wild animals belonging to schedule II of the Act have become dangerous to standing crops, they may be hunted as provided in these rules.

4. The State Government shall, on the advice of the Chief Wild Life Warden of the State, notify the species to which these rules apply.

5. **Authorised officer:** An officer in charge of a territorial forest division, to be called the authorised officer, shall be the authority to constitute hunting blocks, determine hunting quotas of notified species, issue hunting permits, and take all other ancillary actions under these rules. Provided, however, that the State Government can invest all or any of the functions of the authorised officer in any other officer or person as it may consider appropriate.

6. **Hunting Block**

(a) The gram sabha of any village suffering crop damage from wild animals may apply to the authorised officer to constitute a hunting block over the agricultural and other fallow lands of the village. The application shall be accompanied by a resolution of the gram sabha.

(b) On receipt of an application from a gram sabha, the authorised officer, after making necessary enquiries and assessments, may constitute a hunting block in the village.

(c) A hunting block may consist of the lands of one or more adjoining villages as may be specified in the order of the authorised officer.

(d) Hunting blocks shall not include any lands in reserved forests, protected forests, wildlife sanctuaries, or national parks.

(e) Constitution of a hunting block shall amount to the permission of all the owners of the lands included in a hunting block to allow unimpeded access to the hunting parties, forest officers, and any other persons associated with the conduct of hunting, to their lands.

(f) Every hunting block shall have a committee constituted by the gram sabha for consultations with the forest officials as may be needed regarding the conduct of hunting.

7. Hunt Coordinator

    (a) The authorised officer shall appoint, in consultation with the gram sabha, one or more persons, preferably out of the residents of the same village, who have good knowledge of the terrain and wildlife of the area, as hunt coordinators for each hunting block.

    (b) The hunt coordinator shall be responsible for facilitating the hunting activities in his block and maintenance of records as may be directed by the authorised officer.

    (c) Remuneration of the hunt coordinator shall be payable by the hunter in addition to any other fees payable under these rules, at the rates decided by the authorised officer from time to time.

8. Hunting Permit

    (a) Any person desirous of hunting notified wild animals in the state shall require a hunting permit issued by an authorised officer.

    (b) Only a person who is authorised to possess and use firearms as per the provisions of the Arms Act, 1959 and has hunted wild animals in India or abroad before, shall be qualified to apply for a hunting permit. First-time hunters may, however, be issued a hunting permit if they have accompanied a hunter on a hunt on at least two occasions before.

    (c) An application for a hunting permit shall be submitted to the authorised officer in Form H-1, along with the specified fee and supporting documents.

    (d) The hunting permit shall be in Form H-2. The authorised officer may, however, refuse to issue a hunting permit for reasons to be recorded in writing.

    (e) The hunting permit shall be valid only for the period and hunting block specified therein. However, no permit shall be issued for a period of less than three days.

    (f) A hunting permit shall expire on the day the bag limit is reached or on the expiry of the period mentioned in the permit, whichever is earlier. The hunting period may however be extended or changed by the authorised officer on the payment of additional fee as may be prescribed. There will be no more shooting after the expiry of the permit but it will not affect the operations ancillary to hunting such as skinning or dressing of the carcass, transportation, etc.

    (g) Not more than two hunters, whose names and addresses shall be specified on the permit, shall hunt against one hunting permit, and not more than four non-hunting persons will accompany the hunters as assistants or observers. Children under 12 years of age shall not be allowed to join a hunting party. Skinners, butchers, cooks, camp followers, and any labour required to process the carcass shall not be treated as part of the hunting party.

    (h) Only one hunting party shall be allowed to hunt in a hunting block at any given time.

    (i)   The hunters shall carry a copy of the hunting permit with him/her throughout the period of hunt and shall produce it to any forest officer or police officer on demand.

9.   **Fees:** Following kinds of fees shall be payable by the hunters at the rates prescribed by the state government from time to time:

    (a) Permit fee

    (b) Royalty

10. Hunting Quota

    (a) The Chief Wild Life Warden shall determine the hunting quota of each block depending upon the severity of crop damage and abundance of the notified species in the landscape adjoining the hunting block.

    (b) The authorised officer shall widely advertise the hunting quotas of various blocks in his jurisdiction through appropriate means, sufficiently before the beginning of the hunting season.

11. Legal Weapons and Ammunitions: Minimum calibre of the hunting weapon to be used for hunting under these rules shall be .275 bore (7mm) rifle, or 12/16 bore shotgun with single slug bullets. The use of buck shots is prohibited.

12. Hunting Procedure and Conditions

    A hunter shall hunt wild animals specified in his permit in accordance with the procedure and conditions given hereinafter:

    (1) After obtaining a hunting permit from the authorised officer, and on payment of all applicable fees, the hunter shall present his permit to the hunt coordinator of the concerned hunting block on or before the date of starting the hunt.

    (2) The hunt coordinator shall, after satisfying himself that all dues have been paid by the hunter, and after collecting his own dues as prescribed under rule 7, sign the hunter's permit to allow the hunt to proceed.

    (3) The hunt coordinator shall explain to the hunter the boundaries and other salient features of the hunting block and apprise him/her of the conditions, precautions, and procedure of hunting, as well as possible. The first/sole hunter, however, shall be responsible for acquainting himself and members of his party with the conditions of his permit before commencing hunting.

    (4) The boundaries of the hunting block shall be marked by coloured flags or by any other suitable means, during the hunting season, for the benefit of the hunter as well as of the local people.

    (5) The hunting season shall be announced in the village(s) by the beat of drum or any other reasonable means.

    (6) The hunter shall give a list of the assistants and observers included in his hunting party to the hunt coordinator before commencing the hunt.

(7) Every hunter shall submit a declaration in Form H-3 to the hunt coordinator before starting the hunt.

(8) Hunting shall be carried out only in the presence of the hunt coordinator who will accompany the hunting party throughout its stay in the hunting block and shall guide the hunters regarding the presence and movement patterns of notified animals in the block.

(9) Snares, nets, arrows, poison, and dogs shall not be used in hunting.

(10) A female animal accompanied by young ones shall not be hunted unless the young ones are also taken.

(11) The hunter shall only shoot to kill the animal. Every effort shall be made by the hunter to follow, kill, and recover an injured animal. In case an injured animal is not recovered after all possible efforts, written information to that effect shall be submitted to the nearest forest office.

(12) A hunter may enter the forest area adjoining the hunting block to bag an injured or dead animal shot outside the forest. However, he will not enter the forest without the permission of the forest range officer of the area. The permission, if taken over phone or through any other electronic medium must be recorded in writing by the hunt coordinator.

(13) A hunter shall not enter any private property outside the hunting block to kill or recover an injured animal without the permission of the owner of the property.

(14) An animal that is injured but not killed shall also be counted against the bag limit of the hunter.

(15) Hunting shall be carried out at least 200 metres away from a human settlement.

(16) The hunter shall not fire in the direction of a human settlement, house, shop, compound, road, footpath, or any other spot where men or domestic animals are likely to be present.

(17) A hunter may construct a *machaan*, pit, or hide with the permission of the landowner at his own expense. All such structures shall be dismantled by the hunter before leaving the hunting block if the landowner so desires.

(18) Every hunting block shall have a suitable place designated for camping by the hunting parties. Hunters shall set up their camps at their own cost and shall be responsible for keeping the site clean.

(19) A tag in Form H-4 shall be secured through the ear or leg of each hunted animal with a flexible wire before removing it from the kill site. This tag must stay with the carcass until it is disposed of. The tag shall be provided by the hunt coordinator on site. The

tag shall authorise the hunter to transport the carcass within the state.

(20) The hunter shall obtain a transportation permit from the relevant forest office, for transporting the animal, its meat, or any other parts outside the state. The transit permit shall be in Form H-5. The transit permit shall be issued on site as far as possible and the hunt coordinator may be authorised to issue the transport permit if necessary.

(21) The hunter shall be entitled to the ownership of the hunted animal and all its parts but he shall not sell or barter any parts of the animal. The hunter may, however, give the whole carcass or its meat, skin, or any other part to the concerned gram sabha who can dispose of the material as appropriate. The gram sabha shall be deemed to be a licensed dealer under Section 44 of the Act for this purpose. The proceeds from the sale of meat etc. shall be the property of the gram sabha.

13. Management Hunts

If an adequate number of paying hunters are not available to utilise the hunting quota of a block, the authorised officer shall be competent to engage paid hunters as may be necessary to hunt the requisite number of animals. All the meat, skins, and other products accruing from such hunts shall be treated as the property of the gram sabha to be disposed of as prescribed under sub-rule (21) of rule 12 above. The expenses related to such management hunts may be met out of the proceeds of hunting in accordance with a procedure to be determined by the authorised officer.

All the conditions mentioned under rule 12 shall be applicable to the management hunts, *mutatis mutandis*.

14. Hunting Income

(a) The income from the permit fee shall be treated as government revenue but to be spent on wildlife conservation in the state.

(b) The income from hunting royalty shall be the property of the respective gram sabhas. It shall be deposited in a special account of the Divisional Forest Officer and shall be transferred to the accounts of respective gram sabhas within three months after the end of the hunting season. Income from the sale of meat, skins, trophies, etc. or any other income accruing from hunting, shall be directly credited to the accounts of the gram sabha.

(c) The gram sabha shall be free to use this income as it deems appropriate. However, the first charge on this income shall be the payment of compensation for the crop losses suffered by farmers.

(d) If a hunting block consists of the lands of more than one village, the income shall be divided between the concerned gram sabhas in proportion to the land area contributed by each.

15. Refund of Fees

(a) The permit fee once paid shall not be refunded.

(b) Fifty percent of the royalty may be refunded by the authorised officer on a written application for the cancellation of the hunting permit before the hunting period authorised in the permit.

(c) Fifty percent of the royalty in respect of the animals not bagged during the validity period of the permit may be refunded by the authorised officer after making such enquiries as he may deem necessary.

16. Powers of the Chief Wild Life Warden

The Chief Wild Life Warden may issue necessary directions and guidelines to the authorised officers regarding the smooth implementation of these rules and removal of any difficulties. Any directions issued by the Chief Wild Life Warden in this regard shall be deemed to be a part of these rules.

17. Liability of the Hunter

(a) The first/sole hunter shall submit the information related to the animals killed or injured by him to the hunt coordinator before leaving the block in Form H-6.

(b) The hunter shall exercise extreme caution in the use of firearms and shall be responsible for causing death or injury to any person or domestic animal in the course of hunting.

(c) The hunter shall take necessary care to avoid damage to standing crops due to trampling.

(d) The first/sole hunter shall be responsible for the actions or negligence of all the members of the hunting party.

(e) The hunter completely indemnifies the state government, its employees and associates, and the members of the gram sabha on whose land the concerned hunting block may be constituted, against any death, injury, or loss suffered by any member of the hunting party due to any accident or on account of *force majeure*.

18. Maintenance of Records

The authorised officer shall maintain such records regarding the permits issued and animals hunted or injured etc. as may be prescribed by the Chief Wild Life Warden.

19. Arms Act 1959

The Arms Act 1959 shall be applicable to the possession and use of the weapons and ammunition for hunting under these rules.

20. Electronic Permits

The Chief Wild Life Warden shall develop appropriate systems for electronically issuing hunting permits as soon as possible.

21. Bulk Sale of Hunting Permits: Nothing in these rules shall prevent the bulk sale of hunting permits or hunting blocks to *shikar* agents by means of a procedure that may be determined by the State Government.

22. Penalties

(a) Any violation of these rules or that of the orders or directions of an authorised officer regarding compliance with these rules, shall be deemed to be a violation of the Wild Life (Protection) Act, 1972 and shall be punishable accordingly.

(b) The authorised officer may cancel a hunting permit in case of a violation of these rules or any provisions of the Act. Such cancellation shall be in addition to any other penalty that the violation of these rules may invite. All hunting activity shall cease forthwith in case of such cancellation. Any dues paid by the hunter shall stand forfeited.

(c) Penalty for killing or injuring an animal of the notified species above the permitted bag limit shall be double the royalty imposed by an officer, not below the rank of a forest ranger. Killing or injuring an animal of any other species shall invite a penalty under sub-rule (a).

(d) Any animals hunted in violation of these rules, along with their meat, skins, trophies, etc. shall be the property of the gram sabha.

No penalty under clause (b) (c) or (d) shall, however, be imposed without giving the hunter an opportunity of being heard.

23. **Report of the Chief Wild Life Warden:** The Chief Wild Life Warden shall assess the trends in wildlife abundance and crop damage in the hunted landscapes every five years through a competent scientific institution and submit a report to the State Government on the impact of hunting on the abundance of hunted species and crop damage.

24. These rules shall come into force with effect from the date of their publication in the official gazette. All existing rules, regulations, and orders related to the hunting of wild animals considered dangerous to standing crops shall stand repealed with effect from the date of coming into force of these rules.

Attached: Forms H-1 to H-6.

By order and in the name of the Governor.

Sample Notification for Specifying the Species That can be Hunted Under Rule 4 and Prescription of Fees Under Rule 9.

Government of ----- (State)
Forest Department

Notification No.------------------------ Date-----------------. In exercise of the powers conferred by rule 4 of The ----- (state) Crop-Raiding Wild Animals (Hunting) Rules, 2021, the Government of ---- (state) hereby orders that the following species of wild animals shall be the notified species for the purpose of these rules and can be hunted where they have become dangerous to standing crops, namely:

1.   Blue Bull or Roj (*Boselaphus tragocamelus*)
2.   Wild Pig or Wild Boar (*Sus scrofa*)

In exercise of the powers conferred by rule 9 of the said rules, the Government prescribes the following rates of fees for hunting wild animals in accordance with these rules, namely:

1.   Daily Permit Fee

Category	Nationality	Rate (Rupees)	Remarks
Hunters	Indian	500	1.Minimum duration of the hunting permit shall be 3 days.
	Other Nationalities	2,000	
Non-Hunting members of the hunting party	Indian	250	2.Validity of the permit can be extended on payment of additional permit fee.
	Other Nationalities	1,000	

2.   Fee for change of hunting dates or extension of permit validity: Rupees 1,000.
3.   Royalty (Per animal):

Species	Category	Indian Nationals (Rupees)	Other Nationalities (Rupees)	Remarks
Blue Bull	Either sex (Except Trophy males)	15,000	60,000	

Species	Category	Indian Nationals (Rupees)	Other Nationalities (Rupees)	Remarks
	Trophy Male	25,000	1,00,000	Horns 8.5 inches or longer.
Wild Pig	Either Sex (Except Trophy Males)	10,000	40,000	
	Trophy Male	15,000	60,000	Weight 100 kilograms or above.

Any difference in royalty paid in advance and the actual amount due shall be payable on the spot of hunting and shall be credited to the account of the gram sabha concerned.

These rates shall come into force with effect from the date of their publishing in the official gazette.

By order and in the name of the Governor.

Form H-1

(See rule 8)
APPLICATION FOR HUNTING PERMIT.

To,

Divisional Forest Officer,

---- State.

I am interested in hunting wild animals in accordance with The ----- (state)Crop-Raiding Wild Animals (Hunting) Rules, 2021 in your division. Therefore, you are requested to issue a hunting permit as per the details given below.

Hunter	Name	Father's Name	Full Address	Nationality	Age
First/Sole Hunter					
Second Hunter					

Animals and Hunting Block Applied for:

Species	No.	Name of Hunting Block	Period of Hunting

I have read and understood The ----- (state)Crop-Raiding Wild Animals (Hunting) Rules, 2021 and I undertake to abide by the same.

I am not required/ I am required to get my name registered under Section 34 of the Wild Life (Protection) Act, 1972 and the registration has been done by the officer in charge of the................ Sanctuary/ National Park.

I am qualified to possess and use firearms under the Arms Act, 1959.

Enclosures:

    (1) True Copy of Registration u/s 34 of the Act.
    (2) Proof of identity (Passport for foreign nationals)
    (3) Proof of Previous Hunting Experience
    (4) Photograph of the Hunter (4 copies)

Yours faithfully,
(Signature of the applicant)

Name:
Full Address:
Telephone: E-mail:

Form H-2

Book No.---------- Page No.-------

(See Rule 8)

------ (State) HUNTING PERMIT

OFFICE OF THE DIVISIONAL FOREST OFFICER, --------
DIVISION,---- (State)

No. Division/Block/Year/------ Date--------

In accordance with rule 8 of The ----- (state)Crop-Raiding Wild Animals (Hunting) Rules, 2021, the person/persons mentioned below are hereby permitted to hunt wild animals in this division as per details given below:

Hunter	Name	Father's Name	Full Address	Nationality	Age
First/Sole Hunter					
Second Hunter					

Permitted Animals

Species	Number	Hunting Block	Hunting Period

Number of Non-Hunting Members Allowed in the Party:
Note: Additional royalty for trophy animals shall be payable on the spot. Male blue bulls with horns 8.5 inches or longer, and wild pigs weighing 100 kilograms or more, shall be treated as trophy animals.
Sd/Authorised Officer
Seal
Attached: Payment Details
CC:

1. First/Sole Hunter
2. Range Officer
3. Hunt Coordinator

Photograph of the Hunter

Form H-3

{See Rule 12 (7)}

DECLARATION TO BE SUBMITTED BY A HUNTER

To

The Divisional Forest Officer

---------- Forest Division

----- (State).

Sir/Madam,

I ----------------------- the first/sole hunter hereby solemnly declare as follows:

(1) I will abide by The ----- (state)Crop-Raiding Wild Animals (Hunting) Rules, 2021in letter and spirit.

(2) I understand that hunting is a dangerous activity and all members of my hunting party are entering the hunting block at their own risk. I completely indemnify the government of -----, its employees and associates, or any other person associated with the conduct and regulation of hunting in my block against death, injury, or a loss that any member of my hunting party may happen to suffer during the course of hunting.

(3) All members of my hunting party are fully aware of the boundaries of the hunting block.

(4) I shall be responsible for the good conduct of all members of my hunting party as long as they are in the hunting block.

(5) I shall abide by the instructions/advice of the forest officers or any other person designated to supervise and facilitate the hunt by the authorised officer.

     Signatures

     Name of the First/Sole Hunter

     Hunting Permit No. and Date

     Hunting Block.

     Date.

Names and Signatures of Other Members of the Hunting Party

1. --
2. --
3. —
4. —

Form H-4

Book No.---

Page No.---

(See Rule 12)

**SITE TAG FOR IDENTIFICATION OF LEGALLY HUNTED
ANIMAL**

Name of the Hunter
Permit No.
Hunting Block
Forest Range
Forest Division
Date of Hunting
Time of Hunting
Species
Sex
Size
Weight of the Animal
Horn/Tush size (If applicable)

Signatures of the Hunter
Signatures of the Hunt Coordinator
Note: This tag authorises the transportation of the quarry within the
state of -----.

(This tag must be tied through the ear or the leg of the quarry with the
help of a flexible wire before removing it from the place of harvesting).

Form H-5

Book No.------   Page No.-----

(See Rule 12)

TRANSPORTATION/POSSESSION PERMIT FOR LEGALLY HUNTED ANIMALS AND ANIMAL PARTS

Certified that the person mentioned below has legally hunted the animals mentioned below and is permitted to transport/possess the animal/parts mentioned below as per the following details:

Hunter	
Name	
Address	
Permit No.	
Hunting Block	
Date of Hunting	

	Materials					Remarks
Species	Complet e Carcass	Meat (Kg)	Head	Ski n	Any Other Part	Distinctive Characters if any.

Date of Issue		Remarks.
Starting Point		
Destination		
Starting Date		
Valid up to		

Signatures

(Issuing Officer)
Seal of Office

Form H-6

(See rule 17)
REPORT OF WILD ANIMALS KILLED OR INJURED BY A LEGAL HUNTER

Name of the Hunter -----
Hunting Permit No. ------
Hunting Block ----,
Hunting Period: --------
Forest Range -------,
Forest Division ----.
Description of Animals Killed

Species	Sex	Weight	Horn/Tush Size	Weapon Used	Date of Killing (Harvest)

Description of Animals Injured but not recovered

Species	Sex	Adult/Juvenile /Young	Weapons Used	Date of Injury

I hereby declare that the information given above is correct and that no other wild animal or bird was killed or wounded by me during the validity of my permit.

Hunter's Signatures.

Date   Signatures of Hunt Coordinator.

APPENDIX-2

Rules for Hunting Predators

Government of -------- (State)
Forest Department

Notification No.----------------- Dated -------------------In exercise of the powers conferred by Section 64 of the Wild Life (Protection) Act, 1972 (53 of 1972), the State Government hereby makes the following rules for permitting the hunting of wild animals which may be dangerous to human life, namely: -

1. These rules shall be called ------ (name of the state) Dangerous Wild Animals (Hunting) Rules, 2021. They shall be applicable to the whole of the state.

2. In these rules: -

    (1) "Act" means the Wild Life (Protection) Act, 1972 as amended from time to time.

    (2) "Dangerous Animal" means an animal that has recently caused human death or injury or is likely to do so in the future due to its aggressive behaviour, physical disability, presence near human habitation, overpopulation, or for any other reason.

    (3) "Hunter" means a person who is authorized to fire a gun at a wild animal as per a hunting permit issued under these rules.

    (4) "Hunting" has the same meaning as in the Act, but its scope here is limited to killing with the help of firearms.

    (5) "Hunting Agent" means a person or organisation in the business of outfitting hunters and appointed by the Chief Wild Life Warden (CWLW) to facilitate the hunting of an animal specified in a hunting permit issued under these rules.

    (6) "Hunting Block" or "Block" means the general area of occurrence, identified by natural and man-made landmarks, of the animal permitted to be hunted under these rules.

    (7) "Hunting Party" means the hunters, their helpers, guides, assistants, and observers who are authorized to enter the forest to hunt a wild animal as per a hunting permit issued under these rules.

    (8) "Prescribed" means prescribed by the State Government or by an officer authorized by the Government to do so.

(9) "Shooting" means discharging a firearm at an animal with the intention to kill it.

(10) "Wild Animal" means a tiger, leopard, lion, gaur, elephant, or crocodile but may include any other species which may have become dangerous to human life, as defined under (2) above, in the opinion of the Chief Wild Life Warden.

(11) Any terms not defined here shall have the same meaning as in the Act.

3. As provided under Section 11 of the Act, the wild animals that have become dangerous to human life in the opinion of the CWLW shall be hunted as provided in these rules.

4. The Chief Wild Life Warden shall take all necessary steps to have any wild animal captured or killed as expeditiously as possible, using all possible means at his disposal, if he/she is satisfied that it has become dangerous to human life for any of the following reasons, namely:

   (a) An animal has deliberately killed or injured a human being and is likely to kill or injure more people.

   (b) An animal is so weak or disabled that it is likely to be unable to hunt its natural prey.

   (c) An animal is living too close to human habitation, or frequently visits human habitation or cultivation, or shows a behaviour pattern that indicates imminent danger to human life.

5. The CWLW may permit the hunting of the wild animals which are deemed dangerous to human life, for the following reasons: -

   (d) Repeated cases of human death or injury have been noticed in encounters with wild animals; or

   (e) The size, density, structure, and growth rate of a population of a species of wild animals in an area poses a danger to human life.

6. The Chief Wild Life Warden may permit the shooting of any wild animals mentioned in rule 4 and rule 5 if he/she is satisfied that:

   (a) capturing such animals is likely to be difficult or delayed; and any delay in the removal of the animal from the area is likely to endanger more human lives; or

   (b) the rehabilitation of the captured animals in the wild is technically not feasible and is likely to endanger more human lives.

7. Any wild animal captured in accordance with the provisions of Section 11 of the Act, which cannot be rehabilitated in the wild for any reason, may be euthanized unless it is required for display, breeding, or any other like purpose.

8. The Chief Wild Life Warden shall permit the hunting of the animals mentioned in rule 5 and 6 only in accordance with the following procedure:

   (a) The CWLW shall, through a competent institution or expert, conduct an annual assessment of the population size, structure, and growth rate of the target species in the target area.

   (b) The CWLW shall determine, in consultation with competent institutions and experts, the maximum population size for the target area keeping in view the safety of the people and the viability of the population of the species in the area. The safety of the local people shall be given priority over any other considerations in this assessment.

   (c) Shooting of animals likely to be surplus may be permitted on an annual basis or as and when necessary. The animals to be hunted in any year shall be selected in accordance with any of the following criteria, as far as possible:

      (i) Animals living closer to human habitations;

      (ii) Old, sick, injured, handicapped, or malformed animals;

      (iii) Animals showing dangerously aggressive behaviour in human presence;

      (iv) Past-the-prime, non-breeding animals, preferably males.

      (v) Any other animal likely to enter categories (i) to (iv) in near future.

   (d) All animals to be hunted in a particular year or season shall be individually identified and described on the basis of their distinguishing features and general area of occurrence as far as possible.

   (e) In case such hunting is proposed inside a sanctuary or a national park, it shall be allowed only in consultation with the State Board for Wild Life or the National Board for Wild Life, respectively, as the case may be.

9. **Hunting Season:** All hunting under these rules shall be done during the hunting season to be notified by the State Government each year.

10. **Hunting Permit**

(a) Any person desirous of hunting wild animals under these rules shall require a hunting permit issued by the CWLW in the form that may be prescribed.

(b) Only a person who is authorised to possess and use firearms as per the provisions of the Arms Act, 1959 and has hunted wild animals in India or abroad before, shall be qualified to possess a hunting permit. First-time hunters may, however, be issued a hunting permit if they have accompanied a hunting party on a carnivore or elephant hunt on at least two occasions before. Children under 12 years of age shall not be allowed to join a hunting party.

(c) A hunting permit shall be valid only for one hunting season.

(d) The hunter shall carry a copy of the hunting permit with him/her throughout the period of the hunt and shall produce it to any forest officer or police officer on demand.

12. **Hunting Agents:** Hunting permits for the identified animals may be sold to hunting agents either for a fixed fee or through a competitive procedure that may be prescribed. The hunting agents shall be free to transfer the permit to qualified hunters but shall be fully responsible for ensuring that hunting is done in accordance with these rules.

13. **Legal Weapons and Ammunitions:** Minimum caliber of the hunting weapon to be used for hunting under these rules shall be a .375 H&H rifle. The use of lighter guns and buck shots is prohibited.

14. **Hunting Procedure and Conditions**

Hunting of wild animals under these rules shall be subject to compliance with the following procedure and conditions:

(1) After obtaining a hunting permit from the CWLW, and on payment of all applicable fees, the hunting agent shall present his permit to the Forest Range Officer of the area in which a hunting block occurs and shall provide the details of the members of the hunting party.

(2) The Range Officer shall, after satisfying himself with the necessary paperwork, sign the permit to allow the hunt to proceed. The Range Officer shall designate an official to supervise and coordinate the hunt.

(3) The Range Officer shall explain to the hunting party the boundaries and other salient features of the hunting block, and apprise him/her of the conditions, precautions, and procedure of hunting, as well as possible. The hunting agent and the hunters, however, shall be responsible for acquainting themselves and members of the party with the conditions of his permit before commencing hunting.

(4) The boundaries of the hunting block shall be marked by coloured flags or by any other suitable means, during the hunting season, for the benefit of the hunters as well as of the local people.

(5) The hunting season shall be announced in the nearby villages by the beat of a drum or any other reasonable means.

(6) Every hunter shall submit a declaration, indemnifying the state government and its associates against any loss, death, or injury suffered by the hunter in the course of hunting, in the form that may be prescribed, to the Forest Range Officer before starting the hunt.

(7) Only one hunting party shall be allowed in a hunting block at any given time.

(8) The hunting agent shall appoint an experienced hunter as his/her representative to guide and assist the hunters during the hunt. Hunting shall be carried out only in the presence of such authorized representative of the hunting agent who will accompany the hunting party throughout its stay in the hunting block and shall guide the hunters regarding the presence and movement patterns of the target animal in the block.

(9) The hunter shall only shoot to kill the animal identified by the representative of the hunting agent. Every effort shall be made by the hunter to follow, kill, and recover an injured animal. In case an injured animal is not recovered after all possible efforts, written information to that effect shall be submitted to the nearest forest office.

(10) A hunter shall not enter any private property without the permission of the owner.

(11) An animal that is injured but recovered shall be counted as taken.

(12) Hunting shall be carried out at least one kilometer away from a human settlement.

(13) The hunter shall not fire in the direction of a human settlement, house, shop, compound, road, footpath, or any other spot where men or domestic animals are likely to be present.

(14) A hunter may construct a *machaan*, pit, or hide with the permission of the Forest Range Officer at his own expense. No live trees shall be cut for this purpose. All such structures shall be dismantled by the hunter before leaving the hunting block.

(15) No live bait shall be used to attract a carnivore towards a hunting party.

(16) Every hunting block shall have a suitable place designated for camping by the hunting party. Hunters shall set up their camps at their own cost and shall be responsible for keeping the site clean.

(17) A tag in a form that may be prescribed shall be secured through the ear or leg of each hunted animal with a flexible wire before removing it from the kill site. This tag must stay with the carcass until it is disposed of. The tag shall authorise the hunter to transport the carcass or any part of it within the state.

(18) The hunter shall obtain a transportation permit, in the prescribed form, from the concerned Forest Range Officer, for transporting the carcass, its meat, or any other parts outside the state.

(19) An animal hunted in accordance with these rules, and all its parts, shall be the property of the hunter but he shall not sell, transfer, or barter any parts of the animal to any other person.

(20) The Chief Wild Life Warden may impose any additional conditions or waive any of the conditions prescribed in this rule, in the case of crocodile hunts.

15. Management Hunts

If, for any reason, an adequate number of paying hunters are not available to utilise the hunting quota in any year, the CWLW may engage paid or volunteer hunters as may be necessary to hunt the requisite number of animals. All the conditions mentioned under rule 14 shall be applicable to the management hunts, *mutatis mutandis*.

16. Hunting Income

All the income accruing to the Government under these rules shall be used for the conservation of wildlife and welfare of the people living in and around the forests of the concerned forest division in accordance with the procedure that may be prescribed.

17. Powers of the Chief Wild Life Warden

The Chief Wild Life Warden may issue necessary directions and guidelines to any person, officer, or authority regarding the smooth implementation of these rules and removal of any difficulties. Any directions issued by the Chief Wild Life Warden in this regard shall be deemed to be a part of these rules.

18. Liability of the Hunting Agent and Hunter

(a) The hunting agent shall submit the information related to the animals killed or injured by him to the concerned Forest Range Officer before leaving the block in a form that may be prescribed.

(b) The hunter shall exercise extreme caution in the use of firearms and shall be responsible for causing death or injury to any person or domestic animal in the course of hunting.

(c) The hunter and hunting agent shall be jointly responsible for all acts of omission or commission of all the members of the hunting party.

19. Arms Act 1959

The Arms Act 1959 shall be applicable to the possession and use of the weapons and ammunition for hunting under these rules.

20. Cancellation or Suspension of Hunting Permits

The CWLW, or an officer authorized by the State Government in this regard, may cancel or suspend a hunting permit for any of the following reasons, namely:

(a) Death or capture of the target animal due to any reason.

(b) Violation by the hunting agent or any member of the hunting party of any provisions of these rules, or of the Act or any order issued by a competent officer.

(c) For any other reason to be recorded in writing.

(d) No cancellation or suspension under sub-rule (b) or (c) shall be done without giving the hunting agent an opportunity of being heard.

(e) Any person aggrieved by the order of cancellation or suspension issued under this rule may appeal to the State Government against such an order as per the procedure that may be prescribed.

(f) All fees paid by the hunting agent shall be refunded in case of cancellation of a permit except when such cancellation is for reasons specified under sub-rule (b) of this rule.

21. Refund of Fees: The CWLW may refund up to 50% of the hunting fee in case of an unsuccessful hunt provided he is satisfied that the failure to bag the animal was not on account of lack of intent, effort, skill, or faulty equipment. The State Government may prescribe the procedure for processing refund claims.

22. Penalties

(a) Any violation of these rules or that of the orders or directions of the CWLW regarding compliance with these rules, shall be deemed to be a violation of the Wild Life (Protection) Act, 1972 and shall be punishable accordingly.

(b) Any dues paid by the hunter shall stand forfeited on conviction.

(c) Penalty for killing or injuring an animal not specified in the hunting permit shall be fine, not less than double the amount of fee payable for an authorised animal of that species. This penalty shall be in addition to the penalty specified under sub-rule (a).

23. These rules shall come into force with effect from the date of their publication in the official gazette. All existing rules, regulations, and orders related to the hunting of wild animals considered dangerous to human life shall stand repealed with effect from the date of coming into force of these rules.

By order and in the name of the Governor.

Note: These rules can also be used to regulate the hunting of elephants.

APPENDIX-3

Wildlife Law for the Future

In Chapter 1, we have proposed the revamping of WLPA as a part of the proposed HWC management strategy for the country. The outline of the revised law is briefly discussed there. Presented in the following pages is the actual draft of the amended sections and chapters in accordance with the need discussed there.

The draft shows how the sections mentioned here need to read (post amendment) in order to facilitate the effective implementation of this strategy. Other sections which do not need any modification have not been mentioned.

As mentioned there, by and large, we need to bring back the original character of the Act, as it was passed by the parliament in 1972. That would provide all the freedom to the states to deal with conflict situations as they emerge from time to time. However, the draft also contains some new elements proposed in the light of the need to make it obligatory for the State to prevent and mitigate HWC and also to make the communities the owners of any benefits that HWC management strategy may produce from time to time (Sections 9 and 10). This vision did not exist in WLPA when it was promulgated in 1972, nor it does today. In view of this new orientation of the proposed law, the title of Chapter III itself has been changed. Another novel feature of the proposed draft is its linkage with CITES (Section 43-A). Although this feature is not directly linked to HWC management, export of trophies may require dealing with CITES authorities if hunting is ever accepted as the principal HWC management tool.

The Wild Life (Protection) Act, 1972

Chapter I
Preliminary

Section 2. Definitions. —

(16)"hunting", with its grammatical variations and cognate expressions, includes,—

(a) capturing, killing, poisoning, snaring, and trapping of any wild animal and every attempt to do so;

(b) driving or baiting any wild animal for any of the purposes specified in sub-clause (a) and every attempt to do so;

(c) injuring or destroying or taking any part of the body of any such animal or, in the case of wild birds or reptiles, damaging the eggs of such birds or reptiles, or disturbing the eggs or nests of such birds or reptiles.

Chapter III
Management of Human-Wildlife Conflict

Section 9. Obligation to manage human-wildlife conflict

Notwithstanding anything contained elsewhere in this Act or any other law, it is mandatory for the State Government to take steps as deemed necessary from time to time to control danger caused by wild animals to human life and property while ensuring the long-term survival of the species causing, or likely to cause, such danger.

Section 10. Hunting of wild animals

(1) No person shall hunt any wild animal specified in Schedules I or Schedule II except as provided in this Act and in accordance with the rules that may be made in this regard.

(2) The first charge on any benefits accruing from the hunting of wild animals shall be of the local communities.

Section 11. Hunting of dangerous or disabled wild animals.

(1) Notwithstanding anything contained in any other law for the time being in force, the Chief Wild Life Warden or the authorised officer may, by an order in writing, permit any person to hunt wild animals or cause such animals to be hunted in any manner deemed fit, if he is satisfied that any wild animal or a group of wild animals

(a) has become dangerous to human life, buildings, crops, infrastructure, or any other property; or

(b) is so disabled or diseased as to be beyond recovery.

(2) The killing, driving, or wounding in good faith of any wild animal in defence of a person or property, including standing crops, except by snaring, trapping, food explosives, poisoning, or electrocution, shall not be an offence.

Provided that nothing in this sub-section shall exonerate any person who, when such defence becomes necessary, was committing any act in contravention of any provision of this Act or any rule or order made thereunder.

(3) Any wild animal killed or wounded in accordance with sub-section (2) shall be Government property.

Section 12. Hunting of wild animals for special purposes

Notwithstanding anything contained elsewhere in this Act, it shall be lawful for the Chief Wild Life Warden, to grant a permit, to a person, institution, community-based organisation, or any other entity, on payment of such fee as may be prescribed, and subject to such conditions as may be specified therein, to hunt any wild animal or animals specified in such permit, for the purpose of:-

(a) education;

(b) research;

(c) collection of specimens for recognised zoos, museums, and similar institutions;

(d) collection or preparation of snake-venom for the manufacture of life-saving drugs; and

(e) population management.

Section 13: Refusal, suspension, or cancellation of a hunting licence

The Chief Wild Life Warden or the authorised officer may, subject to any general or special orders of the State Government, for good and sufficient reason, to be recorded in writing, refuse to grant a licence or suspend or cancel any permit granted under this Chapter.

Provided that no such refusal, suspension, or cancellation shall be made except after giving the holder of the licence a reasonable opportunity of being heard.

Section 14: Appeal from an order under Section 13

(1) An appeal from an order refusing to grant a licence, or an order suspending or cancelling a licence under Section 13, shall lie,—

(a) if the order is made by the authorised officer, to the Chief Wild Life Warden, or

(b) if the order is made by the Chief Wild Life Warden, to the State Government.

(2) In the case of an order passed in appeal by the Chief Wild Life Warden under sub-section (1), a second appeal shall lie to the State Government.

(3) Subject as aforesaid, every order passed in appeal under this section shall be final.

(4) No appeal shall be entertained unless it is preferred within fifteen days from the date of the communication to the applicant of the order appealed against:

Provided that the appellate authority may admit any appeal after the expiry of the period aforesaid, if it is satisfied that the appellant had sufficient cause for not preferring the appeal in time.

Section 15. Hunting of young and females of wild animals

No person shall, unless specially authorised by a licence, hunt the young of any wild animal, other than vermin, or any female of such animal, or any deer with antlers in velvet.

Section 16. Declaration of closed time

(1) The State Government may, by notification, declare the whole year or any part thereof, to be a closed time throughout the State, or any part thereof, for such wild animal as may be specified in the notification and no hunting permits under Section 12 shall be issued during the said period, in the area specified in the notification.

(2) The provisions of sub-section (1) shall not apply to vermin unless otherwise specified by the State Government in this behalf.

Section 17. Restrictions on hunting

(1) No person shall, for the purpose of sub-section (e) of Section 12,—

(a) hunt any wild animal, from or by means of, a wheeled or a mechanically propelled vehicle on water or land, or by aircraft;

(b) use an aircraft, motor vehicle, or launch for the purpose of driving or stampeding any wild animal;

(c) hunt any wild animal with chemicals, explosives, nets, pitfalls, poisons, poisoned-weapons, snares, or traps, except in so far as they relate to the capture of wild animals under a Wild Animal Trapping Licence;

(d) hunt any wild animal other than with a rifle, unless specially authorised by the licence to hunt with a shot-gun using single-slug bullets;

(e) for the purpose of hunting, set fire to any vegetation;

(f) use any artificial light for the purpose of hunting, except when specially authorised to do so under a licence in the case of carnivora over a kill;

(g) hunt any wild animal during the hours of night, that is to say, between sunset and sunrise, except when specially authorised to do so under a licence in the case of carnivora over a kill;

(h) hunt any wild animal on a salt-lick or water hole or other drinking place or on path or approach to the same, except sandgrouse and water-birds;

(i) hunt any wild animal on any land not owned by Government, without the consent of the owner or his agent or the lawful occupier of such land;

(j) hunt any wild animal during the closed time referred to in Section 16;

(k) hunt, with the help of dogs, any wild animal except waterbird, *chakor*, partridge, or quail.

(2) The provisions of sub-section (1) shall not apply to vermin or if specially exempted in the case of other species for reasons to be recorded in writing.

Section 29. Hunting in a sanctuary

Notwithstanding anything contained elsewhere in this Act, no licence to hunt any wild animals under Section 12 shall be issued in a sanctuary without the previous approval of the State Government. Further, no licence for the purposes of sub-sections (d) and sub-section (e) of Section 12 shall be issued and no permission for the diversion or destruction of wildlife habitat in a sanctuary shall be granted for any purpose except in consultation with the State Board for Wild Life.

Section 35 (6). Hunting in a national park (other sub-sections are not related to hunting)

Notwithstanding anything contained elsewhere in this Act, no licence to hunt any wild animals under Section 12 shall be issued in a national park without the previous approval of the State Government. Further, no licence for the purposes of sub-section (d) and sub-section (e) of Section 12 shall be issued and no permission for the diversion or destruction of wildlife habitat in a national park shall be granted for any purpose except in consultation with the National Board for Wild Life.

Section 39. Wild animals, etc. to be Government property

(1) Every-

(a) wild animal, other than vermin, which is hunted under Section 11 or bred or kept in captivity, or hunted in contravention of any provision of this Act or any rule or order made thereunder, or found dead, or killed by mistake; and

(b) animal article, trophy or uncured trophy or meat derived from any wild animal referred to in clause (a) in respect of which any offence against this Act or any rule or order made thereunder has been committed;

(c) ivory imported into India and an article made from such ivory in respect of which any offence against this Act or any rule or order made thereunder has been committed;

shall be the property of the State Government, and, where such animal is hunted in a sanctuary or National Park declared by the Central Government, such animal or any article, trophy, uncured trophy, or meat derived from such animal shall be the property of Central Government.

(2) Any person who obtains, by any means, the possession of Government property, shall, within forty-eight hours of obtaining such possession, make a report as to the obtaining of such possession to the nearest police station or authorized officer and shall, if so required, hand over such property to the office in charge of such police station or such authorised officer, as the case may be.

(3) No person shall, without the previous permission in writing of the Chief Wild Life Warden or the authorised officer-

(a) acquire or keep in his possession, custody or control, or

(b) transfer to any person, whether by way of gift, sale or otherwise, or

(c) destroy or damage such Government property.

Section 40. Declarations

(1) Every person having at the commencement of this Act the control, custody, or possession of any captive animal specified in Schedule 1 or animal article, trophy, or uncured trophy derived from such animal or salted or dried skins of such animal or the musk of a musk deer or the horn of a rhinoceros, shall, within thirty days from the commencement of this Act, declare to the Chief Wild Life Warden or the authorised officer the number and description of the animal, or article of the foregoing description under his control, custody, or possession and the place where such animal or article is kept.

(2) No person shall, after the commencement of this Act, acquire, receive, keep in his control, custody or possession, sell, offer for sale, or otherwise transfer or transport any animal specified in Schedule 1 or any uncured trophy or meat derived from such animal, or the salted or dried skins of such animal or the musk of a musk deer or the horn of a rhinoceros, except with the previous permission in writing of the Chief Wild Life Warden or the authorised officer.

(3) Nothing in sub-section (1) or sub-section (2) shall apply to a recognised zoo subject to the provisions of Section 38I or to a public museum.

(4) The State Government may, by notification, require any person to declare to the Chief Wild Life Warden or the authorised officer any animal or animal article or trophy (other than the musk of a musk deer or the horn of a rhinoceros), or salted or dried skins derived from an animal specified in Schedule I in his control, custody, or possession in such form, in such manner, and within such time, as may be prescribed.

Section 40-A. To be omitted

Section 43. Regulation of transfer of animals etc.

(1) Subject to the provisions of sub-section (2), sub-section (3), and sub-section (4), a person (other than a dealer) who does not possess a certificate of ownership shall not—

(a) sell or offer for sale or transfer whether by way of sale, gift, or otherwise, any wild animal specified in Schedule I or any captive animal belonging to that category or any animal article, trophy, uncured trophy or meat derived therefrom;

(b) make animal articles containing part or whole of such animal;

(c) put under a process of taxidermy an uncured trophy of such animal, etc. except with the previous permission in writing of the Chief Wild Life Warden or the authorised officer.

(2) Where a person transfers or transports from the State in which he resides to another State or acquires by transfer from outside the State any such animal, animal article, trophy, or uncured trophy as is referred to in sub-section (1) in respect of which he has a certificate of ownership, he shall, within thirty days of the transfer or transport, report the transfer, or transport to the Chief Wild Life Warden or the authorised officer within whose jurisdiction the transfer, or transport is effected.

(3) No person who does not possess a certificate of ownership shall transfer or transport from one State to another State or acquire by transfer from outside the State any such animal, animal article, trophy, or uncured trophy as is referred to in sub-section (1) except with the previous permission in writing of the Chief Wild Life Warden or the authorised officer within whose jurisdiction the transfer or transport is to be effected.

(4) Before granting any permission under sub-section (1) or sub-section (3), the Chief Wild Life Warden or the authorised officer shall satisfy himself that the animal or article referred to therein has been lawfully acquired.

(5) While permitting the transfer or transport of any animal, animal article, trophy, or uncured trophy, as is referred to in sub-section (1), the Chief Wild Life Warden or the authorised officer—

(a) shall issue a certificate of ownership after such inquiry as he may deem fit;

(b) shall, where the certificate of ownership existed in the name of the previous owner, issue a fresh certificate of ownership in the name of the person to whom the transfer has been effected;

(c) may affix an identification mark on any such animal, animal article, trophy, or uncured trophy.

(6) Nothing in this section shall apply—

(a) to animal articles or trophies made out of feathers of peacocks;

(b) to any transaction entered into by a public muscum or recognised zoo with any other public museum or zoo.

Section 43-A. Import and export of specimens of wildlife specimens: -

(1) For the purposes of this section, the words 'species' and 'specimen' carry the same meaning as in the Convention on International Trade in Endangered Species of Wild Flora and Fauna (CITES) of the United Nations.

(2) From the day of commencement of this Act, no person shall import, export, re-export, or introduce from sea any specimens of a species of wild animals or wild plants, or a species included in any of the Appendices of CITES, except in accordance with the provisions of CITES as applicable to India and the rules that may be made in this behalf.

(3) Quarantine certificate, issued by the appropriate authority of the country of export shall be produced for each imported wild animal or wild plant, upon arrival at customs port of entry.

Chapter VA. (Section 49-A to Section 49-C).Prohibition Of Trade Or Commerce In Trophies, Animal Articles, Etc., Derived From Certain Animals.

(To be omitted)

Section 61. Power to alter entries in Schedules.—

(1) The State Government may, if it is of opinion that it is expedient so to do, by notification, add or delete any entry to or from any Schedule or transfer any entry from one Part of a Schedule to another Part of the same Schedule or from one Schedule to another.

(2) On the issue of a notification under sub-section (1) the relevant Schedule shall be deemed to be altered accordingly, provided that every such alteration shall be without prejudice to anything done or omitted to be done before such alteration.

Section 62. Declaration of certain wild animals to be vermin.—

The State Government may, by notification, declare any wild animal specified in Schedule II to be vermin for any area and for such period as may be specified therein and so long as such notificaiton is in force, such wild animal shall be deemed not to be included in Schedule II for such area and for such period as specified in the notification.

APPENDIX-4

Economics of Hunting Crop Raiders

The purpose of these calculations is to bring home to the reader the enormity of the loss that the country is incurring by not treating these species as a natural resource. Even if a small fraction of this potential is realized, it will go a long way in making conservation a tool for human well-being rather than the one for destruction of our rural economy. The economic potential of only two species, i.e. nilgai (blue bull) and wild pig is discussed here while a few other species can also be sustainably hunted over large parts of the country.

For estimating potential income from hunting, one needs to know the size of the hunted population of the target species. The population size depends on the huntable area and the average density of the species. While the area available for hunting outside government forests can be estimated from government land records, we need proper scientific studies to estimate the population densities. However, until such studies are done, crude estimates can be made on the basis of densities reported in similar landscapes elsewhere. Financial estimates can be arrived at on the basis of the hunting quota and rates of fee proposed in the hunting rules presented in Annexure-I above.

These calculations are for Madhya Pradesh. Similar estimates can be created for other states as well.

I Estimate of Huntable Area

It is presumed in these calculations that agricultural lands adjoining government forests are more prone to crop-raiding and therefore shall be available for hunting. An estimate of the huntable area in the state can be arrived at, based on government records, as follows:

(a) Total agricultural land holding: 1,58,36,000 Ha.
(b) Culturable wasteland: 9,37,000 Ha.
(c) Total fallow land: 10,29,000 Ha.
(d) Total huntable area outside state forests: 1,78,02,000 Ha (a+b+c).(https://www.mpinfo.org/MPinfoStatic/English/factfile)
(e) Total number of villages in the State: 51,527.

(f) Area available for hunting per village: 345.48 Ha (d÷e).

(g) Number of villages highly vulnerable to crop damage (Situated within 5 km of forest boundaries as per MPFD estimate): 22,000.

(h) Total huntable area in vulnerable villages: 76,00,560 Ha or approx. 76,000 sq km (345.48 X 22000).

II Estimate of Huntable Populations

There are very few scientific reports on densities and growth rates of wild animals in agricultural landscapes in India. However, some cautious estimates of huntable populations can be made from the following reports based in India and abroad.

Singh (1995) has estimated the nilgai density for the state of Haryana as 5.67 animals per sq km. Ansari (2017) has reported blue bull density between 144 and 176 per sq km in Surajpur reserve forest of Gautam Buddh Nagar district of Uttar Pradesh close to Delhi. Prasad *et al.* (2020) counted 407 nilgais in seven herds residing in an area of 431.10 acres of a government cattle breeding farm in Buxar district of Bihar. This gives a local density of over 240 animals per sq km.

Khan & Khan (2016) reported overall blue bull density in 9 forest patches of Aligarh district of Uttar Pradesh as 38 per sq km. Local densities in forest patches were found to be as high as 132 animals per sq km, while the overall density in the entire district, which has very little forest cover, was estimated as 0.49 animals per sq km. This paper also mentions that nilgai densities in Ranthambhore, Sariska, Keoladeo, and Panna national parks have been determined to be 6.98, 5.19, 7.00, and 6.02 animals per sq km, respectively, in other studies.

Bajwa and Chauhan (2019) report the nilgai density of up to 6.94 per sq km in the Abohar wildlife sanctuary of Punjab. The sanctuary is primarily a privately owned cropland also inhabited by some 5,000 heads of blackbuck.

No Indian density or population estimates of the wild pig are available. However, the following studies indicate the prevailing scenarios in other countries.

Timmons *et al.* (2012) estimated that the average feral hog (pig) density in Texas ranged from 8.9-16.4 hogs/square mile and the state-wide population to be between 1.8 and 3.4 million, with the average being 2.6 million. They estimated 18-21% annual population growth.

Timmons *et al.* (2012) also reported that the estimated harvest of pigs in Texas in 2010 was 7,53,646 or 29% of the estimated population. According to them, without harvest, the feral hog population was expected to triple within five years, with a 28% annual growth rate. With low harvest (15% of the population), the population was expected to increase 2.51 times within five years, with an annual growth rate of 22%. Further, with an average harvest of 28% of the population, the feral hog population was expected to double every five years (2.02 times the initial population), with a 16% annual growth rate. Their model suggested that an annual harvest of 66% was required to hold the population stable.

Another report (Anonymous 2007) says that the pig population in South Carolina grew from less than 1,00,000 to over 15,00,000 (mean values) between 2002 and 2009, despite the increase in annual harvest from approximately 20,000 to just below 40,000 over the same period.

Sweitzer *et al.* (2000) reported that mean population densities ranged from 0.7 to 3.8 wild pigs/km^2 in North and Central California in 1994.

Tack (2018) has reported that the wild pig population is growing all across Europe despite heavy hunting in almost every single country. Annual hunting bags reached as high as 50,000 in Austria, 1,50,000 each in Czech Republic and Hungary, 2,00,000 each in Spain, Italy, and Poland, 6,00,000 in France, and 7,00,000 in Germany by 2010.

Khanom (2019) states that "wild boar population shows an increasing tendency for 34 years in Bavaria, where the north-west part holds the highest density of population (44/km^2)".

Vetter *et al.* (2020) found that about 30% of all females need to be harvested per year to achieve a stable wild boar population size.

Croft *et al.* (2020) report wild pig density in the Castelporziano Preserve (Italy) between 38.6 and 42.9 wild boar per km^2 in 2018. The proportion of wild boar culled per year fluctuated between 15% and 55% of the estimated population. However, typically it is maintained between 30% and 40%.

The same study reports an average density of 21.1 wild boar per km^2 at the Forest of Dean Estate (England). The proportion of wild boar culled per year fluctuated between 15% and 31% of the estimated population with the average maintained close to 25%. The number of boars killed in traffic accidents and found dead was estimated to be approximately 10% of the population.

Croft *et al.* (2020) conclude that, because any amount of recreational hunting and culling has not halted pig population growth, using contraceptives on 40% of the population to complement the culling of 60% of the animals, halved the time to achieve their target reduction compared with culling only and was cost-effective too.

Discussion: All the examples of blue bull density given above are from India, while those about the wild boar are from other countries. Nearly all the density estimates of the blue bull are from forest areas, except the figure for Haryana, while our concern here is to estimate the huntable populations outside forests. Another important point about blue bull is that densities in forest patches without predators (Haryana, UP) are extremely high compared with those in tiger reserves like Ranthambhore, Sariska, and Panna. The highest blue bull densities are reported from small patches of forests scattered across croplands while low densities are from large forest blocks. While only a small portion of the blue bulls living in large PAs may be involved in crop-raiding, most of those living in small patches of forests can be presumed to be available for hunting in croplands. Apart from occasional poaching incidences, the blue bull is under little hunting pressure in India, because of the religious connotations of its vernacular name (nilgai, the blue cow). However, occasional reports of mass killing for crop protection also come to light in some places.

In the light of this summary of facts, we have to make a reasonable guess about the number of huntable animals available per unit huntable area. As we have seen above, the species reaches unbelievable densities around croplands. These estimates relate only to the areas of the forest patches but the available habitat to the species is much more than the area scanned for estimation. However, large numbers of animals have no access to forest patches for shelter and spend all their time in the agricultural fields. The densities of these animals in and around croplands are likely to be higher than the PA examples given above in view of the absence of predators, lack of competition from other species, and the abundance of highly nutritious fodder. The average density of blue bull in the agricultural landscapes adjoining state forests of MP is likely to be somewhere between the highest (38) and the lowest (5.19) densities (landscape level) reported above. On this basis, I am inclined to assume an average density of 10 blue bulls per sq km for the sake of this exercise.

All the above arguments also apply to the wild pig densities in croplands adjoining state forests. However, there is one crucial difference in that all the pig reports are from heavily hunted sites. Most of these reports are national or regional level reports, at scales comparable to the scale in which we are interested. The most interesting part is that even such heavy hunting is unable to stop the growth of these populations. The scale at which they are hunted is unimaginable to us in India. Although the species is believed to be under heavy poaching pressure in India also, which organized hunting is likely to replace, there are clear signs that its population and range are increasing day by day. The highest pig density reported above is 44 per sq km. Perhaps, we can assume an average density of 10 per sq km for the forest-agriculture interface regions of Madhya Pradesh. Although the figure is arbitrary, I think it should be reasonably close to reality as some videos show huge sounders running across farms.

Thus, the average density of huntable populations of blue bull and wild pig for these calculations is assumed to be 10 per sq km on the basis of the above literature review.

III Estimated Income to Gram Sabhas (Royalty)

Based on the annual hunting quota and hunting fees proposed in Appendix-1, the income likely to accrue to the gram sabhas will be as shown below:

Species	Total Huntable area (km²)	Density (Per km²)	Total Estimated Population	Potential Annual Quota (30%)	Rate (INR)	Total (INR)
Blue bull	76,000	10	760,000	2,28,000	15,000	342,00,00,000
Wild boar	76,000	10	760,000	2,28,000	10,000	228,00,00,000
Total Income (INR)						570,00,00,000

The above amount is calculated only at the base price (INR) per animal to keep matters simple. Special rates are proposed in the rules for trophy animals (oversize) and foreign hunters. Additional income to local people from ancillary employment, such as labour, transport, hospitality, guiding, sale of local products shall also be significant.

IV Government Revenue (Daily Permit Fee)

Category	No. of Permits	Rate of Fee (INR)	Total Amount (INR)
Hunters	1,52,000	1,500	22,80,00,000
Non-Hunters	6,08,000	750	45,60,00,000
Total Income			68,40,00,000

Gross Total Income from Hunting: 570,00,00,000 + 68,40,00,000 = 638,40,00,000 (Rs. 638.40 Crore).

Thus, it is obvious that huge incomes can accrue to the villagers and the government from the hunting of only two species occurring outside forests, without any investments. If we add blackbuck to the list, a species that occurs as widely as these two species in the croplands of MP, the incomes can go further up. This income will be comparable to the revenue the state gets from tendu leaf trade which is considered to be the cash cow of the department.

As villagers (gram sabhas) will adopt the scheme slowly, it will take time to realize the full potential of hunting of crop pests in the state. A lot will depend on the way we manage and market the programme. In any case, these calculations are only indicative and will have to be refined on the basis of site-specific data. The income may also be limited by the shortage of qualified hunters in the country. In fact, most countries are facing a shortage of hunters needed to control wild pig populations.

The above estimate does not include the potential income from the sale of meat. Well-known ecologist Prof. Madhav Gadgil believes that wild pig hunting, outside PAs, alone can produce approximately 5 crore kilograms of meat annually. This should be worth at least Rs. 500 crores, even at the most conservative prices. In the above example, that figure would be close to Rs. 100 crores per annum. Moreover, it will help reduce protein deficiency among the rural people.

APPENDIX-5

Guidelines for Ecotourism under FCA

(Draft)
Government of India
Ministry of Environment, Forest and Climate Change (FC Division)
Paryavaran Bhawan, Jorbagh, New Delhi.

No.   Date

Sub: Application of the Forest (Conservation) Act, 1980 to Ecotourism Activities and Infrastructure in State Forests.

In view of the growing recognition of ecotourism as a tool for conservation of forests and wildlife, as well as for improving the well-being of rural communities, the question of liberalising low-impact tourism activities vis a vis the Forest (Conservation) Act, 1980 (FCA) has been under the consideration of the Government for some time. The Wild Life (Protection) Act, 1972 and the National Wildlife Action Plan (2017-2031) already support tourism in protected areas (PAs), and, a comprehensive National Ecotourism Policy is also been developed. Therefore, in supersession of all existing directions and guidelines, the following guidelines are hereby issued in relation to the application of FCA to ecotourism in State forests, namely:

1. Basic ecotourism infrastructure such as hiking/trekking trails, safari roads, campsites, toilets, bathrooms, drinking water facilities, day shelters, etc. shall be considered ancillary to the conservation, development, and management of forests and wildlife.

2. Ecotourism in forest areas shall be allowed and managed in accordance with a detailed management plan conforming to these guidelines and approved by a competent authority designated by the State Government.

3. As far as possible, only existing roads, trails and footpaths should be used for ecotourism. New trails or paths may be created only if absolutely necessary but with minimum disturbance to soil and vegetation.

4. Residential accommodation for visitors should ordinarily be created outside the forests. However, where suitable non-forest land is not available or where overnighting in the forest is considered a part of the ecotourism experience, limited accommodation, and ancillary infrastructure may be developed and operated on forest lands subject to compliance with the following general principles:

4.1. No more than 5 hectares of land shall be used for the creation of accommodation at any one location and each facility shall not have more than 40 beds. Only one such residential facility shall be allowed per forest range (approximately 200 sq km of forest area).

4.2. All residential facilities shall bear a natural look as far as possible and shall cause minimum alteration in natural vegetation and geomorphological features. The same principle shall apply to isolated facilities such as wayside shelters, toilets, refreshment centres, etc.

4.3. The colours and profile of the buildings should merge with nature as far as possible and should preferably be based on local architecture and cultural practices.

4.4. As far as possible, all structures should be such that they can be dismantled and removed at any time without impairing the ability of the site to return to nature.

4.5. Well dispersed tented units or huts/cottages shall be preferred over large monobloc concrete structures.

4.6. If fencing of residential facilities is necessary, barbed wire shall not be used.

4.7. All residential facilities on forest land must follow energy and groundwater conservation practices. No swimming pools shall be allowed. Outside lights in these compounds should be muffled and at a low level.

4.8. Roof-top solar installations, capable of producing at least 60% of the energy requirements, connected to the local grid where possible, shall be mandatory for all residential structures on forest land.

4.9. Adequate and effective arrangements for the storage and disposal of solid waste shall be mandatory for all residential facilities. All plastic and other non-biodegradable garbage must be removed and transported either to a recycling facility or to a designated municipal garbage dump. All kitchen and food waste shall be properly composted and shall at no stage be accessible to wild animals.

    4.10. All abandoned or not-to-be-used sites shall be restored to nature and all debris shall be transported outside the forests.

5. All employment in ecotourism shall preferably go to local communities. At least 90% of the workforce in an ecotourism facility shall be from the revenue sub-divisions (taluks, tehsils etc.) adjoining the subdivision in which the facility is situated. People living in the general impact zone of an ecotourism site shall be given preference in employment and other economic opportunities if any.

6. Foresters (all ranks) should not be involved in the day-to-day management of an ecotourism facility or campsite, as far as possible. All ecotourism services, except regulation and law enforcement, should be provided by specialist staff, communities, or private concessionaires, as the case may be.

7. Public-Private Partnerships (PPP) in ecotourism should be encouraged. State governments shall develop a suitable contractual framework for public-private partnerships (PPP) in ecotourism. The role of the private party in such agreements shall be limited to providing services and facilities and he/she shall have no right over the land or any forest produce, including carbon credits.

8. Local communities shall be free to use PPP areas as allowed under the extant laws and regulations.

9. Forest working plans shall pay special attention to maintaining and enhancing the recreational value of forests, especially the sites in use for ecotourism, in accordance with the National Working Plan Code 2015. Every urban settlement should have an ecotourism forest nearby as far as possible.

10. **Dispersal and Diversification:** As far as possible, and depending upon the potential of a site, attempts should be made to diversify and disperse ecotourism activities, as thinly as possible, over-all available area in order to minimise their impact on nature. To that end, an ecotourism product consisting of multiple activities such as game drives, hiking/trekking, bird watching, cycling, camping, etc. located in different parts of the ecotourism unit, should be encouraged. Dispersal can be both in space as well as in time.

Sensitive sites and species should, however, be protected against any adverse impact due to visitation or infrastructure development.

11. **Visitor Management:** Visitor management in the forests shall be based on the principles of *'Limits of Acceptable Change (LAC)'* as suggested in the comprehensive guidelines issued by the National Tiger Conservation Authority (NTCA) regarding ecotourism in tiger reserves, in 2012. A detailed LAC framework should be generated on a site-specific basis through a formal process of consultation and site visits by competent experts. Some of the parameters and indicators that can be used in this analysis are given in the Annexure to these guidelines. Visitor load and distribution, the nature of activities, site management practices, and land use shall be regularly adjusted in accordance with the observed and acceptable impact on various parameters as recommended by the expert committee mentioned under para 13.

12. **Impact Monitoring**: Impact of ecotourism activities and infrastructure shall be assessed annually in relation to parameters such as the ones given in the **Annexure** and an annual Impact Assessment Report (IAR) shall be prepared for each site. The assessment shall be done by an outside agency or expert and shall be submitted to an expert committee who will suggest remedial action based on the findings of the IAR if necessary. A consolidated summary of the IARs of all sites and the action taken in this regard shall be submitted by the HOFF or any other designated authority of the state to this ministry in the month of July each year.

13. **Guiding and Interpretation**: Good guiding and interpretation are the backbone of an ecotourism experience. Each ecotourism site shall have a sufficient number of trained guides and interpreters who can interpret nature to the visitors competently. Ancillary interpretation facilities such as signages, visitor centres, etc. may be considered as appropriate.

14. **Safety**: The safety of visitors shall be given the highest priority. Risks of entering a forest and taking part in an activity should be carefully conveyed to the visitors and suitable safety drills should be developed for each activity or experience.

15. **Capacity Building**: Each ecotourism site shall have a community capacity building and community engagement plan to ensure that the skills and capacities required for employment in the

ecotourism unit or providing ancillary services are locally available as far as possible.

16. FCA provides that prior approval of the Government of India is mandatory for assigning any forest land to an organisation not owned, managed, or controlled by the government. General approval is hereby granted to all community-based or PPP ecotourism operations operating or proposed in accordance with these guidelines. Site-specific approval shall, however, be required in case a substantial digression from these guidelines is planned or takes place.

17. In view of the recognition of ecotourism as an activity ancillary to the conservation, management, and development of forests and wildlife, as provided in FCA, there shall be no liability to pay the net present value or the cost of compensatory afforestation for the use of forest land for ecotourism activities and infrastructure compliant with these guidelines.

18. HOFF of each state shall be responsible for ensuring compliance with these guidelines.

Issued with the approval of the competent authority.

Sd/

Inspector General of Forests (FC)

Attached: Indicative Framework for Visitor and Site Management.

Annexure to Appendix-5

Indicative Framework for Visitor and Site Management for Ecotourism

{Based on 'Limits of Acceptable Change' (LAC) Approach}

Parameters	Indicators/ Criteria	Desired Condition	Management Approaches/Strategies
Wilderness Quality	Wild Looks and Pristine Scenery, wild animals, no trampling, no erosion.	Preservation, preferably Improvement	No off-roading, control over illicit felling and overgrazing, no major permanent and conspicuous infrastructure in forest land, selection felling for regeneration of trees, as per working/management plan.
Wildlife	Numbers and Density of animals	Improvement	Effective antipoaching operations, more waterholes, habitat management to improve fodder availability and distribution, local support.
Community Benefits	Income, jobs and businesses	Improvement	Guiding jobs to be reserved for locals, training and financial support for community businesses in hospitality and handicrafts, share in govt. revenue.
Community Involvement	Role in decision making, Frequency of consultations	Improvement	Approval of JFM/ecodevelopment committees to all major decisions, regular information dissemination, monthly briefings, and consultations.
	Staff Quality	Courteous, efficient,	Training, orientation, and motivation.

Parameters	Indicators/ Criteria	Desired Condition	Management Approaches/Strategies
Visitor Experience		and well informed	
	Information/inte rpretation availability,	Improveme nt, adequate	Literature, guiding service, Visitor Briefings, interpretation/visitor centres.
	Convenience	Reasonable	Sensitive staff, adequate facilities for toilets, resting and eating places.
	Safety	Assured	Risk information, safety-conscious and experienced guides, Safe infrastructure, Regulation, enforcement.
	Crowding	Minimal	Site-specific and activity-specific carrying capacity, group size limits on group activities (e.g. walking), activity-wise zonation, additional areas to be opened if needed.
	Pollution, dust, noise	Minimal	Low density/intensity traffic, speed limits, visitor education (e.g. no horns, no loud talking), enforcement.
	Garbage (inside the forest)	Zero	Visitor education, monitoring, enforcement, collection and disposal system.
	Garbage (Outside the forest)	Minimal	Visitor Education, Community Education, Monitoring, Collection and disposal System.
	Wildlife (mammals) sightings	Improveme nt	Strategic location of waterholes, Guide/Naturalist training, Promoting growth in population (of animals).
	Exposure to other life forms (Birds, butterflies, spiders, and other arachnids, snakes, Plants,	Desirable	Guide/Naturalist training, visitor orientation, intelligently laid walking/biking trails, literature.

Parameters	Indicators/ Criteria	Desired Condition	Management Approaches/Strategies
	etc.), and scenery		
	Diversity of Experience (game drives, walking, hiking, trekking, biking (cycling), camping, hides/machans, etc.)	Desirable	Combo entry/activity permits, infrastructure (trails, campsites, hides/machans, etc.) for all activities, Guide/Naturalist training, Literature, staff training.
	Exposure to local culture, cuisine, arts and crafts	Desirable	Community training, product development, marketing,
	Quality of Guiding	Progressive Improvement	Guide training and motivation, code of conduct, enforcement.
	Grievance Redressal	Easy, Quick	Transparency, communication with clients, empowerment of local officials/committees, accessibility/availability of senior officers (on phone or email).
Infrastructure	Availability	Assured	Only minimal development in the forests, suitably located, modest.
	Quality	Reasonable	Local architecture, local materials, low cost, unobtrusive.
Impact on Resources	Erosion, trampling	Minimal	Prevention, maintenance, and repairs (road, trails, etc.), regulation of the intensity of use, visitor discipline.
	Deforestation	None	No cutting of trees to be allowed
	Degradation	None	No off-roading, regulation of the intensity of use of sensitive sites, rotation/closure of sites/routes if necessary, visitor/guide education.
	Garbage	Zero	Visitor education, monitoring enforcement,

Parameters	Indicators/ Criteria	Desired Condition	Management Approaches/Strategies
			collection and disposal system.
	Reduction in animal or bird populations,	None	Population monitoring, habitat restoration, supplementation, reintroduction.
	Changes in Animal Behaviour	Minimal	No human contact. Some habituation to human presence will improve visitor experience, no feeding or luring by visitors to be allowed, No edible garbage around eating places.
	Water Quality	No deterioration	Careful location of campsites and vegetal cover, no chemicals, no garbage (plastics, etc.).
	Forest Offences	Progressive Reduction	Likely to decline due to visitor presence, better protection/patrolling using local revenues.
Impact on Communities and Surrounding Environment	Degradation of local infrastructure (e.g. roads, water bodies)	Minimal	Repair and Maintenance, education, commercial houses to pay more for maintenance, regulation of access to water bodies.
	Garbage	Minimal	Education, Collection and disposal systems, regulation.
	Clustering of shops in the villages (e.g. near the gate)	Minimal	Permit system, dispersal of activities to as many locations as possible, regulation.
	Clustering (mushrooming) of Lodges (Outside Villages)	Minimal	Permit system, dispersal of activities, multiple entry points, regulation.
	Noise, Dust	Minimal	Education, regulation.
	Water Quality	No Deterioration	No solid waste disposal in water bodies, No disruption in flow due to plastic waste.

APPENDIX-6

Design of Burn Trials

(Determining Appropriate Type, Intensity, Season and Frequency of Fire for Tiger Reserves in Madhya Pradesh, India)
(Recommended by Trollope *et al.* 2012 to CWLW, MP).

INTRODUCTION

Currently, there is a serious deficiency of knowledge on the fire ecology and effects of burning on grassland and tree/shrub communities in the Kanha, Bandhavgarh, Panna, and Pench Tiger Reserves in Madhya Pradesh State, India. Fire ecology refers to the response of the biotic and abiotic components of the ecosystem to the season, frequency, type, and intensity of fire (Trollope, 1981). This information is essential for the formulation of suitable fire regimes for prescribed burning in the vegetation types where fire is recommended for the removal of moribund and unpalatable grass material, and the prevention and control of encroaching tree/shrub vegetation. Following the visit by the Working On Fire International team to the different Tiger Reserves, it became clearly apparent that prescribed burning is a necessary and essential management practice in the grassland and grass-dominated forest communities to maintain the vegetation in a palatable and available condition for utilization by the different ungulate species in the four Reserves. This lack of information on the fire ecology and effects of fire provides the motivation for the conducting of a field trial to generate this information and make it available for formulating ecologically appropriate prescribed burning programs for managing the vegetation in the Reserves. While there is a significant similarity in the botanical composition and ecology of the vegetation in the different Reserves with similar vegetation communities in southern and east Africa it is strongly recommended that this essential information on fire ecology be generated locally rather than depend on the scientifically known effects of fire in African grasslands and savannas. The climatic and edaphic environments are particularly different especially with regard to annual rainfall received in the Tiger Reserves which is markedly higher than that in Africa.

OBJECTIVES

The objectives of the trial are to:

- Determine the effect of season and frequency of burn and type and intensity of fire on the botanical composition, basal cover, and re-growth of the grass sward;
- Determine the effect of season and frequency of burn and type and intensity of fire on the density and phytomass of trees and shrubs present in the grassland communities;
- Determine the behaviour of the fires in terms of rate of spread, fire intensity, and flame height as influenced by the fuel load and moisture content of the grass sward and the effects of air temperature, relative humidity, and wind speed of the atmosphere;
- Based on the resultant fire behaviour data rate of spread, fire intensity, and flame height models that can be used to formulate prescribed burning guidelines for managing the grassland and grass-dominated communities in forested areas.

HYPOTHESES

Based on fire ecology data for African grasslands and savannas It is postulated that:

- The intensity of head fires burning with the wind has no significant effect on the regrowth of the grass sward because the growing points of grasses are located at ground level away from the release of heat energy in the canopy of the sward;
- Different intensities of head fires will have no significant effect on the mortality of trees and shrubs because trees and shrubs have dormant buds located below ground level in the collar region and are protected from the release of heat energy from above ground level in the grass sward;
- Increasing fire intensities will have a significant effect on the topkill of stems and branches of trees and shrubs because the growing points of the woody vegetation will suffer greater damage from the greater rate of release of heat energy;

- Increasing flame heights will cause a greater topkill of stems and branches in trees and shrubs because the growing points of the woody plants are located in the canopies of the trees and shrubs and are therefore subjected to a greater direct release of heat energy;
- Increasing grass fuel loads will result in greater fire intensities because of the greater availability of fuel for combustion;
- Increasing fuel moisture will result in lower fire intensities because greater quantities of moisture need to be boiled off during the combustion process;
- Increasing air temperatures will result in greater fire intensities because less heat energy is required to raise the grass fuel to its ignition point;
- Increasing wind speeds will result in greater fire intensities because of the greater availability of oxygen for the combustion process.

PROCEDURE

The following procedure comprising treatments and pre- and post-treatment measurements will be conducted during the trial:

Treatments:

a. Season of Burn:

- Burning after the monsoon in early winter during November/December when the grass curing is greater than 65% - BEW;
- Burning in mid-winter during February/March when the grass sward is fully cured i.e. greater than 75% - BMW;

b. Frequency of Burn
- Annual Burn - B1
- Biennial Burn - B2
- Triennial Burn - B3
- Quadrennial Burn - B4

c. Control treatment – no burn – K.

d. Fire Regime

<u>Type of Fire</u>: Head fire burning with the wind;
<u>Fire Intensity & Season of Burn</u>:

Early Winter Burn (BEW)– *November/ December*	Mid-Winter Burn (BMW) – *February/ March*
Low Intensity Fire - <1000 kJ/s/m;	High Intensity Fire - >2,000 kJ/s/m
Grass Curing – 65%	Grass Curing – >80%
Air Temperature - <20 C^0	Air Temperature - >25 C^0
Relative Humidity - >40%	Relative Humidity - <30%
Wind Speed - ≤10km/h	Wind Speed - <10km/h

Frequency of Burn: Annual, Biennial, Triennial, & Quadrennial burning treatments.

The treatments will be replicated three times and the plot size will be 50m x 50m arranged in a Randomised Block Design. Twenty metre wide firebreaks between plots will be constructed in order to contain the burning treatments. The size of the trial will be 370m x 230m = 85,100m^2 = 8.51 ha. The trial will be conducted in the absence of grazing and will be fenced to exclude wild ungulates. The reason for this is to determine the effect of fire alone on the grass sward and tree/ shrub vegetation.

Treatment Summary:

TREATMENTS
B1 – BEW - Annual Burn – Early Winter - *Nov/ Dec*
B1 – BMW – Annual Burn – Mid Winter – Feb/ Mar
B2 – BEW – Biennial Burn – Early Winter- *Nov/ Dec*
B2 – BMW – Biennial Burn – Mid Winter– Feb/ Mar
B3 – BEW – Triennial Burn – Early Winter – Nov/ Dec
B3 – BMW – Triennial Burn - Mid Winter – Feb/ Mar
B4 – BEW – Quadrennial Burn – Early Winter – Nov/ Dec
B4 - BMW– Quadrennial Burn – Mid Winter – Feb/ Mar
K – Control – No Burn

Measurements:

Grass Sward – The botanical composition and basal cover (Point To Tuft Distance – PTTD) will be recorded with a 100 point quadrat survey arranged in four transects down the centre of each quarter of the plot at approximately 2 m intervals using the technique developed by Trollope (1990) in the Kruger National Park. Pre-burn and post-burn grass fuel loads will be recorded with a Disc Pasture Meter (100 Disc Hts. at 2 metre intervals recorded along the same transects as used for the point quadrat survey). The fuel loads will be estimated by the Kruger National Park calibration developed by Trollope & Potgieter (1986). The post-burn grass fuel loads will be conducted annually in each plot at the end of the monsoon rains in October/ November.

Trees & Shrubs – The pre-burn and post-burn density and phytomass of trees and shrubs will be recorded in each plot using the Adapted Point Centre Quadrat (APCQ) technique developed by Trollope *et. al.* (2011). The PCQ circular quadrats will comprise 40m diameters located in the centre of each of the trial plots. The post-burn APCQ surveys will be conducted annually in each plot at the end of the monsoon rains in October/ November.

Fire Behaviour

The burning treatments will be applied according to the procedure developed by Trollope (1978) and the rate of spread, fire intensity, and flame heights of the fires will also be recorded according to the procedure developed by Trollope (1978). These data will be used to develop the Rate of Spread, Fire Intensity, and Flame Height Models, and the relationship of these fire behaviour parameters and the response of the vegetation.

Dear Reader, if you have enjoyed the book and found it useful, would you care leaving a brief review at your retailer's website and at your social media pages?

Bibliography

1. Anand Shaurabh and Sindhu Radhakrishna (2017). Investigating trends in human-wildlife conflict: is conflict escalation real or imagined? Journal of Asia-Pacific Biodiversity 10 (2017) 154-161.

2. Animal Use Affairs Committee of International Association of Fish and Wildlife Agencies (IAFWA) 2005: Potential Costs of Losing Hunting and Trapping as Wildlife Management Methods.

3. Anonymous, 2019. Identification Of Prone Forest Areas Based On GIS Analysis Of Archived Forest Fire Points Detected In The Last Thirteen Years. Technical Information Series Volume I No. 1 2019. Forest Survey of India.

4. Anonymous. 2007. Harvest Trends & Distribution of Feral Pigs in SC. South Carolina Department of Natural Resources. Life's Better Outdoors – dnr.sc.gov.

5. Anonymous. 2016. Eco-friendly Measures to Mitigate Impacts of Linear Infrastructure on Wildlife. Wildlife Institute of India, Dehradun, India.

6. Anonymous. 2017. State of the Forest Report 2017. Forest Survey of India, Dehradun.

7. Anonymous. 2019. ENVIS Centre on Wildlife & Protected Areas. Protected Areas of India. Wildlife Institute of India, Dehradun. http://www.wiienvis.nic.in/Database/Protected_Area_854.aspx (08.02.2019).

8. Ansari, Nasim Ahmad. 2017. Status of mammals with special reference to population estimation of Nilgai Boselaphus tragocamelus and suggest mitigation measures to prevent crop damage in and around Surajpur reserve forest, Uttar Pradesh, India. Journal of Entomological and Zoology Studies. E-ISSN: 2320-7078 P-ISSN: 2349-6800 JEZS 2017; 5(4): 1085-1091 © 2017 JEZS.

9. Assessment of Forest Burnt Area in India using Resourcesat-2 AWiFS Data." Current Science 112, no.7: 1521-1532.

10. Bajwa & Chauhan. 2019. Distribution of Nilgai antelope (Boselaphus tragocamelus) and its interaction with local communities in the Abohar wildlife sanctuary, Northwestern India. Journal of Wildlifc and Biodiversity3(4):27-35 (2019).

11. Busse, Matt D. and DeBano Leonard F. 2005. Soil Biology. In: Neary, Daniel G.; Ryan, Kevin C.; DeBano, Leonard F., eds. 2005. (revised 2008). Wildland fire in ecosystems: effects of fire on soils and water. Gen. Tech. Rep. RMRS-GTR-42-vol.4. Ogden, UT: U.S. Department of Agriculture, Forest Service, Rocky Mountain Research Station. 73-91.

12. Champion H.G. & S.K. Seth (1968). General Silviculture for India. Government of India, Publications Branch, Department of Printing and Stationery, Delhi-6.

13. Chapman, H. H. 1912. Forest fires and forestry in the southern states. American Forests. 18: 510-517.

14. Chundawat, R. S, Merten, J. Agasti, S. Sharma, K. Raju U. and Matthews, J. 2017. Value of wildlife tourism for conservation and communities: a study around four tiger reserves in Madhya Pradesh (Part-1, Tourism infrastructure and revenue). Bagh Aap Aur VAN (BAAVAN) and TOFTigers.

15. Croft, Simon; Barbara Franzetti, Robin Gill & Giovanna Massei. 2020. Too many wild boar? Modelling fertility control and culling to reduce wild boar numbers in isolated populations. PLoA ONW 15 (9): e0238429.

16. Dogra Pyush, Andrew Michael Mitchell, Urvashi Narain, Christopher Sall, Ross Smith, and Shraddha Suresh. 2018. "Strengthening Forest Fire Management in India". World Bank, Washington DC.

17. Gera, Mohit (2017). Likely Impacts Of Climate Change On Forest Fires And Adaptation Strategies. Indian Forester, 143 (8) : 729-736, 2017. ISSN No. 0019-4816 (Print) ISSN No. 2321-094X (Online).

18. Ghosh, Sonali (2015). Drivers of Change - a Geospatial Study on Fires in Terai Grasslands of Manas Tiger Reserve and World Heritage Site, India. In Rawat, G.S. and Adhikari, B.S. (Eds.) 2015. Ecology and Management of Grassland Habitats in India. ENVIS Bulletin: Wildlife & Protected Areas. Printed in 2015; Wildlife Institute of India, Dehradun-248001, India.

19. Hiremath Ankila J. and Bharath Sundram (2005). The Fire-Lantana Cycle Hypothesis in Indian Forests. Conservation and Society, Pages 26-42, Volume 3, No. 1, June 2005.

20. Johnsingh, A.J.T. and Murali, S. 2021 (unpbl). The Last Lions. 19 pictures, 1 map, and 24 pages.

21. Karanth KK, Gopalaswamy AM, DeFries R, Ballal N (2012) Assessing Patterns of Human-Wildlife Conflicts and Compensation around a Central Indian Protected Area. PLoS ONE 7(12): e50433. doi:10.1371/journal.pone.0050433.

22. Karanth Krithi K. & Kudalkar Sahila (2017) History, Location, and Species Matter: Insights for Human-Wildlife Conflict Mitigation From India, Human Dimensions of Wildlife, 22:4, 331-
346, DOI: 10.1080/10871209.2017.1334106.

23. Karanth, K.K., Gupta Shriyam, Vanamalai (2018). Compensation payments, procedures and policies towards human-wildlife conflict management: Insights from India. Biological Conservation 227. September 2018, doi:10.1016/j.biocon.2018.07.006.

24. Khan, Khursid A., and Khan, Jamal A. 2016. Status, abundance, and population ecology of Nilgai (Boselaphus tragocamelus Pallas) in Aligarh District, Uttar Pradesh, India. J. Appl. & Nat. Sci. 8 (2): 1080 - 1086 (2016).

25. Khanom, Tanzinia. 2019. Impact of Climate Change on Wild boar (Sus scrofa) population in Bavaria, Germany.Master's Thesis. Technische Universitat Munchen.

26. Kitchener, A. C.; Breitenmoser-Würsten, C.; Eizirik, E.; Gentry, A.; Werdelin, L.; Wilting, A.; Yamaguchi, N.; Abramov, A. V.; Christiansen, P.; Driscoll, C.; Duckworth, J. W.; Johnson, W.; Luo, S.-J.; Meijaard, E.; O'Donoghue, P.; Sanderson, J.; Seymour, K.; Bruford, M.; Groves, C.; Hoffmann, M.; Nowell, K.; Timmons, Z. & Tobe, S. (2017). "A revised taxonomy of the Felidae: The final report of the Cat Classification Task Force of the IUCN Cat Specialist Group" (PDF). Cat News (Special Issue 11): 71–73.

27. Kittur B. H., S. L. Swamy, S. S. Bargali, Manoj Kumar Jhariya (2014). Wildland fires and moist deciduous forests of Chhattisgarh, India: divergent component assessment. Journal of Forestry Research (2014) 25(4): 857–866 DOI 10.1007/s11676-014-0471-0.

28. Kodandapani Narendra, Cochrane Mark A. and Sukumar R. (2004). Conservation Threat of Increasing Fire Frequencies in

the Western Ghats, India. Conservation Biology. Pages 1553-1561. Vol. 18 No. 6. December 2004.

29. Kodandapani Narendra, Cochrane Mark A. and Sukumar R. (2008). A comparative analysis of spatial, temporal, and ecological characteristics of forest fires in seasonally dry tropical ecosystems in the Western Ghats, India. Elsevier. Forest Ecology and Management 256 (2008) 607-617.

30. Kumar Harish, Lehmukhl J.F., and Mathur P.K. (2015). Grassland Communities of Terai Conservation Landscape: Effects of Management Practices and Conservation Strategies. In Rawat, G.S. and Adhikar, B.S. (Eds.) 2015. Ecology and Management of Grassland Habitats in India. ENVIS Bulletin: Wildlife & Protected Areas. Printed in 2015; Wildlife Institute of India, Dehradun-248001, India.

31. Lamarque, F., J. Anderson, P. Chardonnet, R. Fergusson, M. Lagrange, Y. Osei-Owusu, L. Bakker, U. Belemsobgo, B. Beytell, H. Boulet, B. Soto, and P. Tabi Tako-Eta 2008. Human-wildlife conflict in Africa: An overview of causes, consequences and management strategies. Working Paper – ILO.

32. MILWARD R. C. The Indian forest service: Its origin and progress. Unasylva Vol. 3. No. 1. The Empire Forestry Review, Vol. 26, No. 2, 1947.

33. Ministry of Environment, Forest and Climate Change, 2017: India's National Wildlife Action Plan (2017-2031).

34. Mondal Nandita and Raman Sukumar (2014). Fire and soil temperatures during controlled burns in seasonally dry tropical forests of southern India. CURRENT SCIENCE, VOL. 107, NO. 9, 10 NOVEMBER 2014.

35. Mondal, N. and R. Sukumar. 2015. "Regeneration of Juvenile Woody Plants After Fire in a Seasonally Dry Tropical Forest of Southern India." BIOTROPICA 47, no. 3: 330-338.

36. Mondal, N. and R. Sukumar. 2016. "Fires in Seasonally Dry Tropical Forest: Testing the Varying Constraints Hypothesis across a Regional Rainfall Gradient." PLOS ONE 11(7): e0159691. doi:10.1371/journal.pone.0159691.

37. Muruthi, P. 2005. Human-Wildlife Conflict: Lessons Learned from AWF's Africa Heartlands. African Wildlife Foundation Working Papers.

38. Pabla, HS, 1992: Handling a Young National Park in the Dry Tropics of India. Tropical Ecosystems: Ecology and

Management. Editors: K.P. Singh and J.S. Singh, pp. 197-205, 1992, Wiley Eastern Limited, New Delhi.

39. Pandey, R.K. 2015. Dynamics of Grassland Communities in Kanha Tiger Reserve, Madhya Pradesh: Ecological and Management Implications. In Rawat, G.S. and Adhikar, B.S. (Eds.) 2015. Ecology and Management of Grassland Habitats in India. ENVIS Bulletin: Wildlife & Protected Areas. Printed in 2015; Wildlife Institute of India, Dehradun-248001, India.

40. Pandav B., Natrajan L., Kumar A., Desai A. and Lynkghoi B. 2021. Household perceptions and patterns of crop loss by wild pigs in north India. Human–Wildlife Interactions 15(1): EarlyOnline, Spring 2021 • digitalcommons.usu.edu/hwi.

41. Phillips, J.F.V., 1965. Fire - as a master and servant: its influence in the bioclimatic regions of Trans - Saharan Africa. Proc. Tall Timbers Fire Ecology Conf. 4: 7-10.

42. Prachar, Randy; Sage, R. W., Jr.; Deisch, M. S. 1988. Site occupancy, density, and spatial distribution of beaver colonies in burned and unburned areas in the Adirondacks. Transactions, Northeast Section of the Wildlife Society. 45: 74.

43. Prasad, Suday; Singh D.K. and Chowdhury, SK. 2020. Residential Population Structure and Abundance of Nilgai, Boselaphus tragocamelus, (Pallas) in Bihar, India. Current Journal of Applied Science and Technology. 39(13): 110-117, 2020 Article no. CJAST.56969 ISSN: 2457-1024; June 2020.

44. Q. Qureshi, S, Saini, P. Basu, R. Gopal, R. Raza, Y. Jhala, 2014. Connecting Tiger Populations for Long-term Conservation. National Tiger Conservation Authority & Wildlife Institute of India, Dehradun. TR2014-02.

45. Rangarajan, Mahesh, Ajay Desai, R Sukumar, PS Easa, Vivek Menon, S Vincent, Suparna Ganguly, BK Talukdar, Brijendra Singh, Divya Mudappa, Sushant Chowdhary and AN Prasad. Gajah. Securing the Future for Elephants in India. The Report of the Elephant Task Force, Ministry of Environment and Forests. August 31, 2010. New Delhi: Ministry of Environment and Forests, 2010. http://www.environmentandsociety.org/node/2697.

46. Rawat, G.S. and Adhikari, B.S. (Eds.) 2015. Ecology and Management of Grassland Habitats in India. ENVIS Bulletin: Wildlife & Protected Areas. Printed in 2015; Wildlife Institute of India, Dehradun-248001, India.

47. Ray Tapas, Dinesh Malasiya, Radha Rajpoot, Satyam Verma, Javid Ahmad Dar, Arun Dayanandan, Debojyoti Raha, Parvaiz Lone, Praveen Pandey, Pramod Kumar Khare & Mohammed Latif Khan (2020): Impact of Forest Fire Frequency on Tree Diversity and Species Regeneration in Tropical Dry Deciduous Forest of Panna Tiger Reserve, Madhya Pradesh, India, Journal of Sustainable Forestry. https://www.tandfonline.com/loi/wjsf20.

48. Reddy, C. Sudhakar; Alekhya, V L Padma; Saranya, K R L; Athira, K; Jha, C S; Diwakar, P G and Dadhwal, V K. (2017). Monitoring of fire incidences in vegetation types and Protected Areas of India: Implications on carbon emissions. J. Earth Syst. Sci. 92017) 126: 11. DOI 10.1007/s12040-016-0791-x.

49. Reddy, C. Sudhakar; Bird, Natalia Grace; Sreelakshmi, S. T.; Manikandan, Maya; Asra, Mahbooba; Hari Krishna, P.; Jha C. S.; Rao, P. V. N. and Diwakar, P. G.(2019) Identification and characterization of spatio-temporal hotspots of forest fires in South Asia. Environ Monit Assess (2019) 191 (Suppl 3): 791.

50. Reddy, C. Sudhakar; Jha, C.S.; Manaswini, G.; Alekhya, V.V.L. Padma; Vazeed; S. Pasha and Satish, K.V. (2017). Nationwide Assessment of Forest Burnt Area in Using Resourcesat-2 AWiFS Data. CURRENT SCIENCE, VOL. 112, NO. 7, 10 APRIL 2017.

51. Rodgers, W.A. 1986. "The Role of Fire in The Management of Wildlife Habitats: A Review." The Indian Forester. Volume 112, Issue 10, October 1986.

52. Saberwal, V., Gibbs, J.P., Ravi Chellam andJohnsingh, A.J.T. 1994. Lion-human conflict in the Gir forest, India. Conserv. Biol. 8: 501-507.

53. Saha Sonali and Henry F. Howe (2003). SPECIES COMPOSITION AND FIRE IN A DRY DECIDUOUS FOREST. Ecology, 84(12), 2003, pp. 3118–3123 q 2003 by the Ecological Society of America.

54. Shilla U. & Tiwari B.K. (2015). Impact of fire and grazing on plant diversity of grassland ecosystem of Cherrapunjee. Keanean Journal of Science Vol 4 2015 67-7.8. ISSN 2321 – 6077.

55. Singh, H.S. (2017). Dispersion of the Asiatic lion Panthera leo persica and its survival in human-dominated landscape

outside the Gir forest, Gujarat, India. CURRENT SCIENCE, VOL. 112, NO. 5, 10 MARCH 2017.

56. Singh, R. (1995). Some studies on the ecology and behaviour of Nilgai with an assessment of damage to agricultural crop and development of strategy for damage control in south western Haryana. Ph.D. Thesis, Aligarh Muslim University, Aligarh.

57. Sinha, Samir Kumar, Behera Subrat Kumar, Bodhankar Smita, Choudhury BC, Kaul Rahul. (2015). Ecology and Management of Grasslands in Valmiki Tiger Reserve in the Himalayan Foothills, India. In Rawat, G.S. and Adhikari, B.S. (Eds.) 2015. Ecology and Management of Grassland Habitats in India. ENVIS Bulletin: Wildlife & Protected Areas. Printed in 2015; Wildlife Institute of India, Dehradun-248001, India.

58. Sriramamurthy, R.T, R.S. Bhalla and M. Sankaran. 2020. Fire differentially affects mortality and seed regeneration of three woody invaders in forest-grassland mosaics of the southern Western Ghats. Biological Invasion, 22: 1623-1634.

59. Sundaram B., Siddhartha Krishnan, Ankila J. Hiremath & Gladwin Joseph. Ecology and Impacts of the Invasive Species, Lantana camara, in a Social-Ecological System in South India: Perspectives from Local Knowledge. Hum Ecol (2012) 40:931–942. DOI 10.1007/s10745-012-9532-1

60. Sundaram, B., Krishnan, S., Hiremath, A.J. *et al.* Ecology and Impacts of the Invasive Species, Lantana camara, in a Social-Ecological System in South India: Perspectives from Local Knowledge. HumEcol 40, 931–942.

61. The Corbett Foundation (2017). Dynamics of Human–Sloth Bear Conflict in the Kanha-Pench Corridor, Madhya Pradesh, India. The Corbett Foundation. Mumbai, India.

62. Sweitzer, Richard A. Dirk Van Vuren, Ian A. Gardner, Walter M. Boyce and John D. Waithman 2000. Estimating Sizes of Wild Pig Populations in the North and Central Coast Regions of California. The Journal of Wildlife Management. Vol. 64, No. 2 (Apr., 2000), pp. 531-543 (13 pages).

63. Tack, J. (2018). Wild Boar (Sus scrofa) populations in Europe: a scientific review of population trends and implications for management. European Landowners' Organization, Brussels, 56 pp

64. Thekaekara Tarsh, Vanak Abi Tamim, Hiremath Ankila J, Rai Nitin D, Ratnam Jayashree, Sukumar Raman 2017. Notes

from the other side of a forest fire. Economic and political weekly · June 2017. Vol. LII Nos. 25 & 26.

65. Thekaekara, Tarsh, Abi Tamim Vanak, Ankila J Hirema, Nitin D Rai, Jayashree Ratnam, and Thomassen, J., Linnell, J. & Skogen, K. 2011. Wildlife-Human Interactions: From Conflict to Coexistence in Sustainable Landscapes. Final report from a joint Indo-Norwegian project 2007-2011. - NINA Report 736. 83 pp.

66. Timmons, J.B; Higginbotham, B.; Lopez, R.; Cathey, J.C.; Mellish, J.; Griffin, J.; Sumrail, A. and Skow, Kevin. 2012. Feral Hog Population Growth, Density and Harvest in Texas. Texas A&M AgriLife, Texas A&M University. SP-472, August 2012.

67. Trollope Winston S.W. & Trollope Lynne A. (2007). FIRE ECOLOGY AND MANAGEMENT OF AFRICAN GRASSLAND AND SAVANNA ECOSYSTEMS. Associates – Working On Fire International, 38 Durban Street Fort Beaufort, 5720, South Africa.

68. Trollope Winston S.W., Trollope Lynne A, Austin Chris de Bruno. 2012 (Unpubl.). Assessment of the Ecological Status and Necessity for Prescribed Burning in the Grassland and Forest Communities in the Kanha, Bandhavgarh, Panna, and Pench Tiger Reserves in Madhya Pradesh, India. January 2012. Working on Fire International, Nelspruit, South Africa.

69. Trollope Winston S.W., Trollope Lynne A, Austin Chris de Bruno, 2012. (Unpubl.) Burn Trials for Determining Appropriate Type, Intensity, Season and Frequency of Fire For Tiger Reserves in Madhya Pradesh State, India. Working on Fire International, Nelspruit, South Africa.

70. Trollope, W S W., 1978. Fire behaviour - a preliminary study. Proc. Grassld. Soc. SthAfr. 13: 123-128.

71. Trollope, W S W., 1981. Recommended terms, definitions, and units to be used in fire ecology in Southern Africa. Proc. Grassld. Soc. Sth Afr. 16: 107-109.

72. Trollope, W S W., 1990. Development of a technique for assessing veld condition in the Kruger National Park. J. Grassld. Soc. South. Afr.7, 1:46-51.

73. Trollope, W.S.W., 2011. Assessment of Veld Condition Using the Adapted Point Centred Quarter Method. Special Report: Working On Fire International, Nelspruit, South Africa: 1-20.

74. Tyagi A. 2007. Thunderstorm climatology over Indian region. MAUSAM, 58, 2 (April 2007), 189-212. 551.58 : 551.515.4 (540).

75. Vasu Niranjan K. Singh G. (2015). Grasslands of Kaziranga National Park: Problems and Approaches for Management. In Rawat, G.S. and Adhikari, B.S. (Eds.) 2015. Ecology and Management of Grassland Habitats in India. ENVIS Bulletin: Wildlife & Protected Areas. Printed in 2015; Wildlife Institute of India, Dehradun-248001, India.

76. Verma Satyam, Dharmatma Singh, Sathya Mani and Shanmuganathan Jayakumar (2017). Effect of forest fire on tree diversity and regeneration potential in a tropical dry deciduous forest of Mudumalai Tiger Reserve, Western Ghats, India. Ecological Processes (2017) 6:32 DOI 10.1186/s13717-017-0098-0.

77. Verma Satyam, Jayakumar S. 2012. Impact of forest fire on physical, chemical, and biological properties of soil: A review. Proceedings of the International Academy of Ecology and Environmental Sciences, 2012, 2(3):168-176.

78. Verma Satyam, Jayakumar S. 2014. Impact of forest fire on diversity, stand structure and regeneration of woody species in a tropical deciduous forest of Western Ghats. Conference Paper. Dept. of Ecology & Environmental Sciences School of Life Sciences Pondicherry University, Puducherry.

79. Vetter, Sebastian G. Asofia Puskas, Claudia Bieber & Thomas Ruf 2020. How climate change and wildlife management affect population structure in wild boars. University of Veterinary Medicine, Vienna, Research Institute of Wildlife Ecology, Savoyenstr.

About the Author

Harbhajan Singh Pabla is the former Chief Wild Life Warden of Madhya Pradesh. Apart from doing the usual things that an Indian forester does, he nurtured his love for the wild while managing national parks like Kanha, Panna and Bandhavgarh. Along the way, he developed a penchant for challenging the stereotypes that have ruled the conservation mindset in the country so far.

He introduced a culture of active wildlife management in India. When Panna lost all its tigers, he developed and implemented the tiger reintroduction plan that has given the world the confidence that wild tigers will always be around. He also reversed the local extinctions of gaur, blackbuck and barasingha through reintroductions. Thousands of animals have been moved between Indian parks since then, on the strength of the learnings from his initiatives. Despite his retirement from IFS, he still dreams of seeing the white tiger back in the wild. His wish list also includes seeing Indian foresters using horses for patrolling the wilderness. He believes that India will not be able to conserve its wildlife unless it becomes a tool for creating jobs for rural people and human-wildlife conflict is managed effectively.

He has also worked as a forestry and wildlife management consultant in Sri Lanka, Bangladesh and Nepal.

Currently, he lives in Bhopal, India and can be contacted at:
E-mail: pablahsifs@gmail.com
Cell: +91-9425007850

By the Same Author

Road To Nowhere
(Wildlife Conservation in India-1)

Wardens In Shackles
(Wildlife Conservation in India-2)

Laws At War
(Wildlife Conservation in India-3)